"There is an unseen but very real crisis affecting masculinity and men everywhere. This book offers an intelligent, thoughtful look at the causes of this crisis and the ways we can move beyond it. *The Warrior's Journey Home* makes sense on a personal and societal level."

—Marvin Allen, author of *In the Company of Men*,
Director of the Texas Men's Institute

"One of those books that takes a minute to read a paragraph, and ten minutes to reflect on the richness and impact of the thoughts. Get this book!"

—Peter Alsop, Ph.D., author, singer, songwriter, father

"Rush Limbaugh and Howard Stern, Pat Buchanan, Pat Robertson and Jesse Helms should all read *The Warrior's Journey Home.* They may not like it, but they will benefit from exposure to Jed's information and perspectives. Jed's book will enlighten, amuse, and surprise you."

—Donald B. Ardell, Ph.D., publisher of *Ardell Wellness Report*

"Jed Diamond takes his place among those speaking up on behalf of our threatened earth. He takes us back before warriors, to a time of hunters and gatherers in search of a home for people today, so displaced from the earth."

—Professor Shepherd Bliss, Psychology Department,
John F. Kennedy University

"Diamond continues his important work of infusing the alcohol and recovery literature with a heightened awareness of male socialization. Men's recovery will be greatly enhanced when the insights of Diamond's book are appreciated."

—Gary R. Brooks, Ph.D., Co-Coordinator, Society for
the Psychological Study of Men and Masculinity

"A timely book—honest, unpretentious, and compassionately REAL! Jed Diamond's personal journey will touch many people; and the essence of recovery and healing will resonate with us all."

—Chungliang Al Huang, Living Tao Foundation,
author of *Embrace Tiger Return to Mountain*

"A must read for all men and women who want to understand why men are the way we are. Get copies for everyone you know!"

—Stan Dale, Director of the Human Awareness
Institute

"Jed's fluid approach to addictions as individually defined and his creativity in treating them offer much hope to the many men and women who are turned off by the rigidity of other programs. His model of the rings of addiction is one of the most useful recovery tools I have ever seen."

—Robbie Davis-Floyd, Ph.D., author of *Birth as an American Rite of Passage*

"*The Warrior's Journey Home* is a fine contribution to the new road map for living outside of limiting concepts of manhood. The world needs men who are free at every level to serve. This book can help men make the transition from making a living to making a life."

—Joe Dominguez, author of *Your Money or Your Life*

"Don't miss chapters six, seven, and eight."

—Ken Druck, Ph.D., author of *The Secrets Men Keep*

"Clear, complete, simple, powerful! A must read for men looking to move their recovery forward."

—Bob Earll, author of *Lonely All the Time*

"The men's movement meets the earth! Based on 28 years of experience, Jed offers us a blueprint for survival."

—John Enright, Ph.D., recovering psychologist, poet, and Earth-lover

"There are important new ideas in this book; and you can tell the author discovered them by living his life fully, with eyes and mind wide open."

—Bob Frenier, founding publisher of *Wingspan: Journal of the Male Spirit*

"A warm, thoughtful, compassionate, and balanced approach to our human tendency to become 'addicted' to just about anything. Offers practical, straightforward steps we can take to identify our addictions and then grow beyond them."

—Douglas Gillette, co-author of *King, Warrior, Magician, Lover*

"Jed Diamond does a fine job of combining personal, environmental, and psychological healing in making an original and fascinating statement about men and the direction they need to go if we are going to survive and thrive."

—Herb Goldberg, Ph.D., author of *The Hazards of Being Male*

"Jed Diamond draws a compelling thread between the loss of our warrior values, the desecration of the planet, and our pervasive addictions. He then outlines a set of clear and pragmatic practices that can return us to a deeper connection to ourselves and the natural world. This book is equally important for woman as it is for men."

—Richard Strozzi Heckler, Ph.D., author of *In Search of the Warrior Spirit*

"This is a very important book. It goes right to the heart of our present problems and shows us how to heal ourselves, our relationships, and the fragile planet we all share. I highly recommend it for both men and women."

—Gerald Jampolsky, M.D., author of *Love Is Letting Go of Fear* and *Change Your Mind, Change Your Life*

"Offers us the vital distinction between the shamed, powerless soldier and the healthy masculine identity of the true warrior spirit."

—Bill Kauth, co-founder of the New Warrior Training, author of *A Circle of Men*

"Jed Diamond's call to action on behalf of men's psychological, physical, and spiritual renewal is the key to protecting the earth and reweaving the broken threads of our social fabric."

—Aaron Kipnis, Ph.D., author of *Gender War/Gender Peace: The Quest for Love and Justice Between Women and Men*

"Diamond draws the best from the recovery movement as well as from psychotherapy while creating his own, original views of addictions, the recovery process, and that other necessary ingredient for success: a spiritual side to life."

—Terry Allen Kupers, M.D., author of *Revisioning Men's Lives: Gender, Intimacy and Power*

"Jed's work not only bridges the Men's and Recovery Movements like no other book has done, but in the process he takes the reader by the hand, the throat, the heart, and the soul and ushers us into a new possibility where masculinity is life affirming. The soldier is no longer needed because the Warrior of the Spirit has finally found a home."

—John Lee, author of *The Flying Boy* and *At My Father's Wedding*

"Explores with great compassion and understanding those dimensions of men's secret self that have been consigned by multitudes of walking wounded to silent despair."

—Hanny Lightfoot-Klein, author of *Prisoners of Ritual: A Women's Odyssey into Female Genital Circumcision in Africa*

"As a mother who did not know enough to protect my own babies from the fires of the first physical/psychological wounding—circumcision—I am grateful to have *The Warrior's Journey Home* to offer my sons."

—Marilyn Fayre Milos, R.N., Executive Director, National Organization of Circumcision Information Resource Centers

"Diamond has produced a comprehensive and clearly written guide which awakens men to our full potential for healing ourselves and the world we inhabit—a valuable and inspirational contribution to both men's and recovery movements."

—Robert Pasick, Ph.D., author of *Awaking from the Deep Sleep*

"Jed Diamond's homeward journey of awakening has taken him far into the mystery of being male and human—dangerous territory in an age when being male and human is practically a crime. Speaking as a member of the gender and the race, I found much here that I didn't know, hadn't been able to figure out (and had even been afraid to look at or think about)."

—Daniel Quinn, author of *Ishmael*

"Addresses all the major issues that trouble thoughtful men and women, including addictions, violence toward others, destruction of our environment, and the longing for father's love. A highly recommended book which women, too, will find very informative."

—Jennifer P. Schneider, M.D., author of *Back From Betrayal*

"Stripping away our addictions, returning to our true core, Diamond clearly shows that our future lies in going back to the time when men's sacred duty was the preservation of the earth.

—John Stokes, Director, The Tracking Project

THE
WARRIOR'S
JOURNEY
HOME

HEALING MEN,
HEALING THE PLANET

JED DIAMOND, L.C.S.W., C.A.S.

NEW HARBINGER PUBLICATIONS, INC.

Publisher's Note

This publication is designed to provide accurate and authoritative information in regard to the subject matter covered. It is sold with the understanding that the publisher is not engaged in rendering psychological, financial, legal, or other professional services. If expert assistance or counseling is needed, the services of a competent professional should be sought.

Library of Congress Catalog Number: 93-086801
ISBN 1-879237-60-1 Paperback
ISBN 1-879237-61-X Hardcover

Copyright © by Jed Diamond
New Harbinger Publications, Inc.
5674 Shattuck Avenue
Oakland, CA 94609

Printed in the United States of America on recycled paper
Original cover art by SHELBY DESIGNS & ILLUSTRATES
Original cover photo by Roger Kose, Standing Stone Productions, Ltd.

First printing 1994, 5,000 copies

Contents

Acknowledgments

I want to thank my wife, Carlin, and our children—Jemal, Angela, Aaron, Dane, and Evan—for loving me just the way I am. To Edith, my mother, and to Morris, my father, I think I've finally stopped blaming you for the things I thought you should have given. You gave me my life, and though you gave me much more, that was enough to set me on my path. The men in my men's group—Tom, Dick, John, Ken, Denis, Tony, Kellie, and Norman—have been a source of support since we first began meeting in 1979. They continue to teach me what it means to be a man. In having the courage to confront their own wounds and heal themselves, my clients have aided me in my own recovery in more ways than they will ever know. Though details have been changed to protect their identity, many of their stories are given in the book.

Reflecting on the roots of my growth as a man and my work with men, I'd like to acknowledge my debt to a number of other people. When I read Betty Friedan's *The Feminine Mystique,* in 1964, I knew that freeing women from restrictive sex roles would free me as well.[1] Herb Goldberg taught me that there were hazards to being male and that the price we paid for being "top dog" in society was too great.[2] Warren Farrell showed me how to stand beside women in our quest to dismantle the male roles that were harming women, children, and ourselves. His example also showed me that we needed to disengage and confront those women who confused "women's liberation" with blaming men for all that is wrong in our world.[3]

Joseph Pleck taught me that I could be a feminist without being anti-male, and that there was a place for sound scholarship and good manners in the emotional debate on gender roles and relationships.[4] In Fred Hayward I found a man who was willing to stand up for men's rights and who wasn't afraid to use humor to show the anti-male bias in the media.[5] Anne Wilson Schaef was one of the first to write about the relationship between our restrictive sex roles and the kinds of addictions we develop.[6]

Robert Bly introduced me to poetry, myth, and storytelling. Through Bly I met the Wild Man, Iron John, and the mythical man within, who led me to my roots as a two-million-year-old hunter-warrior.[7] John Lee has taught me that two men with different styles and backgrounds could work together and learn to love one another.[8] Shepherd Bliss has offered support and friendship from the beginning. His fierce gentleness has been of great help in my journey.[9]

I want to acknowledge my agent Candice Fuhrman for her knowledge, sound advice, good humor, and support beyond the call of duty. The staff of New Harbinger Publications have been most professional, accessible, generous, kind, and flexible—qualities that have become all too rare in the business of publishing. I particularly want to thank Pat Fanning, Barbara Quick, Mary McCormick, Gayle Zanca, Tracy Powell, Barbara Butler, Stacy Clarke, Karen Mallannao, Barrett Jones, Dana Landis, Mary Lee Cole, Dorothy Smyk, and my indexer, James Minkin.

Thank you all, and many others unnamed.

Notes

1. Betty Friedan is one of the leaders of the women's movement. Her book, *The Feminine Mystique* was an inspiration for women and men. It was published in 1963 by Dell Publishing Company in New York.

2. Herb Goldberg is one of the leaders of the men's movement. His book, *The Hazards of Being Male*, was widely read. It was published in 1977 by New

American Library in New York.

3. Warren Farrell has been an inspirational leader in both the women's and men's movements. He is the only man ever elected three times to the Board of the National Organization of Women (NOW) in New York. His first book, *The Liberated Man*, was published in 1974 by Random House in New York. His most recent book *The Myth of Male Power*, was published in 1993 by Simon & Schuster in New York.

4. Joseph Pleck has been an active supporter of the women's and men's movements for many years. He has written many articles and a number of books, including *The Myth of Masculinity*, published in 1981 by M.I.T. Press in Cambridge, Massachusetts.

5. Fred Hayward is a long-time supporter of men's rights and gender justice. He is the founder and director of Men's Rights, Inc., in Sacramento, California.

6. Anne Wilson Schaef has written a number of books including *When Society Becomes an Addict*, published in 1987 by Harper & Row in San Francisco.

7. I first met Robert Bly in 1983 when I sent him a copy of my book *Inside Out: Becoming My Own Man*. He had just begun focusing his attention on men after more than a decade leading conferences on The Goddess. Since that time he has emerged as a leading writer, poet, and storyteller in the men's movement. His book *Iron John* was published in 1990 by Addison-Wesley Publishing in Reading, Massachusetts.

8. John Lee is a good friend and has emerged as a leader in both the men's and recovery movements. He is the author of a number of books including *The Flying Boy*, published in 1987, and *At My Father's Wedding*, published in 1991 by Bantam in New York.

9. Shepherd Bliss has been active in the men's movement since the early 1980s when I first met him. We have been friends and colleagues ever since. He has contributred to numerous books and coined the term "mythopoetic" to describe the "soul" work that he and others like Robert Bly were developing.

Introduction

If we believe the media, the men's movement is something of a joke, and recovery is a passing fad.

Yet if we could get inside the hearts and souls of the over 80 million men in this country whose manhood is constantly under attack, and who continue to be confused about what it means to be a man, we would know a different reality.

If we could feel the pain of the nearly 50 million men who are suffering from addictions, most in "manly" silence, we would know a different reality.

If we could hear the cries of women who work with, live with, and love these wounded warriors, and must deal with their deadly outbursts of rage and stony silences, we would know a different reality.

If we could sense the sorrow of the earth as another bulldozer rips through its flesh in the name of progress, we would know a different reality.

Why is there such a discrepancy between the view that the issues of men and recovery are passe and the deeper reality that we have only scratched the surface? The answer, I believe, is that those who are most invested in the status quo—particularly, government and business leaders—are afraid to acknowledge the power of the men's and recovery movements. Such leaders dismiss the movements as passing fads, not because they are insignificant, but rather because they so strongly call into question the assumptions of our present reality.

The coming together of the men's movement and the recovery movement signals the beginning of real healing for men, women, children, and the planet itself. It also signals the end of civilization as we have known it, a civilization that has been built on domination, consumption, and addiction. That is the truth that many are afraid to hear. That is the reality that the *Warrior's Journey Home* tries to bring to light.

Untreated addictions continue to grow like cancer. Twenty-eight years ago, when I first began working in the field, men were dealing mostly with alcohol and heroin addictions. In recent years, there has been an addictions explosion. Men are now struggling with everything from homemade amphetamines to designer drugs, compulsive sex to destructive work, overspending to overeating. There are now over 250 different 12-step recovery programs, each dealing with a different addiction.

Many of us have become desperate with an insatiable desire for "more"; addictions are spreading throughout the planet. "I believe," says Vice-President Al Gore, "that our civilization is, in effect, addicted to the consumption of the earth itself. This addictive relationship distracts us from the pain of what we have lost: a direct experience of our connection to the vividness, vibrancy, and aliveness of the rest of the natural world."

I wish there weren't a need for this book. I wish that the problems addressed by the other books on men and recovery had been dealt with and solved. But that is not the case. From birth to death, males continue to be subjected to stresses that lead to the devastation of our masculine souls and a myriad of addictions which attempt to cover the pain of our loss. The following findings point to a few of the realities that males face today:

- Mothers talk to, cuddle, and breastfeed male infants significantly less than female infants.

- Male infants suffer a 25 percent higher mortality rate than females.

- Sixty percent of newborn males (over 3,300 every day) have their normal, healthy foreskins literally torn from their sensitive penises before being forcibly amputated, usually without anesthesia. Many clinicians now consider circumcision to be a form of child sexual abuse.

- Male children are treated more roughly and punished more harshly and frequently than female children.

- By age nine, most male children learn completely to repress all their feelings (except anger, which is sometimes considered acceptable if directed toward other males).

- All male children, unlike their female playmates, grow up knowing that they must be prepared to kill other men and be willing to die at the hands of other men. Every 18-year-old male must "do what a man's gotta do" and register to be a soldier.

Aaron Kipnis, psychologist and author of *Knights Without Armor*, says that males account for:

- 70 percent of all assault victims
- 80 percent of homicide victims
- 85 percent of the homeless
- 90 percent of persons with AIDS
- 93 percent of persons killed on the job
- 95 percent of incarcerated persons

Kipnis concludes by saying, "In general men have higher sickness, accident, suicide, substance abuse, and violent victimization rates than women. Yet the majority of our social and psychological services are predominantly geared to meet the needs of female clients."

The Warrior's Journey Home explores the origins of addictions and the ways in which men lost the primal connection with their masculine selves. Generic recovery programs don't go far enough to heal these wounds: there is a need for programs that speak to the unique experience of men. This book details ten tasks of mature masculinity and seven stages of recovery that men can use to guide them in their return to a more powerful and authentic experience of manhood.

It's my intention to demonstrate the necessity of bringing into the same place of focus men's issues, addiction and recovery issues, and planetary healing. Addictions can be traced not just to the beginning of the industrial age, when, some assert, we lost connection with our healthy roots, but back 10,000 years, to the very inception of civilization. This was when we stopped being hunter-gatherers and began domesticating plants and animals. There is a relationship between the loss of manhood that came about when men no longer lived as hunters, and the beginnings of our addictive search to fill ourselves from the outside.

When we stopped being hunter-gatherers, we changed more than just the way we got our food. We began seeing the nonhuman world—plants, animals, the earth itself—as resources to be exploited by mankind, and we lost our spiritual connection with these resources. Our I-thou relationships became I-it relationships, and the sacred began to vanish from our lives. Having lost our intimate connection with the earth, a void was created in our masculine souls. The emptiness inside turned us into addicts, forever looking outside ourselves for the substance or activity that we hoped would fill the black hole within.

Cut off from our source, feeling damaged at the core of our being, we began relating to others with fear and anger. Our relationships, even the most intimate ones, came to be based on competition and domination rather than cooperation and partnership.

In learning about the ancient hunters, I began to realize that they were the first warriors. These were men who revered life, but were not afraid to embrace death. They knew that other living things must die so that they might live. They also accepted that their own deaths were required for life to continue.

It is only in our "civilized" society that death has become separated from life, and both life and death are feared rather than embraced by men. In our obsessive denial of death we also, unknowingly, destroy life. It is no coincidence that two of the primary by-products of civilization are armaments and addictions. Young men are no longer taught to become warriors, but rather are trained to be soldiers whose primary purpose is to kill other men.

Meditation master Chogyam Trungpa says that we must separate the life of the warrior from the destruction of war. "Warriorship here does not refer to making war on others," he says. "Aggression is the source of our problems, not the solution. Here the word 'warrior' is taken from the Tibetan *pawo* which literally means 'one who is brave.' Warriorship in this context is the tradition of human bravery, or the tradition of fearlessness." Trungpa concludes by saying, "Warriorship is not being afraid of who you are."

In rediscovering the ways of the original warriors—the hunter-gatherers—I believe I have found a key to unlock our own recovery from addictions, and to aid in the reemergence of mature masculinity and the healing of the planet.

The Warrior's Journey Home: Healing Men, Healing the Planet expands on what we have learned about individual recovery, offers new information on healing our relationships, and shows how we can broaden the meaning of recovery to include the whole planet. Developing mature masculinity also requires dealing with our addictions. Both types of recovery must occur before we can achieve health and wholeness: we must recover our lost manhood and recover from our debilitating addictions.

Herb Goldberg wrote, "The male has paid a heavy price for his masculine 'privilege' and power. He is out of touch with his emotions and his body. He is playing by the rules of the male game plan and with lemming-like purpose he is destroying himself—emotionally, psychologically and physically." When I first read these words, I cried. I felt that someone finally understood my pain and anger. We've come a long way since Goldberg wrote *The Hazards of Being Male* in 1976. The healing process, which began as a trickle, is now a sizable river that is getting larger each day. Many of us began our healing journey because someone close to us felt that we were in trouble. Increasingly now, we are taking charge of our own recovery.

Some of you may worry that joining with other men may entail denying your need for relationships with women. This is not true. An interval of separation from women is needed if we are to find our masculine selves. Grounded in the authentic experience of mature masculinity, we can begin to relate to women as loving equals.

As the original guardians of the animals and the land, men ought to feel a deep sense of grief and shame at what we are doing to the planet. Our true warrior spirit will increasingly be reflected in our willingness to protect and heal the earth.

John Seed, the Australian founder of the Rainforest Information Centre, tells of a meeting he had with a group of Australian Aborigines in Sydney. After the meeting, they stepped outside into the night air. The great city spread out before them. One of the native Australians asked, "What do you see? What do you see out *there*?"

John looked at the pulsating freeways, towers of anodized glass and steel, ships in the harbor, and replied, "I see a city, lights, pavements, skyscrapers ..."

The native Australian said quietly, "We still see the land. Beneath the concrete we know where the forest grows, where the kangaroos graze. We see where the platypus digs her den, where the streams flow. That city there ... it's just a scab. The land remains alive beneath it."[1]

Some of you, I know, may be concerned about my use of the term "warrior." You believe that we definitely *do not need* more war in the world, and would like to find a different metaphor for describing the emerging male. I agree that we need to end the threat of war on our planet; but I also believe that men need to reclaim the ancient spirit of the warrior and reclaim the power from those who would use the warrior mystique to draw people into battle. There is a crucial difference, I believe, between *soldiers* and *warriors*.

The soldier seeks to destroy an external enemy. The warrior seeks peace with the enemy within. To heal ourselves and the planet will take all our courage and strength. It is necessary that men develop and embrace the power of peaceful warriors.

A Note to Women

Although focused on men, this book is for you, too. One of the tragedies I see in my counseling practice is the increasing number of women who are suffering from what traditionally have been men's addictions. There is an increasing number of women addicted to cocaine, nicotine, sex, power, and gambling. (I see a similar trend with men who now suffer from bulimia, anorexia, valium addiction, and codependency.) Many women have been successful in shedding their old gender roles only to take on the most destructive aspects of the male role.

It is my hope that this book will help you heal from these addictions and also keep you from going down the same addictive path that has killed so many men. I do not see it as progress, for instance, that women can now die with men as fellow soldiers.

Healing the male spirit also involves the female spirit. Each woman has within her a masculine side that must be healed if she is to become whole. As you read of the men who talk about their lives in these pages, the male spirit in you may also be touched. Just as I recognized that the women's movement wasn't only for women, but had something important to teach me, I hope you will see that the men's movement is about your own healing as well. Truly, men's liberation and women's liberation are opposite sides of the same coin, and will be achieved together or not at all.

Some women are frightened of the men's movement. They fear that men who become even more powerful will use their power to hurt women. Many women know all too well that those who use their power to dominate others often take out the worst of their rage on women and children. As I hope you will see, domination and violence can result when men are abused and grow up feeling vulnerable and weak. Men who express power in positive ways are those who have healed their wounds and know how to nurture themselves and others. These men will be the true allies of women and children.

A Personal Note From the Author

My interest in recovery began in 1965 as I sat fascinated in the audience at U.C. Berkeley, listening to two men and two women talk about their history of drug addiction and how their lives had improved since joining a rehabilitation program called Synanon. Started in 1958 by Charles Dederich, a recovering alcoholic who had become sober in Alcoholics Anonymous (A.A.), Synanon used the recovery principles of A.A. to help drug addicts as well.

When Synanon announced that they were going to offer the "Synanon game," as their therapy groups were called, to interested students at the University, I immediately signed up. I had no idea what the Synanon game was, but I was impressed with the emotional honesty of the recovering addicts I'd heard speak, and on some deep level of my being I felt they had something to teach me.

After a year of involvement in these groups, I was shocked to discover that I, too, was an addict. My drug was not heroin or alcohol. It was women. I had to admit that my behavior was just as compulsive, out of control, and destructive as any drug addict's when I "fell in love." This discovery marked the beginning of my own recovery.

The men's movement began for me in the delivery room of Kaiser hospital, in November 1969. My wife was pregnant with our first child and I had spent the last nine hours coaching her in the Lamaze breathing techniques we had been taught. When I began the classes, I wasn't sure I wanted to be part of the birth process, afraid I might pass out at the sight of blood or become overly concerned with her pain and be more problem than support.

When she was wheeled into the delivery room and the doctor asked me to leave, I experienced a mixture of sadness and relief. Following doctor's orders, I dutifully squeezed my wife's hand, turned, and walked down the long hallway, toward the exit sign leading to the waiting room, to sit with the other expectant fathers. Yet, in the eternity of those few moments it took to make the short walk, something shifted in me. I felt a call from some deep part of myself—or maybe it was from the life preparing to come into the world. It was a call that could not be denied.

I turned around and walked back into the delivery room and took my place at the head of the table. There was no question of asking permission, no chance I would leave if asked. I was simply there. I felt a wonderful sense of calm come over me and unbelievable wonder as my son, Jemal, came into the world. My tears flowed freely as I joined in the magic of life and silently made a commitment to myself and my son that our relationship would be different than my father's had been with me. Following my internal sense of what was right rather than the dictates of external authority was the first step on my healing journey.

Wherever you are in the recovery process, just exploring or deeply involved, I encourage you to open yourself to the process outlined in this book. Take what is useful and leave the rest, and know that the knowledge is being offered with a great deal of love and appreciation for your willingness to embark on the journey.

I write the kind of books I like to read. I want a book to be personal and expressive, but also authoritative. I want to know what people actually do that works, not just the theory of what is supposed to work. If there are things that touch me, I like to explore them in greater depth and respond to the author.

Throughout the book I've used examples from my own life as well as from my therapy practice. Since my own experience is that of a white, middle-class, heterosexual male, most of my examples reflect that background. Yet I believe that much of what I say will speak to people of different classes, races, or sexual preference.

This book includes a bibliography for further reading, and a list of resources for getting more involved in men's issues, recovery issues, and planetary healing.

Since healing involves the emotions and spirit as well as the mind, I've included what I call "love darts" at the beginning of chapters and throughout the book. These are short sayings or quotes that have touched me and deepened my understanding. I recommend that you pause when you come to one, read it out loud or to yourself, and take a few moments to meditate on its possible relevance in your own life.

There are notes at the end of each chapter. Any reference sources not cited there can be found in the bibliography.

 It is not easy to find
happiness in ourselves,
and it is not possible to
find it elsewhere.

—Agnes Repplier,
The Treasure Chest

The People

Before telling you about the recovery process, I'd like to introduce you to some of the men whose experiences are interspersed throughout the book. They're all upper middle-class heterosexual males—but their experiences can easily be extrapolated to other economic and cultural lifestyles. All have gone through the process of recovery or are "on the path." You will hear more about their lives later, but, for now, a brief sketch may help you empathize with their healing journey.

Carlos. Thirty-seven, owns his own catering business, married with two small children. "I've used most all drugs, whatever was available, at various times in my life. Alcohol has often been a problem. Work has always been a major part of my life, and only recently have I seen my tendencies to work addictively. I was overweight growing up, and food has been a problem for as long as I can remember."

Daniel. Thirty-eight, computer salesman, divorced with one child. "The first addictions I dealt with were drugs and alcohol, which I had used since I was a kid. In my earlier days, narcotics were my drugs of choice, though I've used most everything at one time or another. I'm a compulsive worker, though I'm not sure I would call it an addiction, and I know I'm not ready to change it. More recently I've recognized my sexual addictions."

Ron. Forty-five, certified public accountant and small business consultant, married for the second time, with a teenage daughter and two-year-old son. "Work has been my primary addiction—being successful and making money. I've also become preoccupied with sex, mostly fantasies. In trying to please others, I've developed a lot of codependent symptoms and too easily give up my own needs in trying to please my wife and daughter."

Jamie. Forty-two, owns his own private elementary school. "I never felt I had any addictions until a friend recommended I attend Alanon meetings. The woman I had been living with finally joined A.A. to deal with her drinking, and I was going crazy trying to fix her. From Alanon, I learned about codependency, and realized I've spent my whole life taking care of women and children. Like my father, I've turned self-sacrifice into an addiction—and it's killing me."

Joseph. Thirty-three, organizational consultant, single. "I never would have considered myself an addict before I began in therapy. I was just an all-American boy who loved sex and worked his ass off to become successful. Only since I've been able to talk about the tremendous shame I've felt about all aspects of my sexual life, have I came to realize what a problem it was. It's only recently that I realized how much of my drive for success comes from boyhood rules about fear of failure that have kept me locked into work I don't liked."

Tony. Twenty-seven, attorney, single. "I started using drugs and alcohol when I was 13 or 14 and it progressed steadily. I wouldn't let myself believe I had a problem, even though I was getting wasted every weekend and I had drugs hidden all over my room and a few other places in the house. I probably would have died saying things were fine if my parents hadn't intervened when I was 20 and told me I needed to get into treatment or move out of the house."

Kevin. Fifty-three, licensed psychologist, real estate developer, divorced with three children. "My understanding of my addictions has changed over time. I first recognized I had a drinking problem, then learned about my compulsive work habits and my preoccupation with getting more and more money. Most recently I began to see that my sexual and romantic activities were also addictive."

Writing this book has been a delight. It has taken me into places I never dreamed I'd go and has deepened my love for myself, for you the reader, and for the planet that gives us all life. If you'd like to respond to anything I've written, I would be pleased to hear from you. I wish you peace, joy, and laughter on your journey.

Notes

1. Quote taken from Foreman, Dave, *Confessions of an Eco-Warrior*, Harmony Books, New York, 1991. p. 7.

1

The Rings of Addiction and the Ten Tasks of Mature Masculinity

 "Try not to become a man of success, rather become a man of value."
—Albert Einstein

It had been 20 years since Kevin first walked into my office. I could still remember the day. He had been referred originally by a mutual friend who was concerned about Kevin's drinking. When I came out to meet Kevin, I was greeted by a sandy-haired man in his early thirties, with restless blue eyes and a smile that seemed to hide deeper feelings. His handshake was firm, but his voice was shaky. "I've been drinking since I was a teenager," he told me during our first hour, "but I never thought much of it. Problem drinking was something that happened to someone else, not to a successful psychotherapist. I've done my damnedest to deny what my family and friends keep telling me, but now I know I need help." The two years of our intensive work together went by quickly.

Now, sitting in my office, having returned for one of our twice yearly "fine-tuning" sessions, Kevin looked younger than his 53 years. His air was quietly happy as he reflected back on his torment before be came for treatment, and the difficult process of recovery itself.

"You know, the thing that stands out for me," he commented, "is that people can trust me now." He stretched out his long legs and looked directly into my eyes—a complete contrast from the man I met so long ago. "When I first came to see you, I never could understand why people would come to me for help and then leave abruptly. I thought I was covering my own problems so well. I might have a drink or two during lunch, so I could face the pressures of the afternoon; but I took great pains to brush and gargle, and I was sure no one knew." Kevin at first laughed and shook his head as he recalled those earlier days, but then his face became serious.

"I never felt clean inside, and I guess people picked that up. Now there are fewer inconsistencies between what's going on inside and what I express on the outside. Things aren't perfect—I don't expect they ever will be; but it's wonderful to know that I don't have to hide who I am."

One of the advantages of having been a therapist for more than 25 years is that I can see people's progress over a long period of time. When I was just starting out in the field, I was sure that addictions could be "cured" in a year, or two at most. I was also naive and arrogant enough to believe that the recovery process began when the person first came into my office. Prior to that magic moment, the person was "sick"; after that moment, he was on a steady path to health and well-being.

Everything changed for me when I recognized that I, without being aware of it, had chosen to work with addictions because I needed to work on myself. The founders of A.A. believed that everyone is both the helper and the person needing help. It's been a tremendous burden on "professional helpers" that our training often teaches us to deny our own needs and to believe that we help best when we keep our own problems hidden.

"I've told you," Kevin emphasized, "that your help was absolutely crucial to my recovery, particularly your personal sharing of your own struggles. There was even a time when I didn't think I could survive without your support. But looking back on things now, I can see that there were many people who were crucial to my recovery. At the time, I was so angry and afraid, all I could see were people who didn't give a damn about me."

Kevin smiled wistfully. "One of the greatest gifts I ever received was my first wife telling me that she loved me but couldn't live with me another day. I never believed she'd do it, but the next day she left, taking my son and daughter with her. I cried for weeks and hated the friends who came by to comfort me. Remember how I stopped coming to see you after only four sessions?"

I nodded, remembering so many people, like Kevin, who had dropped out of therapy, only to be confronted with some new experience that resulted in a renewed commitment to their recovery.

"I'll never forget Matt," said Kevin, "the only friend who wouldn't put up with my sniveling after I'd drink myself into oblivion and wake up hung over the next day. His words were tough, but they were also loving, and they jarred me out of the self-pity I was lost in. 'Kevin, I love you too much to watch you kill yourself. I'm going to an A.A. meeting tonight. I'll pick you up at seven and I don't want to hear any excuses.'"

Kevin's eyes filled with tears as he remembered his friend. "You know he died of cancer, don't you? He was just 50. He overcame his alcoholism and helped so many others, but couldn't kick his addiction to cigarettes. I still miss him."

At the time when Kevin returned to therapy, he had been going to A.A. meetings for six months; and though he had stopped drinking, and his life was more stable, he still hadn't dealt with his feelings. Kevin didn't realize it, but his addictive tendencies had not been healed: they were simply redirected to his work. Kevin spoke of those years.

"I thought if I just stopped drinking, everything would be okay," he said with a sigh. "But putting a plug in the jug didn't solve my problems. I felt I had lost so much time during my drinking years that I had to catch up fast."

"Work became my new drug. I became just as obsessed with 'building my practice' as I had once been with drinking. But now, instead of people looking at me funny, they applauded and told me how great I was. In my spare time, I got into commercial real estate and really began to make money. My success in business seemed to make me more attractive to women. Without confronting the pain of losing my wife and family, I went after every woman I could find."

In addition to attending his A.A. group and doing therapy with me once a week, Kevin joined a Workaholics Anonymous group. "I learned I didn't have to do it all now, that there was actually plenty of time to accomplish everything I wanted to do. And, besides, what's the use of saving myself from death by drinking if I have a heart attack in the process?" Later, as our counseling progressed, Kevin joined SLAA (Sex and Love Addicts Anonymous) and began sorting out his addictive love life.

Once Kevin had stabilized and healed his intimate relationships, we were able to move ahead and begin working on the trauma from his past. We dealt with issues of low self-esteem, abandonment, and shame as we began moving slowly back through Kevin's family history.

After taking thousands of people through the recovery process, I have evolved a model that fits my own understanding of what works and has proven helpful to the people who have sought me out.

The Rings of Addiction and Recovery

Here is a model that describes my basic ideas about the layers of addiction that are present in all addicts, no matter what substance or practice they're addicted to.

This model summarizes my experience over many years of working with addiction. Visualizing the problem this way helps me understand how addictions develop, how they are related to one another, what kinds of addictions often accompany the male role, and what steps are necessary for recovery. Each ring represents a stage of the recovery process. Within each stage, there are

The Rings of Addiction

tasks that men must accomplish if they are to develop and deepen a mature version of their masculinity.

In subsequent chapters, each of the stages will be developed in more detail, drawing on the actual experiences of men in recovery. Addiction is the "dis-ease" of lost selfhood. The image I have is of a stone being thrown into the center of a calm, clear lake. As the stone breaks the surface, it causes rings to radiate out from the center. In like manner, the serenity of an individual is disturbed by traumatic events from childhood. The resulting behavior patterns are the individual's often misguided attempts to deal with the pain of his trauma, as well as to find the self that was lost. I summarize the process as follows:

The first ring represents the true self.

We are conceived as perfect beings, with all the ingredients necessary to be a loving, valuable, productive human being. Though our true self can be covered over and forgotten, it can never be lost.

The second ring represents the black hole.

Although we are born perfect, most of us come into a family in which our basic needs for safety and security are not well met. We come to believe that something essential is missing in us. In order to survive in our families, we "forget" our true self. In its place, we feel a terrifying emptiness, a hole where our sense of substance and worth once resided.

The third ring represents the band of shame.

Believing that we are damaged goods, we come to despise ourselves. Unable to believe that it is our parents—our life-support system—that is faulty, we blame ourselves. If we are hurt by our parents, we assume that it must be because we are so horrible.

The fourth ring represents the false self.

The experience of constant shame is so overwhelming that we would kill ourselves if we did not do something to dispel it. In order to survive, we develop an "as if" personality meant to convince others that we're okay. We contrive a pleasing mask which we hope will hide the horror of who we believe ourselves to be.

The fifth ring represents the addictive core.

Living within a black hole, surrounded by a band of shame, covered by a false self, we become very lonely. At this layer we finally lose hope about finding healing comfort by looking within. We come to believe that the way to soothe our pain is to look for something "out there." The hunger generated by this addictive core sends us on a journey away from our true selves in search of our missing parts.

The sixth ring represents the sex and love addictions.

Having lost trust in our ability to find love and acceptance within ourselves, we try to fulfill these needs through others. Believing that we need the attention of others to survive, we develop excessive attachments. Afraid to get hurt, on the other hand, we keep others at a distance. Our relationships often alternate between obsessive attachment and detachment

The seventh ring represents the inanimate objects of our desire.

Since people can, and often do, disappoint us, we try to fill the void and lessen the pain through relationships with inanimate things. We turn to drugs, alcohol, T.V., food, money, work, etc. It's as though we say to ourselves, "People can hurt me, but Miss Alcohol or Lady Cocaine will never let me down." When one thing fails, we try another. Ultimately, nothing works and we either continue feeding our addiction until we die or we begin to recover.

The rings of addiction and recovery give us a structure for understanding what is happening in our lives and what to do about it. They show us that addictions develop from the inside out, but must be treated from the outside in.[1] They also remind us that everyone with an "outer-ring" addiction must also deal with all the issues contained in the inner rings.

Thus, every alcoholic also has love addictions of one kind or another that he must heal. He must also deal with his addictive core, false self, band of shame, black hole, and true self. Though every sex and love addict may not have the outer-ring addictions, he still must deal with all those issues in the inner rings.

The Ten Tasks of Mature Masculinity

In the past, recovery programs rarely dealt with issues of masculinity, and men's programs rarely focused on recovery issues. I have found that both must be dealt with if men are to develop healthy and joyous lives. In working on my own issues, and with thousands of men over the years, I have found the following 10 tasks to be crucial for men.

Task 1. *Balance our desire to "do" with our need just to "be."*

For men on the recovery path, the first thing we need to learn to do is to resist the temptation to do something. We are forever trying to fix things before we've taken time to read the directions; we're always trying to remedy our family's problems before listening to hear what family members need. As John Bradshaw put it in his book *Homecoming*, we become "human doings," rather than "human beings."

In one of our first therapy sessions, Ron expressed the longing so many of us have just to *be*. "I've spent my whole life working; always producing, always fighting to stay ahead, forever pushing myself." Ron's eyes filled with tears and his face twisted with frustration. "Damn it, I'm tired of killing myself. I wish I could just rest, kick back, and be me. I want to be accepted for who I am, not what I do. But if I stopped, I'm afraid I'd lose the respect of my wife and kids."

Finding the balance is the first task of mature manhood.

Task 2. Understand and heal our confusion about sex and love.

"My intellect tells me that sex and love should be a normal part of life, like eating and sleeping," said Daniel in one of our therapy sessions. "But they're really charged for me—with excitement, desire, fear, longing. I'm never really comfortable with thoughts about sex, but I think about sex constantly; and I'm not even sure I know what love is. Women turn me on, just with a look—even women I know I shouldn't be having these thoughts about. My cock seems to have a will of its own."

Studies from the late '70s show that men think about sex an average of six times an hour; that's 750 times a week, not counting dreams.[2] By contrast, the average married couple has sex 1.5 times a week.[3] Given such a degree of male sexual frustration, it isn't surprising that *Playboy* and *Penthouse* are the most popular men's magazines, with combined sales of nearly 6 million copies a month, and pornography is a billion dollar growth industry. Yet men often feel guilty about sex, and wonder how to integrate their sexual desire with a need for love and intimacy. Our sex and love lives often feel separate from each other.

Understanding, accepting, and integrating sex and love into our lives is the second task of mature masculinity.

Task 3. Transform our ambivalent feelings toward women and children.

"I was making love with Judy," admitted Carlos, "feeling close and warm. Then she said something that set me off and I felt like hitting her. I don't understand where these feelings come from."

Most men know the perplexing feelings of loving, needing, and caring for a woman at one moment; then hating, hurting, and fearing her the next.

Some of us are also aware of the confusion we feel toward our children. They are at once the most precious and valuable beings in our lives, and also the focus of some of our most destructive rages.

Ron expressed his confusion and shame about his anger toward his two-year-old boy. "Most of the time, Jason is the love of my life. I cry with joy to watch him play. But at other times, a rage comes over me, and I feel like I want to hurt him. The thought that I might do something to him terrifies me."

Uncovering the roots of our ambivalence, and developing a foundation for love and support, is the third task of mature masculinity.

Task 4. Express our grief over the absence of our fathers, and risk getting close to other men.

The absence of strong and loving fathers in our lives is so pervasive that we often take it for granted. For many of us, it just seemed natural to have a dad who was gone, or one who was too tired and withdrawn after a day at the office to be emotionally available. For others, the presence of father was a source of fear. When we heard, "Wait til' your father gets home!" we knew we could expect a punishment, not a loving embrace.

Yet this absence leaves deep wounds, and our unwillingness to accept and deal with the depth of our pain ensures that our sense of longing remains unhealed. We grow up to become adult children forever trying to please a father who was never there. Our relationships with other men remain competitive and shallow, because we're never really relating to *them*.

Expressing our grief and learning to get close to other men is the fourth task of mature masculinity.

Task 5. Change our self-hatred to self-actualization.

With all the emphasis on men as the "top dogs" in society, the self-hatred that is so pervasive in men's lives often goes unnoticed. We may be told we are top dogs, but we are dogs nonetheless.

From our earliest nursery rhymes, in which we're told that little boys are made of "snips and snails and puppy-dog's tails," to our adult movies, in which men are portrayed as mindless killers, we are given ample reason to hate ourselves. We are rarely given healthy and wholesome male models to guide our paths of growth.

Relinquishing our self-hatred and learning to actualize ourselves is the fifth task of mature masculinity.

Task 6. Acknowledge our wounds, and heal our bodies and souls.

"I always wished my body would disappear," explained Tony, a tall, good-looking young man. "I was taught that the body was dirty, a necessary evil for supporting the loftier aspects of the human intellect." Tony continued with a look of pain and disgust. "My 'body image,' if you could call it that, was of a stone pedestal that held up my head. I needed to dust it off at times, but its only purpose was to support my brain."

We think of women as being the ones who have problems with body image, always trying to lose weight or look prettier. But men also feel ashamed of their physical beings. Shame, in all its various forms, manifests itself on a physical level. Men ignore their bodies and the feelings that go with them—which is one of the reasons why we die seven years earlier than women. Our spirit and soul cannot develop and thrive in a body that is damaged.

Acknowledging our wounds, and healing our bodies and souls, is the sixth task of mature masculinity.

Task 7. Uncover the roots of our basic insecurity.

We often seem so sure of ourselves that it is difficult to imagine how deeply insecure most men really are. "I don't think

I've ever felt secure in my life," confided Carlos. He looked up toward my office ceiling and sighed. "I've always felt a sense of impending doom, like no matter how hard I try or how fast I go, I won't make it. I never feel I'm good enough, and no one could really love me the way I am."

The key to understanding the insecurity men feel is to recognize that we have become separated from our physical world. We have lost our connection to a sense of place, to the experience of belonging somewhere. We feel like orphans cast out into a dangerous world. Getting to the roots of our basic insecurity is the seventh task of mature masculinity.

Task 8. *Acknowledge and heal our hidden childhood abuse.*

"My dad often spanked me with a board that I had to get myself," said Daniel. "If it was too small, he screamed at me and made me get a bigger one." Carlos remembers experiences with his mother: "She used to fondle my genitals when I was little, and fed me sweets whenever I felt sad—which messed up my attitudes about food."

As Carlos recounted his experience, he shared a view that is common among adults who were abused as children. "You know, I forgot that those things ever happened. When I did remember, I didn't see my mother's behavior as particularly abusive. It just seemed kind of normal, like whatever she did was probably done for my own good."

Accepting and working through the ways in which we were abused is the eighth task of mature masculinity.

Task 9. *Explore the origins of our violence and change our destructive behavior.*

"There are times when I lose it," Joseph told me. "I see myself as a gentle, peaceful man, but the truth is, I've been pretty abusive. With one of my girlfriends, I remember pushing her so hard, she fell on the floor. I've come close to date-raping two women— one I knew, and the other I picked up drunk at a bar. I've gotten so angry at times, I've choked my dog, Buddy, who I really love."

The violence men keep bottled up periodically explodes outward, but more often it is directed toward themselves. Joseph remembered becoming so enraged that he would break windows and furniture and even hit his head against the wall.

Getting to the roots of our violence, and changing our destructive behavior, is the ninth task of mature masculinity.

Task 10.   Return to the spirit of true warriors.

Our human ancestors have been on the planet for at least two million years. For 99 1/2 percent of human history, every man on the planet lived as a hunter-gatherer. The true warrior spirit is not to be found in the violent images of Rambo. It is not to be found in the latest technological innovations of the Pentagon. Rather it will be found by examining the outlook and experience of the ancient hunters.

We can learn from those few living exemplars of the hunting cultures that have survived into modern times. These include the Pygmies of the African rain forest, the !Kung San of the Kalahari Desert, the Australian and Tasmanian aborigines, the Eskimos, and the many tribes of native peoples of the Americas.

Reconnecting with the warrior spirit of our hunter-gatherer ancestors is the tenth task of mature masculinity.

What is Addiction?

When I began working in the field in 1965, addiction was a pretty straightforward and simple matter. It was seen as the compulsive desire to use a drug, most often alcohol or heroin. There were certain drugs that were considered to be "addictive." If people used such a drug, they would soon develop a physiological craving which would cause them to use more of the drug.

Now it's generally recognized that addiction involves more than just physiology and isn't at all restricted to the use of heroin or alcohol.

I think of addiction as the disease of lost selfhood. When people come in for help, I explore the ways in which they have lost their connection with seven aspects of the self:

1. *Physiological loss.* How is a person out of touch with his body and its normal functioning?

2. *Psychological loss.* How has the person lost touch with his sense of self-esteem?

3. *Familial loss.* In what ways was the family a person grew up in dysfunctional or abusive?

4. *Interpersonal loss.* Has the need for healthy friendships been replaced by an addictive peer group?

5. *Social loss.* How have social pressures—such as racism, sexism, or social isolation—limited support from the community in which a person lives?[4]

6. *Cultural loss.* How has life in a dominator/domesticator culture cut this man off from his partnership roots?

7. *Spiritual loss.* What are the ways in which this man has lost his connection with the spiritual dimension of life?

Craving for Ecstasy: Two Different Types of Addictions

According to anthropologist Angeles Arrien, there are two universal life energies, which she calls *dynamism* and *magnetism*. The dynamic life energy has to do with starting, initiating, setting things in motion. In shamanic cultures, dynamism is associated with sun energy; in oriental cultures, with *yang*. Jung called it the animus. Magnetic energy has to do with drawing in, receiving, opening, and deepening. In shamanic cultures, magnetism is associated with the energy of the moon; in oriental cultures, with *yin*; and in Jungian psychology, with the anima.[5]

In the introduction to their fascinating book, *Craving for Ecstasy*, Drs. H. Milkman and S. G. Sunderwirth lay the foundation for a more comprehensive understanding of addiction that links perfectly with Arrien's concepts of the dynamic and magnetic.

Addictions can be understood as falling into two categories, depending on whether the substances or activities involved speed up the nervous system or slow it down. The first group are categorized as *arousal* addictions, the second as *satiation* addictions.

Cocaine is the prototypical arousal drug, and heroin is the prototypical satiation drug. Someone on cocaine moves fast, talks fast, thinks fast. When he's high, he's in continual motion. By contrast, the person under the influence of heroin looks half asleep. He nods out. His voice is dreamy and slurred. People who crave satiation drugs and activities are trying to find a way to relax and escape.

Those who become excessively reliant on satiation are liable to use depressant drugs, such as heroin, tranquilizers, or sleeping pills; gorge themselves on food; get hooked on destructive relationships; or watch too much T.V. Their compulsive search for tranquility is a way of maintaining control over their own hostility or other overwhelming emotions. Like babies, such people want to pull all the energy into themselves, metaphorically curling up into a fetal position. Satiation junkies are often introverts who have trouble relating easily to large groups of people.

On the other side of the coin, the arousal or excitement addict is a compulsive thrill-seeker. In Arrien's terms, he has over-developed his "dynamic" qualities. His energy is pushing outward, confronting a world that is perceived as threatening. Arousal types tend to compensate for deep-seated feelings of inferiority by repeatedly trying to demonstrate their physical prowess or intellectual ability. They are often extroverts who thrive on the intensity and excitement of large crowds, parties, and public events.

In addition to getting hooked on such drugs as cocaine, amphetamines, and caffeine, arousal junkies often get hooked on sex, gambling, excessive work, and the preoccupation with making more and more money.

Alcohol is a drug that seems to be *both* stimulating and relaxing for different men, or for the same man at different times. This is one the reasons why it is such a difficult drug to manage for so many people in our society.

Men are traditionally trained to deal with life stresses by overemphasizing the dynamic. In our desire to get high and escape the stresses of life, we most often develop arousal addictions. Yet, as you'll see in subsequent chapters, men are increasingly developing satiation addictions that have traditionally been associated with women.

Twenty-eight Years of Recovery: Four Significant Truths

In looking back at my own recovery and the recovery of the people I've worked with for over a quarter of a century, there are four truths that stand out for me. First, everyone is addicted to something. Second, there should be earlier intervention and lengthier work than is commonly practiced in the therapeutic community. Third, addiction is not all negative, but has a positive aspect that must be acknowledged. Fourth, healing intimate relationships and healing the planet are just as important as healing the individual.

Let's look at these four issues in more depth.

Everyone Is Addicted to Something (or Someone)

Traditionally it's been assumed that addiction was a problem for a small minority of the population. Heroin addicts and alcoholics, we felt sure, were irredeemable members of society, and most likely were to be found among ethnic minorities. Cocaine addicts and workaholics, we knew, were all rich and famous, or striving to become rich and famous. Addicts were always seen as someone other than us.

With this view of addiction so prevalent, it isn't surprising that less than 10 percent of people with addiction problems have sought help. And those were only for the most serious manifestations of addiction. Only about 1 percent sought help for less serious problems.[6]

Increasingly we have come to recognize that addiction is not a disease of the few, but is symptomatic of our modern world: it affects us all. There are now more than 250 different 12-step recovery programs dealing with addictions, from alcohol to work, sex to violence. For many in the recovery community, it is no longer a question of "Are you addicted?" but rather, "What are your addictions?" We can no longer point the finger at "them," but must look at ourselves. To paraphrase the wisdom of that well-known social philosopher Pogo, "We have met the addict and he is us."

We Need to Begin Sooner and Work Longer

The first step of all 12-step programs is to acknowledge that we are powerless over our addiction—that our lives have become unmanageable. This corresponds to Step 8 in my process, which is, I believe, that for most recovery begins much too late. If we are convinced that addiction is a rare phenomenon affecting only someone else—the poor and dispossessed, or the rich and famous—it is easy for us to ignore the early warning signs of our own unhappiness, assuming that it's been caused by something else.

An analogy of going to the dentist may be helpful. Let's say that we believe tooth decay to be a problem only for a tiny minority of the population. We also believe that if you get tooth decay, your life is ruined, but feel that it's inappropriate to seek help until your teeth are so bad you can't eat anymore. Few people would go to the dentist if these beliefs were commonly held.

In reality, we view tooth decay as a near universal problem, and treat it very differently. There is no stigma attached to going to a dentist, since everyone is seen as being at high risk. People are encouraged to go to a dentist for regular checkups rather than waiting for serious problems to manifest themselves. Efforts are directed toward preventing problems before they occur and recognizing problems while they are still minor.

It's really the same story with addiction. We don't have to wait until a person is in crisis and ready to admit that he's powerless before treating him. We can help people look at the process much earlier, before addictions are entrenched and denial is strong.

Much of our current treatment is organized around what insurance will pay for rather than on what people need. Thus we have treatment limited to 28-day residential programs with a one-year follow-up. Many veterans of the addictions field recognize that recovery is a long-term process. In my approach, I talk about stages of recovery that occur over a period of seven years and longer.

There Are Positive Sides of Addiction

At first, most clients think it is ludicrous when I ask them to tell me all the positive things their addiction does for them. They see their addiction as a cancer—something that is not part of them, and needs to be removed quickly and completely. Yet after we talk more, and they begin to see how tightly they have held on to their habit, treating it like a cherished lover or friend, they begin to see that their addiction means more to them than they originally had thought.

Kevin broke down in tears when he could accept that his relationship with alcohol was not all bad. "I had turned to her in good times and in bad. She was there for me when no one else was. Even though things became destructive in the end, we had some wonderful times together. It was like thinking about an old lover. I knew we could never again be together, that we were destroying each other; but I still mourned the loss and cried for the love that never would be."

Clients almost always express a tremendous sigh of relief when I tell them they don't have to hate their addiction in order to move beyond it. In fact, hating it robs us of the ability to see it clearly and learn what need the addiction served in our lives. Rather than ripping it out, we can respectfully remove it, replacing it with something that will serve us better.

As men get more deeply into the recovery process, they often find confronting their addiction to be a modern rite of passage. They are required to face the idea of death and the loss of their old way of life. As is the case with all rites of passage, the ultimate result is rebirth into a new way of being. Recovery is, for many, a spiritual journey to wholeness.

In a society that has lost its rituals of initiation, recovery is one of the few passages available that men can use to cut away the dead wood of their civilized prison and return to the wild path of the warrior. Addiction can be seen as both a refusal to be "a good little boy" and a misguided attempt to find an authentic ground of being. Just as addiction is the disease of lost selfhood, recovery gives us the opportunity to journey home.

Individual, Relationship, and Planetary Recovery Are Interdependent

The recovery movement has evolved through three periods. Between 1935 (the year in which Alcoholics Anonymous was founded) and 1985, the focus was primarily on individual recovery. The question was, "How can I heal myself?" The second stage began around 1985 as we focused on family issues and codependency. The question then was, "How can I heal my one-to-one relationships?" We focused our attention on the father wound, our broken connections with our mothers, brothers, sisters, children, and mates. In the 1990s, we've reached the third stage as we begin to focus on our addictive society. Now the question is, "How can we heal our fragile planet?"

Individual recovery will never be complete until we heal our interpersonal relationships. Individual and relationship recovery is useless if we continue to destroy our planetary life-support system. All three are necessary for total recovery.

As an example, our eating practices affect the planetary health as well as our personal health. The same transnational corporations that push alcohol and nicotine on young people in the U.S. are cutting down the rain forests in the Amazon. It does little good to recover from our drinking problem only to die because of the depletion of the ozone layer.

Just as Martin Luther King, Jr., realized that freedom for African-Americans required that he focus beyond the plight of individual men to the political and economic forces that were sending them off to the war in Vietnam, so too recovery requires that we confront the social forces that feed the machine of addiction.

What I've Learned on the Recovery Path

Over the past 28 years, I have worked with over 10,000 people, perhaps 70 percent of them men. It has been a privilege to be part of these people's lives: I've received from them at least as much and likely *more* than I've given. There are a few people with whom I've kept in touch over the entire period, and many whom I've known for 10 to 20 years. Being able to see the recovery process over a relatively long timeframe, I've come to a number of conclusions.

1. Recovery is possible for everyone.

There aren't any problems, no matter how severe, any addictions, no matter how entrenched, that cannot be healed. This reality came home to me when I worked with a man who had multiple addictions and had been the victim of severe sexual abuse as a child. In the course of his therapy, he revealed the intense guilt he felt over having killed a man in a fight, and his shame at having repeatedly abused his own daughter. Treatment was lengthy, but he did recover.

2. Recovery is a lifelong process.

Recovery from addiction is unlike recovery from illness, in that it has a powerful spiritual component. It is more like a journey that we have the opportunity to undertake. A man's recovery from addiction often begins as a rite of passage, and continues as a quest to find his lost self.

3. Recovery is not an event, but a journey through specific stages.

Just as there are certain developmental stages that a person goes through when moving from infancy to toddlerhood, from childhood to adolescence, so too there are stages of recovery. Completing each stage is like peeling off another layer from an onion as we move closer and closer to the nub at the center.

4. Manhood is not achieved simply through biological maturation. There are tasks that all males must accomplish if they are to become authentic, mature men.

In traditional cultures, these tasks were taught to young men by their male elders. In contemporary society, where male initiation is often lacking, men grow up feeling like adult children rather than mature adults. Identifying and completing a specific set of tasks, described later in this book, allows men to develop a sense of mature masculinity.

5. Developing mature masculinity and recovering from addictions are opposite sides of the same coin.

The men's movement and the recovery movement have often been treated separately. I believe them to be intimately related: they must be considered in tandem. Addictions develop as a result of the wounds we experienced as men. As we reverse the effects of our addictions, we also reclaim and heal our masculine selves. As we deepen our experience of manhood, we are impelled to confront and heal our addictions.

6. Each individual is unique: personal timing must be respected in healing a man's addictions.

One person may go quickly through the stages of recovery and tasks of mature masculinity, progressing systematically. Another person may take much longer. He may go from stage one to stage four, then back to three, returning finally to one. He may have many detours in between. There is no right or wrong way to experience recovery.

7. Everything is part of recovery. We can't really "relapse."

I used to think of recovery as being comprised of all the "good" things we do for ourselves—going to meetings, being in therapy, learning about health, and so on. If someone used drugs again, or started getting back into old patterns, I judged them as being outside the recovery process.

But I've found that we learn as much from our slips as we do from our successes. There is a saying that summarizes this view: "If things don't go right, they go left." There is no "good" and "bad" in recovery. All our experiences are part of the process of healing.

8. There are inherent differences between men and women.

In a dominator culture like ours, where "different" often means "inferior," it is not surprising that many people believe inherent gender differences simply don't exist beyond the obvious physiological differences between men and women. But many other men and women feel afraid and tense in one another's presence. The "battle of the sexes" is a painful reality for them: the opposite sex feels like an enemy. There are both men and women who wish that gender differences would disappear to the extent that the sexual dimorphism of our species will allow: that we could all just be people.

And yet we feel the powerful energy of "maleness" and "femaleness" whenever men and women are in each other's presence, and often when groups of men or women are gathered together.

I believe that the resolution to gender conflict is not to be found in developing a unisex approach to life, but rather in recognizing the mystery of male and female, and changing the dominator culture to one of partnership. Only in this way can we allow the differences to enrich our relations, not stifle them.

9. As men, we must honor and develop our masculine functions before we can integrate our feminine functions.

Many men have recognized that there are destructive aspects to the male role. Psychologist Shepherd Bliss calls these "toxic masculinity." In our desire to heal, many of us have tried to find health by drawing on the feminine. If the male role is destructive, we reasoned, maybe women have a better sense of what is healthy. The result has been a poisonous dependency on women, in which we have become locked into destructive relationships and taken on some of the toxic sides of femininity.

Rather than rejecting our masculinity in favor of the feminine, we must go deeper inside ourselves to reconnect with the source of our authentic manhood. This can only be done in the company of other men. Having reclaimed our manhood, we can then enter into healthy relationships with women (who have, ideally, done their own healing in the company of other women), and integrate the feminine into our lives.

10. Although men and women have much in common in their recovery, there are also important differences.

I have found that men and women go through the same stages of recovery. However, the genders differ in the issues that each must confront while moving through these stages. For example, in working through intimacy dysfunction, men often become addicted to sex, while women tend to get hooked on relationships. In going through the band of shame, men often ask, "Am I sufficiently tall and strong?" while women will ask, "Am I sufficiently thin and pretty?" Each gender has different tasks to accomplish in healing their wounds and returning to their true selves.

Before beginning the first stage of your recovery journey, you need to go back in time, back thousands of years, to the point at which the human species started on the road to addiction. Having located where we got off track, you can begin your search for the key to your healing, the key that will open the door to your true warrior spirit.

Notes

1. This is a general rule of thumb and, like all rules, has exceptions. Sometimes a sexual addiction, for instance, must be treated first, since it is so serious or life-threatening that it needs immediate attention. Sometimes we need to treat an outer-ring addiction at the same time as an addiction represented by a more interior ring, since both are equally serious.

2. Shanor, K. (1978) *The Shanor Study: The Sexual Sensitivity of the American Male.* New York: Dial Press.

3. Masters, W., V. Johnson, and R. Kolodny (1985) *Human Sexuality*, 2nd. ed., Boston: Little Brown & Company, p. 247. In the first year of marriage, frequency of intercourse is 3.7 times per week, dropping to 2.2 times in the fourth year, and 1.5 in the sixth, continuing to fall with time together and age.

4. I first began developing this broadened definition of addiction in the 1970s. My first published description of these ideas was in an article titled "Our Anti-Drug Abuse Programs: Pathologies of Defense," in the journal *ExChange*, 1:6, August 1973.

5. Arrien, A. "Healing All Our Relationships" (audio tape). Information on ordering tapes and articles can be obtained by writing to: Angeles Arrien, The Tarot Handbook, P.O. Box 2008, Petaluma, CA 94952.

6. See Cahalan, D., and B. Treiman (1976) *Drinking Behavior, Attitudes, and Problems in Marin County, California*. Berkeley, CA: Social Research Group, School of Public Health, University of California, and Cahalan, D., and R. Room (1974) *Problem Drinking Among American Men*, New Brunswick, NJ: Rutgers Center For Alcohol Studies.

2

When Men Stopped Being Warriors and Became Killers

 "Civilized society in general has been like a rabid dog. Its bite infects the healthy even though it contains the germ of its own destruction."
—Andrew Bard Schmookler

In Search of the Warrior Spirit

"The first fact we need to know about men," says marriage and family therapist Dr. Jonathan Kramer, "is that men have the warrior spirit."

What is the warrior spirit? The answer can't be found in our modern soldier, nor in the spirit of such cultural icons as Rambo. Rather we must look for the warrior spirit in the ancient hunters: it is a cooperative, reciprocal, egalitarian spirit rooted in a sacred respect for all life.

Richard Strozzi Heckler possesses a fourth-degree black belt in aikido and a doctorate in psychology. His 25 years of research about the tradition of men as warriors has taken him from the study of Australian aborigines to the training of army Green Berets. In his most recent book, *In Search of the Warrior Spirit*, he says that warriors throughout human history shared the following virtues: heroism, courage, selflessness, service to others, personal authenticity, lifelong mastery and skill, and a love and reverence for the earth and all its creatures.

Heckler says that these traditional warrior virtues were first found in the behavior of men during the time before agriculture and the domestication of animals, when all men were hunters. The true heart of the warrior was developed during the hunt, when men were at the center of the twin mysteries of life and death, in spiritual union with the animal they pursued.

Robert Bly's book *Iron John* draws the connection between the ancient hunters and the male archetype which he calls the "Wild Man." In ancient times, the Wild Man was known as the Lord of the Animals: "[he] has been associated with the initiation of young men for at least fourteen thousand years."

In retelling the myth of Iron John, Bly says that when the boy goes off with the Wild Man, he learns these things: "That sexual energy is good; that the hunting instinct, which mammals possess without shame, is good; that animal heat, fierceness, and passionate spontaneity is good; and that excess, extravagance, and going with Pan out beyond the castle boundaries is good too."

Bly is saying that this deeply embedded male spirit must be sought outside the bounds of civilization, out in the wild. When men reconnect with the spirit of the Wild Man, they also reconnect with the spirit of the ancient hunters, the first warriors.

John Stokes is a modern-day tracker who gives workshops with Robert Bly. He calls on men to return to the spirit of the original warriors.[1] "Wake up," he says. "Men have traditionally been the guardians of the earth. We need to define the new warriors. Men are now called on to be warriors for the earth. You love this earth so much you would defend it to the death."

In order to recapture the spirit of the warrior, we must go back in time before the advent of agriculture, when all people on the earth were hunter-gatherers.

The Affluent Partnership Society

We generally refer to our early ancestors as hunter-gatherers or gatherer-hunters, since it was the gathering activities of the women that brought in most of the food. A broader, more comprehensive name for this arrangement is "affluent partnership society," since equality, cooperation, and abundant leisure are such key elements in its success. Riane Eisler, author of *The Chalice and the Blade*, contrasts two models that describe social systems. "The first, which I call the *dominator* model, is what is popularly termed either patriarchy or matriarchy—the *ranking* of one half of humanity over the other. The second, in which social relations are primarily based on the principle of *linking* rather than ranking, may best be described as the *partnership* model. In this model—beginning with the most fundamental difference in our species, between male and female—diversity is not equated with either inferiority or superiority."

For hunter-gatherers in the past, as well as those alive now, men and women had quite different roles, yet neither dominated the other. Women generally gathered food while men hunted game animals. Basic needs were generally well met and there was ample leisure time.

In their anthology, *Man the Hunter*, anthropologists Richard Lee and Irvin Devore describe the lives of typical hunter-gatherer women and men. "A woman gathers on one day enough food to feed her family for three days, and spends the rest of her time resting in camp, doing embroidery, visiting other camps, or entertaining visitors from other camps. For each day at home, kitchen routines, such as cooking, nut cracking, collecting firewood, and fetching water, occupy one to three hours of her time. This rhythm of steady work and steady leisure is maintained throughout the year."

Like the women, the men generally go out in groups: "The hunters tend to work more frequently than the women, but their schedule is uneven. It is not unusual for a man to hunt avidly for a week, and then do no hunting at all for two or three weeks.... During these periods, visiting, entertaining, and especially dancing are the primary activities of the men."

For males, the hunt for large animals was not just a matter of getting food, but was a sacred ritual and a key to manhood. Social scientist Paul Shepard tells us in The Tender Carnivore and the Sacred Game, "The whole of man's hunting endeavor must be understood as a symbolic, cultural, and social activity. Though he is a highly capable social predator on large, dangerous mammals, he is singularly without the nutritional necessity of eating meat. He is a polished runner and stalker who eats meat as a sacrament."

If, as many theorists think, true affluence is measured by the absence of need and the enjoyment of extensive leisure time, then the hunter-gatherers are, as anthropologist Marshall Sahlins called them, the original affluent society.

The children of the hunter-gatherer societies led what many modern psychologists would consider idyllic lives. In the first two years of life, the infant is held upright, close to its mother's body. The child is either carried in the mother's arms or in a sling. In these formative years, the baby suckles frequently; in its upright position, it sees and hears the world the mother experiences. The mother is totally responsive to the infant's needs, even while she herself socializes and works with other women.

Anthropologists believe that because the hunter-gatherer woman shares these early years of motherhood with other adults, she feels neither isolated nor deprived of her responsibility, unlike most modern women. Because the mother is happy, the child is happy, and this becomes the basis for a sense of personal security that most hunter-gatherers carry all through their lives.

At the age of three or four, children are weaned from the breast and join other children in small play groups which are closely supervised by adults. The group may consist of from nine to twelve children, ranging in ages from three to thirteen. Because these groups are made up of both boys and girls with a wide variety of ages and skill levels, competitive activities are all but impossible. Like adults, the children learn that cooperation rather than competition is the rule.

Older children tend to look after the younger ones. Since there is continuous contact between adults and children, the children learn not from formal, deliberate lessons, but by watching and imitating the adults. Children become adults, and take on adult responsibilities, between the ages of fourteen and sixteen. Boys begin going out with the men to hunt; girls start going out with the women to gather.

In hunter-gatherer societies, there is not only a healthy partnership between the people, but between the people and the land. Since they are nomadic, their movements ensure that their animal, fruit, nut, and vegetable supplies will never be depleted through overharvesting. Anthropologists estimate that the San peoples of the Kalahari Desert, for instance, have lived in the same area, in balance with nature, for as long as 40,000 years. I shudder to think how much damage I have seen in my own neighborhood since the time I grew up there, a mere 40 years ago.

In *The Tender Carnivore and the Sacred Game*, Paul Shepard describes those who lived in the affluent partnership society: "Although it has long been fashionable to describe it so, the world of the hunting and gathering peoples is not a vale of constant demonic threat and untold fears. It is a life of risk gladly taken, of very few wants, leisurely and communal, intellectual in ways that are simultaneously practical and esthetic. Most pertinent to our time, it is a life founded on the integrity of solitude and human sparseness, in which men do not become a disease on their environment but live in harmony with each other and with nature."

After a lifetime of study, anthropologist Richard Lee concluded in *Man the Hunter*, "To date, the hunting way of life has been the most successful and persistent adaptation man has ever achieved."

Twelve thousand years ago, the entire world population was less than 10 million, roughly the present population of Moscow, and all were hunter-gatherers. Yet, at the same time that these affluent partnership societies were at their peak, events were taking place that would alter the course of history and mark the beginning of the end for hunter-gatherer societies throughout the world.

The Rise of Civilization and the Beginnings of War and Addiction

About 10 to 12 thousand years ago in the old-world area from Turkey to the Caspian basin, and south to the Red Sea and Palestine, the hunting-gathering way of life began to shift. Rather than relying solely on what the earth provided, people began to domesticate animals, using their milk and meat for food. They also began to gather the seeds of some of the wild plants they had been eating and found that they could grow them and have a more abundant food supply. These changes were almost imperceptible at first, occurring over a few thousand years, but they represented a fundamental change in the way humans related to themselves and the world.

We think of the beginning of agriculture as an invention of people who had evolved far enough to develop this wonderful innovation. However, there is ample evidence to show that hunter-gatherers had long had the intelligence and skill to domesticate plants and animals. They simply chose not to do it.

No one knows what prompted the first people to decide to alter their relationship with nature—to manipulate the plants and animals to satisfy human needs, rather than living with what nature offered. Some believe that climatic changes caused traditional food supplies to diminish. My own belief is that the phenomenon represented a loss of spiritual connection with life.

With the shift from hunting-gathering to domestication, there was also a change in religious philosophy. The hunter-gatherer cultures saw human beings as equal partners with all of the natural world. Contrast this view with that of our more modern religion, "And God said, Let us make man in our image, after our likeness: and let them have dominion over the fish of the sea, and over the fowl of the air, and over the cattle, and over all the earth, and over every creeping thing that creepeth upon the earth."

It must have required a great deal of trust to believe that the animals would always be there, that edible roots would always be found underground, that humans could be partners with nature. It's easy to imagine that some people got scared—that they lost faith in the abundance of the universe.

It must have seemed quite innocent at first, and certainly not something that could cause problems. What could be bad about having more food available for the people? We do know that domestication produced the first surpluses. Hunter-gatherers sought food when they needed it, but didn't acquire extra. For the first time, with domestication, people created more than they needed at any one time. They began to "save for a rainy day."

Now men needed storage facilities to keep the grains safe. They needed to build walls to keep the animals from running off, and they needed walls around the community to protect against those who would steal what had been saved. They no longer migrated throughout their territory, but needed to remain close to their crops. Finally, armed men were required to defend the new towns.

Population size increased greatly as people ate more and reproduced more and became more settled. Feeding ever larger populations required more and more exploitation of the land and animals. The cycle continues to this day.

Anthropologist Richard Leakey and biologist Roger Lewin describe what happened when we gave up our hunting-gathering way of life. There occurred, they said in *Origins*, "a dramatic alteration in the relationship people had both with the world around them and among themselves. The hunter-gatherer is a part of the natural order; a farmer necessarily distorts that order. But more important, sedentary farming communities have the opportunity to accumulate possessions, and having done so they must protect them. This is the key to human conflict, and it is greatly exaggerated in the highly materialistic world in which we now live."

Although the reason for the shift from the hunter-gatherer way to domestication is unclear, what's certain is that once the Pandora's box of civilization was opened in one place, its contents spread rapidly throughout the world. It seems that the majority of hunting-gathering peoples did not choose to adopt a domesticating way of life when it became available. When they didn't join the dominant society, they were killed.

Dominator societies, which came to characterize more and more of human life, systematically destroyed the older partnership societies. In *The Primitive Views of the World*, anthropologist Stanley Diamond calls hunter-gatherers "conscripts to civilization, not volunteers." He concludes that "no primitive society has gone to civilization as to a greater good."

Once the first dominator society was born, the violent way of life it demanded spread throughout the world. The psychologist and social analyst Andrew Bard Schmookler reminds us that once one element in society chooses the dominator approach, it will spread throughout the entire society. "Power is like a contaminant," he says in *The Parable of the Tribes*, "a disease, which once introduced will gradually yet inexorably become universal in the system of competing societies."

The birth of civilization also brought us alcohol and drug abuse. It's no surprise that alcohol and drug use were virtually absent during the millenia when our human ancestors lived in partnership with nature. Anthropologist Carlton Coon says, "Before outsiders began bothering them, the vast majority of hunting and gathering peoples were notably free from the use of habit-forming drugs."

It is often said that if you want to get a glimpse of people's true priorities, not just what they profess, you should take a look at how they spend their money. The eminent scientist Carl Sagan tells us, "every year, the world spends one trillion dollars on armaments. In addition, the world spends on illegal narcotic drugs something like half a trillion dollars every year. That is capital otherwise unavailable to the human species. We have decided to spend it on war and drugs."[2]

If we add to the half trillion dollars we spend on illegal narcotic drugs the money we spend on alcohol, nicotine, gambling, pornography, and other forms of addictive escape, I'm sure that the price tag for all our addictions would exceed the trillion dollars we spend on war each year.

Although we can point to a great many valuable things that civilization has brought us, we must be willing to open our eyes. The primary, even though unintended, legacy of civilization has been *violence and addiction*.

Civilization: The Worst Mistake in the History of the Human Race

Without knowing it, the first agriculturists were changing the way in which they viewed the world and themselves. Hunter-gatherers saw themselves as equal partners with the plants, animals, and nonliving parts of the world. They were part of nature, totally embedded within it. They saw themselves as guests, rather than masters. They trusted nature to take care of their needs and therefore didn't fear for the future or need to accumulate "more."

Instead of looking at nature in all its sacred beauty, with the dawn of civilization we began to distill, dismiss, discard and destroy nature. We became interested only in those things that we could use. The rest we threw away.

In domesticating plants, civilized society concentrated on those that produced a large yield, were easily stored, and would last a long time. Other plants came to be viewed as useless weeds that needed to be destroyed. Animals were treated the same way. We bred sheep, cows, chickens, and pigs to produce the greatest amount of edible meat. "Wild" animals were seen as a nuisance; their habitats were destroyed to make room for crops; and they were killed if they preyed on domestic animals. A wolf or a spotted owl thus becomes less valuable than a cow or a chicken, with less of a right to live. Man was suddenly at the center of this hierarchy, occupying its most elevated position.

Pulitzer Prize-winning poet Gary Snyder captures the spirit of the difference between the wild energy of the warrior-hunter and the destructive energy of the civilizing farmer. In a poem called "Spel Against Demons," he says:

> the man who has the soul of the wolf
> knows the self-restraint
> of the wolf
> aimless executions and slaughterings
> are not the work of wolves and eagles
> but the work of hysterical sheep ....[3]

With our romantic view of the family farm, it is difficult to accept the dark side of agriculture. We picture pastoral scenes of contented cows mooing in the fields while happy children play in the hay waiting for Father to come in from his joyous day plowing and planting. Mother is waiting and smiling, having just finished preparing a wondrous feast on her woodburning stove in the vast and hospitable kitchen.

Although this scene may still ring true in some quarters, the reality of the agricultural way of life can be quite different.

"When men cultivate plants and domesticate animals," says Paul Shepard, "their attention is turned to inbreeding. The husbandry system, whose forms underlie the foundations of modern thought, excludes wild nature as chaotic, other, and evil."

The way of life that began with the domestication of plants and animals has reached its zenith with the advent of modern technology. In our desire to see only the good sides of our technological revolution, we have failed to see how totally alienated we have become from nature.

"Where evolution was once an interactive process between human beings and a natural, unmediated world," says Jerry Mander, author of *In the Absence of the Sacred: The Failure of Technology & the Survival of the Indian Nations*, "evolution is now an interaction between human beings and our own artifacts. We are essentially co-evolving with ourselves in a weird kind of intraspecies incest."

For the last 10 thousand years or so, we have been trying to alter and dominate the natural environment and bring it under our control. Our efforts have not produced a better world. Paul Shepard calls the results of our handiwork "Genetic Goofies." Since hearing the term, I've never been able to look at a cow, a car, or a chainsaw without a slight shudder.

An unbiased observer of our "civilized" move to agriculture and domestication might conclude, as did Jared Diamond, one of the world's leading physiologists, that it was "the worst mistake in the history of the human race."[4]

From I-Thou to I-It: From Connection to Addiction

The core experience of the hunter-gatherers is that they love their world. The core experience of the addict is that the world is there to be used.

The philosopher Martin Buber describes two kinds of human relationships: I-It and I-Thou. In relation to nature, ourselves, and God, I-It sees us as separate. Others are to be used for our benefit. I-Thou sees us as involved in a sacred relationship of communion. Others are to be respected and cherished. As Buber says, "Love is responsibility of an I for a Thou."

Hunter-gatherers lived in an I-Thou relationship to their whole world. "The Indians," writes Joseph Campbell in *The Power of Myth*, "addressed all of life as a 'thou'—the trees, the stones, everything." He goes on to suggest to us, "You can address anything as a 'thou,' and if you do it, you can feel the change in your own psychology. The ego that sees a 'thou' is not the same ego that sees an 'it.'"

Campbell goes on to comment, "The Indian relationship to animals is in contrast to our relationship to animals, where we see animals as a lower form of life. In the Bible we are told that we are the masters. For hunting people, the animal is in many ways superior. A Pawnee Indian said: 'In the beginning of all things, wisdom and knowledge were with the animal. For Tirawa, the One Above, did not speak directly to man. He sent certain animals to tell mankind that he showed himself through the beast. And that from them, and the stars and the sun and the moon, man should learn.'"

Contrast the hunter's view of the animals he kills for food with the modern process described in John Robbin's magnificent book, *Diet for a New America*, as terrified, caged animals are killed in factories.

The animals [have] their throats slit, and then—
with tongues hanging limply out of their mouths—
their bodies are unceremoniously hooked behind the
tendons of their rear legs and are swung up into the
air onto the overhead track, which moves them
through the killing room like bags of clothes on a
dry cleaner's motorized rack.

The birth of agriculture and animal husbandry ushered in a shift in human relationships from I-Thou to I-It. Relationships that once were whole became fragmented.

Treating the animals as an it rather than a thou was particularly destructive to the true warrior spirit of men. For thousands of years the animals were men's respected adversaries. When we bred the wildness out of the animals, we lost touch with the wild man in us. Cut off from our own spiritual roots, we could more easily kill other men. Having lost connection with the spiritual values of the hunter, we could more easily embrace the material values of the soldier. Drugs, used as an escape from the pain of our lost selves, became our frequent companions.

The first city-states of Mesopotamia began to expand about 7,000 years ago. Land, which was once seen as sacred, was now a thing to be used, owned, and fought over. The men were taught that it was their duty to go off and kill other men to defend and protect those who owned the land. What would a man, a hunter-warrior genetically programmed to honor life, have to do to become a killer? He would have to cut off his feelings. Drugs, used not as a sacrament but as a painkiller, were necessary.

"Spirit in its human manifestation," says Buber, "is a response of man to his Thou. Spirit is not in the I, but between I and Thou. It is not like the blood that circulates in you, but like the air which you breathe." We are reminded that *spiritus* is the Latin root for the verb "to breathe."

Those who have lost their true spiritual connection attempt to substitute "spirits" in alcohol and drugs for the real thing. But this misguided attempt to relate to a drug does not satisfy man's deeper hunger for a true spiritual commitment. "Man lives in the spirit," says Buber, "if he is able to respond to his Thou. He is able to, if he enters into relation with his whole being."

As we moved away from the hunter-gatherer way of life, characterized by cooperation and partnership, to that of civilization, characterized by competition and domination, our self-esteem began to fall. It's difficult to feel good about ourselves when we see plants, animals, and people only as things to be used. The way we see others is the way we see ourselves.

We flee our loss of connection by becoming inflated with self-importance and propelled by self-will. A key concept in understanding addiction is that recovery begins with surrender—turning one's will over to a higher power. Addiction has its origins in man's transition into willfulness. Buber contrasts the willfulness that leads to addiction with the acceptance that leads to freedom:

> The self-willed man does not believe and does not meet. He does not know solidarity of connection, but only the feverish world outside and his feverish desire to use it.
>
> But the free man has no purpose here and means there, which he fetches for his purpose: he

has only the one thing, his repeated decision to approach his destiny.

The Myth of the Primitive and the Myth of Civilization

Although at times I wish we could turn the clock back 10,000 years and return to our hunter-warrior roots, I know that is impossible. Yet I believe we can reconnect with those roots. We must if we are to survive and develop a world in which people can overcome their addiction to consuming the earth. The first step in recovery is to break through our denial that everything is fine. We can no longer continue with "business as usual," hoping against hope that more civilization will get us off of our destructive path. Yet to be able to see an alternative, we must examine the nature of our denial and our beliefs about our primitive past and our civilized present.

Civilization. The word has such a lofty sound, bringing to mind images of beautiful cities and godlike, magnificent human beings. Primitive, on the other hand, is associated with the rudimentary and unrefined, with discomfort and a lack of amenities. There is a culturally embedded notion about human evolution that things have gotten better over time; that as difficult as times are now, we are a lot better off than our predecessors who lived in caves. If many groups of primitive peoples have been destroyed, this is no great loss to humanity, since they have been replaced by more highly evolved societies. Natural selection kills off the less valuable and leaves those who are better suited to survive.

Anthropologist Ashley Montagu articulates this view then suggests the ways in which it may be flawed. "From the rather self-conscious heights of our own state of equivocal civilization and of that of the community to which we belong, we men of the latest period of human development have traditionally taken the view that whatever has preceded us was by so much the less advanced .... It has been easy to fall into the habit of assuming that the later developed is not only the more evolved but also the better."[5]

This is reflected in our terminology. Civilization is defined as a state of human society characterized by a high level of intellectual, social, and cultural development. To civilize, the dictionary says, is to bring out of savagery. To be civilized is to be humane. A lack of civilization connotes an absence of all that human beings have achieved in the course of their evolutionary development.

Those who lived prior to the advent of agriculture are designated as primitive. The misconception isn't just that our ancestors, and the few intact groups of hunter-gathers, are viewed as simple and unsophisticated; they are also misjudged as savages. Some are romanticized as "noble savages." But most are regarded with caution and fear, as Indian people were viewed by White settlers in North America: as blood-thirsty savages, just waiting to rape our women and steal our children.

In this culture-bound view, people who lived before the dawn of civilization are stereotyped as beetle-browed apes with small brains, bull necks, knock-knees, unintelligible grunt-like speech, and a nasty habit of dragging their womenfolk around by the hair. Civilized man, by contrast, is seen as graceful and well-proportioned, intelligent, articulate, cultured, refined, and resourceful.

However, when we look honestly at so-called "primitives" and compare their lives to our own "civilized" existence, an objective observer would have to conclude that not only are our views of pre-agricultural man and post-agricultural man false, they are actually 180 degrees off.

In his magnificent book *Ishmael*, Daniel Quinn points out that "primitive" cultures, which he calls "Leavers," have lived successfully according to nature's laws for millions of years. "Civilized" cultures, which Quinn calls "Takers," rejected those laws and have rapidly brought the planet to the brink of destruction.

Quinn likens our attempt to build a culture while rejecting time-tested laws of survival to man's early attempts at flight. "Let's suppose," he says "that this trial is being made in one of those wonderful pedal-driven contraptions with flapping wings, based on a mistaken understanding of avian flight.

"As the flight begins, all is well. Our would-be airman has been pushed off the edge of the cliff and is pedaling away, and the wings of his craft are flapping like crazy. He feels wonderful, ecstatic. He's experiencing the freedom of the air. What he doesn't realize, however, is that this craft is aerodynamically incapable of flight. It simply isn't in compliance with the laws that make flight possible—but he would laugh if you told him this. He's never heard of such laws, knows nothing about them. He would point at those flapping wings and say, 'See? Just like a bird!' Nevertheless, whatever he thinks, he's not in flight. He's an unsupported object falling toward the center of the earth. He's not in flight, he's in free fall."

Like Quinn's would-be airman, civilized society has ignored the laws of nature. Though our craft has been in the air for some time, it was doomed from the very beginning. We're like the man in the joke who jumps out of a ninetieth-floor window on a bet. As he passes the tenth floor, he says to himself, "Well, so far so good!"

In our fear and denial, we cling ever more tightly to the madly flapping aircraft of civilization, hoping against hope that somewhere in our civilized tool kit is the one tool that will save us from disaster. "But your craft isn't going to save you," says Quinn. "Quite the contrary, it's your craft that's carrying you toward catastrophe. Five billion of you pedaling away—or 10 billion or 20 billion—can't make it fly. It's been in free fall from the beginning and that fall is about to end."

If our civilized way of life is killing us, is our only hope a return to our primitive past as hunter-gathers? Fortunately, the answer is "no." We could not return to the ways of our Stone Age forbearers, even if we chose to do so. There are just too many humans on the planet to support the hunter-gatherer way of life.

The real problem isn't with the way we get our food, but rather with how we treat ourselves, each other, the animals, the plants, and the land. There have been many so-called primitive peoples who have successfully used agriculture: the Lega in Zaire, the Kubu of Sumatra, the Hopi, Zuni, and Natchez of North America, to name only a few. What is true of these cultures, as opposed to our own consumptive civilization, is that they do not dominate but rather live in partnership with all of life. They take only what they need and leave the rest.

It may help clarify the alternatives to summarize the two kinds of cultures that humans have developed:

Partnership Societies (Leavers)	Dominator Societies (Takers)
1. Small populations	1. Large populations
2. People spread out	2. People concentrated
3. Much leisure time	3. Little leisure time
4. Mobile	4. Sedentary
5. Open country	5. Walled cities
6. Peaceful	6. Warlike
7. Trust nature	7. Fearful of nature
8. Enjoy wildness and diversity	8. Enjoy domesticity and predictability
9. Little emphasis on private property	9. Private property important
10. Giving normal	10. Taking normal
11. Sharing rewarded	11. Hoarding rewarded
12. Cooperative	12. Competitive
13. Guests on the land	13. Owners of the land
14. Honor and respect animals	14. Disdain and exploit animals
15. Leadership advisory	15. Leadership executive
16. Change slow and controlled	16. Change uncontrolled and rapid
17. Relationships based on equality and partnership	17. Relationships based on hierarchy and domination
18. Men and women equal	18. One gender dominates the other
19. High self-esteem	19. Shaky self-esteem
20. Great Spirit is part of nature	20. God is above nature
21. Child abuse rare	21. Child abuse common
22. Connection	22. Alienation
23. I-Thou relationships	23. I-It relationships
24. Free, accept what have	24. Addictive, always wanting more
25. Built to fly	25. Built to crash

In his award-winning book, *The Parable of the Tribes*, Andrew Bard Schmookler writes: "If we were to persist in viewing the great edifice of civilization as structured for the purpose of meeting human needs, civilization would seem to be a gigantic Rube

Goldberg contraption.... If we view social evolution as a result of people continually choosing better ways to meet their needs, civilization becomes a kind of joke."

More than a cosmic joke, some would say that civilization is a potentially fatal disease. Anthropologist Carlton Coon reminds us in *The Hunting People* that "man's gradual conquest of nature has caused him to live in groups of increasing size and complexity, until now the world of men verges on an intricate unity. At the same time man has used up many of the materials on the earth's surface until parts of it lie bare and ravished. To a cosmic geographer with only an objective interest in man, our species might appear to be nothing but a highly organized skin cancer destroying the surface of the earth with growing rapidity."

Back on the Path or the End of the Road?

There are two culture-bound myths that we must overcome if we are to survive into the twenty-first century. The first is that the cure for our ills is more of the same—more civilization, more technology. Underlying that myth is the belief that we are doomed anyway, so we might as well "eat, drink, and be merry...."

Many people feel that even if we acknowledged the old ways to be best, they are lost forever. Such people tell us that we can't go home again and must accept our destiny. They see themselves as realists, simply looking life in the eye and accepting fate. With their civilized view of the world, they would have us believe that we are on a conveyer belt of destruction. Having put the machine in motion, we can do nothing to stop our rapid progress toward the end.

It's true—things do look bad. As we approach the end of the twentieth century, we seem destined to repeating our patterns of death and destruction. I agree with the realists that we can't go back to the past. The reason, however, is not because the past is lost to us. What the realists don't recognize is that the past lives on in each one of us. Men have always been, and still are, hunter-warriors.

Chief Oren Lyons is Faith Keeper of the Turtle Clan of the Oenendaga Nation, and Director of Native American Studies at State University of New York at Buffalo. As someone who has seen the destruction of his people and way of life, he has more reason than most of us to feel pessimistic. Yet he is full of hope. In a Bill Moyers T.V. interview I heard Lyons say, "As long as there is one to sing, and one to dance, and one to speak, and one to listen, life will go on."

Our human ancestors have been on the earth for at least two million years. During the vast majority of that time, we lived as hunter-gatherers. What we call civilization, a period character-ized by our addictive and exploitative patterns of use, is a mere ten thousand years old. Our hunter-warrior roots are built into our genetic makeup. We may have lost connection with who we really are, but this identity can never be destroyed. It is built into the "hard wiring" of our human nature.

In trying to explain the depth of our hunter-gatherer roots, I offer the following visualization: Think of the two million years of human history as having taken place in a single calendar year. On January 1, the human species is born. All the men are hunter-warriors. We are hunter-warriors all through January, February, and March. As the springtime months of April and May come along, we are still hunter-warriors. Through the summer months of June, July, and August, we are still hunter-warriors. As fall ap-proaches, we continue our hunter-warrior ways through Septem-ber and October. As the chilly winds of winter blow, we are still hunter-warriors. It is not until 4 a.m. on December 30th that we begin to domesticate plants and animals, and not until 7 p.m. that we develop armies and begin killing each other in large numbers. All 15,000 wars in human history have been fought between 7 p.m. on December 30th and midnight December 31.

It's easy to conclude that we are, at our very core, still hunter-warriors. Our destructive behavior as civilized human be-ings can be thought of as analogous to the feverish ravings of a person who has contracted pneumonia in the frosty cold of win-ter. Civilization is not who we are: it is an illness that may kill us, or from which we may recover. As hunter-warriors we have a long history and a great deal of strength. Our hope is not to return to a past that has vanished, but to recognize that our war-rior roots are still deep within the soil of the earth. They may be covered with snow, but they are very much alive and present in us all.

The world of the hunter-warrior is not a vision of a lost paradise. Rather it is inevitable, a part of our genetic and spiritual heritage. It is the core of who we are. Our addictions direct us to the road of continued civilization and destruction. Our healthy core beckons us back to the path of our ancestors. We can still decide which call to heed.

Notes

1. Stokes, J. "Finding Our Place on Earth Again." *Wingspan*, Summer 1990.

2. Sagan, Carl, in Vittachi, A. (1989) *Earth Conference One: Sharing a Vision for Our Planet.* Boston: New Science Library.

3. Snyder, G. (1969) *Turtle Island.* New York: New Dimensions Publishing Corporation.

4. Diamond, J. "The Worst Mistake in the History of the Human Race." *Discover*, May 1987.

5. Montagu, A. *The Journal of the American Medical Association.* March 24, 1962. Vol. 179.

3

Healing Our Masculine Compulsions—Alcohol, Cocaine, Narcotics, Steroids, Food, Work, Money

"To do is to be"—Plato
"To be is to do"—Socrates
"Do be, do be, do"—Sinatra

Task 1: Balance our desire to "do" with our need just to "be"

The last chapter offered some ideas about where society first got off track. With these ideas in mind, we can begin to heal our own addictions.

Do you remember the rings of addiction I talked about in Chapter 1? You learned in that section that addictions develop from the inside out, but must be treated from the outside in. The seventh ring contains our addictions to substances and activities, such as alcohol, drugs, work, money, and food. Stage 1 of recovery addresses these addictions.

The first task of healing requires that we learn to develop a greater sense of being—of living life for its own sake, rather than always trying to do more and more. As the love dart at the beginning of the chapter suggests, we need to keep a sense of humor as we begin our recovery.

Finding a New Way To Get High: Reclaiming the Ecstasy and Serenity of True Spiritual Experience

Adrenaline addiction has become endemic for men in this culture. It is the dynamic dimension in men's lives run rampant; the compulsion for bigger, better, faster, harder.

In getting to the root of this addiction, I've noticed that men addicted to arousal seem to need more and more stimulation, novelty, excitement, and danger in their lives. They try to avoid the opposite feelings—stagnation, ordinariness, boredom and passivity—all of which they perceive as leading to death, psychological if not physical.

For an arousal type to hear that he has to give up his drug of choice and behave like an ordinary person feels like a death sentence to him. A treatment approach that doesn't take into account this type of person's need to be special and out of the ordinary just won't work. The trick for therapists is to be able to deflate his ego, so he will recognize that he doesn't have all the answers, while at the same time letting him know that he is unique and important.

If you are dealing with these issues in yourself, the most crucial thing I can tell you is that you can still get high. The fear is that if you give up your arousal addictions, life will be so dull and boring, it won't seem worth living. Many people would rather die than consider a life that is not lived fully, all out, at the extremes.

It helps to think of the dilemma of the addict as existing on a horizontal line, with one end represented by passivity and the other by excitement.

Passivity ←————————————————→ **Excitement**

We put a lifetime of effort into trying to avoid passivity at all cost in our endless search for more and more excitement. When we undertake recovery, the only way we can conceive of giving up our addictive patterns of excitement-seeking is to go to the other extreme, which in our way of thinking will inevitably lead to dullness and death.

Men in our society are conditioned to overdo things and seek the speed and excitement that leads to adrenaline addiction. But a new pattern is emerging that runs counter to tradition. Many women, seeking liberation, have given up their feminine addictions only to find themselves hooked on such traditionally male compulsions as cigarettes, cocaine, and sex. And many men are giving up their macho drives for power and success only to get hooked on such things as food, tranquilizers, and codependent relationships—all of which have been considered in the past to be typically female problems.

Just as I believe that women will find value in books such as this which are focused on "men's" issues, I believe that men would do well to be open to reading "women's" books. I've gotten a great deal of help, for instance, from such books as Robin Norwood's *Women Who Love Too Much* and Patricia Love's *The Emotional Incest Syndrome*.

Many of us turn away from the constant stimulation and excitement of the fast lane and look for drugs and experiences that will slow us down. As an alternative to the dynamic outward energy that leads to arousal addiction, we become dependent instead on the inward-drawing magnetic energy that leads to satiation addiction.

Carlos says that food often served to calm his nerves when he felt overworked. "I would eat when I was anxious and it would make me feel better. Gradually I found that I was using food like a drug, turning to it more and more often to deal with uncomfortable feelings. I would feel terribly uncomfortable and fat, but learned that after I went on a binge, I could make myself throw up and feel better. It became just like the drug cycle of ups and downs."

Those who are hooked on satiation, and seek the safety of passivity, are afraid of going to the other extreme, which threatens them with manic excitement, peril, and, ultimately, death.

Even though our addiction either to arousal or satiation may be killing us, the other extreme continues to exert an even more powerful threat to our sense of well-being. Some of us try to find the balance by staying halfway in between, but this never works.

As addicts, we reject anything that is "halfway." Most of us would certainly agree with William Blake, who said, "the road to excess leads to the palace of wisdom." In fact, many of us have bet our lives on finding wisdom through excess.

When I work with men who are hooked on either extreme, I usually can get their attention when I ask, "Would you be willing to give up a life of excitement if I could offer you ecstasy?" or, "Would you be willing to give up passivity if I could offer you serenity?"

There is another dimension to life that no one may ever have told you about. It exists on a vertical line, with ecstasy at the top end and serenity at the bottom.

Ecstasy

Serenity

Most men are intrigued enough to want to explore the possibilities of this alternative model. They feel less frightened about moving away from excitement when they learn that they'll have a reprieve from boredom: peace and serenity seem to be far more acceptable alternatives. I remember Carlos's fascination in one of our counseling sessions when I told him that the line of ecstasy and serenity allows you to live in the extremes without becoming unbalanced.

"That was like gold for me," Carlos recalls. "Up until then, I believed that I had only two choices. I could live a life of extreme excitement and die from the effects of my addiction, or I could live the good, quiet life and die of boredom. The idea that I could live life fully, take risks, and explore, and still survive and be healthy was like a fire being lighted in my soul."

I explained to Carlos that the reason why this is possible is because each step "up" toward ecstasy automatically produces a step "down" into serenity; and each step into serenity creates a step into ecstasy. You may have experienced this phenomenon when engaged in a moment of spiritual rapture—seeing a magnificent sunset, or bursting with love for another human being. There is simultaneous experience of ecstatic bliss and blissful serenity. In that moment, you occupy both ends of the continuum at the same time. This is the dream of every addict—to live at the farthest reaches of experience. But unlike a life following the horizontal model, in which there are mood swings from one end to the other, here on the vertical plane we can be "far out," but always in balance.

Addicts are people who want to go home. But we are like damaged homing pigeons, flying ever faster but in the wrong direction. In our desire to get high without risking going inside ourselves, we settled for intensity when what we really were searching for was ecstasy.

One of the difficulties in helping men find the right direction home is that most men in America are taught to be compulsive "doers." The very excess that kills us is built into our cultural conditioning.

Being Male in America Is a Competitive Sport

The compulsion to be doing something is inexorably linked to men's seemingly insatiable need to compete. Psychologist Elliot Aronson reminds us in *The Social Animal* of some of the competitive experiences that are so familiar to men. "From the Little League ballplayer who bursts into tears after his team loses, to the college students in the football stadium chanting, 'We're number one!'; from Lyndon Johnson, whose judgment was almost certainly distorted by his oft-stated desire not to be the first American President to lose a war, to the third grader who despises his classmate for a superior performance on an arithmetic test; we manifest a staggering cultural obsession with victory."

"I feel like I always have to be on," says Carlos, as he hurriedly prepares a rush order for a customer in his catering service. "I can never slow down or rest, because I'm afraid I'll fall behind. It's like playing a basketball game where I run full speed up and down the court, except there are no time-outs, no half-time breaks, and the game never ends. I used to think I was just real goal-oriented. Now I realize I've become addicted to the excitement I get from trying to be the best."

"It's a dog-eat-dog world," says another client, Daniel, "and only the strong survive. The lure of money became my drug, along with the occasional excitement of a sexual fling to add a little spice. Life is a gamble and you've got to ride it for all it's worth."

For Kevin, the world of gambling was more than a metaphor. "As a kid I used to bet on anything and everything. We'd toss pennies, pitch dimes, and draw straws. I'd bet on football, baseball, basketball. If there wasn't a game to bet on, I'd bet my brother that the phone would ring within five minutes, or that I'd see a stationwagon within one. For me, the adrenaline rush I'd get when I'd be up against the wire was like the best drug I could find. Beating the odds and beating the other guy made life worth living. I loved to compete, and I never believed I would lose. When I did, it just made me want to win back even more the next time."

Virtually all men are schooled in the commandments of male culture. From older brothers, buddies, sports, T.V., our fathers, and other adults, we learn to strive for success in the outer world, and to disregard conflicting feelings from our inner world. No matter what culture you were brought up in, the phrases that conditioned you and became embedded in your psyche were in essence the same: "No pain, no gain"; "Don't wimp out on me"; "Take it like a man"; "Don't be a sissy"; "Stiff upper lip"; "Boys don't cry"; and so on.

Stage 1 Recovery

The core task of stage 1 of the recovery process is to help men let go of their compulsive need to do something. Most of us were taught that every problem in life can be solved if we will just settle in, buckle our belt another notch, focus our attention on the desired goal, and keep pushing hard.

We are brainwashed to believe that we can take care of whatever confronts us through will-power alone. We are also convinced that we don't need anyone's help. Men rarely recognize that their compulsion to do something often creates more problems.

So, if this sounds familiar to you, close your eyes for a moment, take a deep breath, and tell yourself, "I don't have to take immediate action—I can relax." Our fear tells us that we can't just sit back and do nothing; we must forge ahead. It's often hard to recognize the difference between "doing nothing" and "just being."

The work described in this chapter will help you break out of your cycle of "doing" and help you to simply be more who you are. The process will also help you break out of your isolation and reconnect with others.

During the first stage of recovery you will work on the following issues:

- Exploring the Addictive Process
- Finding a Guide
- Understanding the Different Types of Addictions
- Assessing Danger
- Evaluating the Pros and Cons of Addiction
- Trying the Simple Solution
- Acknowledging Where You Are in the Addictive Process
- Admitting the Need for Help
- Finding an Approach Appropriate to Your Type of Addiction
- Getting Into the Right Support Group
- Developing Safety, Support, and a Personal Definition of Abstinence
- Dealing With Grief, Defenses, and the Meaning of Being an Addict

Let's take a more detailed look at the recovery process, remembering that no one's recovery will proceed in the same manner. Each person is unique, and will work through these issues in his own way.

Exploring the Addictive Process

Long before a man decides that he has an addictive problem, he begins to look at the ways in which he relates in the world. We often feel different from our peers—either superior or inferior to them—and notice that our patterns of escape differ as well. Daniel recalls the time in his college career when he began to drink heavily. "College was a stressful time—away from home for the first time, trying to keep up my grades, trying to prove I was someone special, constantly on the make for women. Getting down and partying relieved the tension. I found I could drink more, and more often, than a lot of my friends. I was proud that I could handle my alcohol better than they could, though in my senior year I began to wonder why I drank so much."

Over time, we recognize that we use our substance or behavior of choice—alcohol, drugs, work, food, and so on—to escape from our inner pain. As our abuse gets more and more out of control, our attempts to control it get more vigorous. Carlos recalls this stage of his recovery: "I knew something was wrong, and I was terrified that it might be my alcohol, drug use, or my obsessive work schedule. These were the very things that seemed to keep me going, and I didn't want to let them go. I was scared to look at my problem, but I couldn't ignore it either."

This initial dawning of insight, which may go on for years and is usually experienced alone, is a time of observing our behavior. Our insights often come in small flashes. We recognize something about our behavior, ask questions about what we are doing with our lives, and begin to notice the relationship between how we feel and our patterns of use and abuse. We often alternate between feeling that something isn't right here, and our blind faith that things will be better tomorrow. We become increasingly confused.

A man has worked through this step when he recognizes that he's not sure whether or not he may have a problem, but knows that he needs some guidance to help sort things out.

Finding a Guide

Finding a guide is crucial for men in recovery. It's also one of the most difficult steps for us to take. We are trained from childhood on to handle our problems ourselves; to see pain as something that will make us stronger. "No pain, no gain" becomes a mantra inducing us to try harder to make things work, even though our lives are becoming increasingly unmanageable (to use the language of A.A.). We long to reach out to someone, but our pride and our fear keep us locked into ourselves.

All men who have an addiction also have a great fear of people. We are survivors and we have survived to this point, we believe, by being on guard. We may have become superficially close to others, but we've always kept our innermost selves protected. Now we have reached the point where we need a guide. What we are doing on our own just isn't working, no matter how hard we try.

"I knew I needed some kind of help," says Ron, reflecting on this stage of his recovery, "but I was scared to reach out. I kept saying to myself, 'Don't be a sissy—you can work it out yourself.' Even when I was ready to accept help, I didn't know where to begin to find it."

Most of us are so well trained to be "Lone Rangers," solving all of life's problems ourselves, that even when we're ready to reach out for help, we don't know where to turn.

Recovery is an ongoing process: you will have many different guides along the way, each one of them just right for you. Be open to guidance in whatever form it takes. Be gentle with yourself. Choose a guide that is appropriate to your emotions and circumstances.

Some guides I have used in my own recovery include:

Reading books. I love to read, and have had the experience of a book seeming to fall off the shelf by accident. When I picked it up, I found that it had a particular meaning—it was just what I needed at the time.

Listening to music. Just the right song or piece of music can often clarify my understanding at a given point in my journey.

A friend. A guide can be someone who just listens to me, who cares without judging, and lets me know I'm not alone.

My inner self. As I child, I used to have imaginary friends to whom I talked constantly for support and comfort. As an adult, I gave up childish things, knowing that my "friends" were just parts of me. Since I learned not to like or trust myself, I stopped talking and listening to myself. Yet there was always some part of me that was wise. When I began listening again, I found that I had a wonderful guide very close at hand.

My higher power. At first we have a very limited, and sometimes negative, view of a higher power. Our first higher power was the parent who refined the limits of our world. All our judgments about spiritual matters are colored by our parents' attitudes and behaviors. Later experiences with organized religion are often negative for many men. Far from being limited to conventional notions of God, though, your "higher power" can be anything outside your own ego. Sure, it can be God, however you understand him. It can be the Goddess, nature, your recovery group, your own intuitive wisdom, or your belief in universal principles. In the same way in which your guide will charge or evolve at different points in your recovery, your conception of your higher power will also undergo refinements and mutations.

A sponsor in one of the 12-step programs. Learning to trust another adult who we do not know well is extremely difficult for many of us. Yet great comfort can be provided by someone who understands in their bones what we have been through because they have been through it themselves.

A professional counselor or therapist. Many of us have had bad experiences with counselors. We sought out a clergyman, psychologist, marriage and family counselor, psychiatrist, or social worker because we thought they would understand. Yet many seemed blind to our addiction, and a few took advantage of our vulnerability and increased our fear of getting close. Some demanded that we give up our addiction too soon, and others allowed us to continue our acting-out behavior too long while we "worked on other things." When we find good counselors—individuals who know themselves, have wrestled with their own problems, have come to understand the addictive process, and have their own program of healing and spiritual development— we are in possession of an important guide.

A "two-hatter." You may be fortunate enough to find a person who is both an excellent psychotherapist or counselor and is also involved in his own program of recovery, having recognized his own addiction and gotten help (of course, this person might as easily be a woman). Such individuals are still relatively rare, but their number is growing. Look for them. It's worth the search.

The best long-range guidance system I have found is a combination of your inner self, your higher power, and a "two-hatter."

If you can't find an individual who wears both hats, look for someone who at least understands both worlds. Seek out a counselor who is open to self-help programs such as Alcoholics Anonymous, and who has attended meetings for at least several months; or look for a seasoned 12-step sponsor who has benefited from counseling or psychotherapy.

Whatever or whoever provides guidance, they help us look at ourselves and the kinds of addictions that run our lives.

Understanding the Different Types of Addictions

Often we are blind to one addiction but can recognize that another aspect of our life is out of control. The traditional view of addiction is one-dimensional—either I'm an alcoholic, a cocaine addict, a compulsive gambler, or whatever. If we don't find addiction in the place where we look, we assume that we're not an addict. But we need to expand our understanding of addictions. The days when people were addicted to only one thing are long past. In a recent study conducted by a colleague and myself on 200 people in recovery, we found the number of addictions they reported to range from 1 to 15, with the average being 7.[1]

Recognizing that a person will usually have more than one addiction can help speed the recovery process. I've seen many men who, at first, are blind to their addiction to alcohol, but recognize that cocaine is a problem. Others who see that their alcohol use is out of control are sure they can still smoke marijuana. As a two-hatter myself, I work with people where they are. Rather than asking, "Are you addicted?" I often ask, "In what areas of your life are you addicted?" When asked in a nonjudgmental way, men will often be able to recognize that they are having problems.

It took Tony a while before he recognized that he had a problem with cocaine; but when he did, he was able to give it up. It took him another six months, however, to give up his drinking and marijuana use. "I knew I had to give up cocaine, even went to Narcotics Anonymous meetings; but I still wasn't ready to stop drinking or smoking pot. I'm just grateful my therapist hung in there with me. He didn't judge me for using, but he didn't let me get away with believing that I could drink and smoke and be okay."

This is the appropriate stage to explore your relationships with substances—such as alcohol, cocaine, heroin, nicotine, caffeine, and food—and behavioral patterns—such as accumulating money, gambling, spending, and work.

Assessing Danger

One way to assess danger in dealing with men's addictions is to do nothing and wait a few years and see how things go. If you have an addiction to cocaine or alcohol or work, for instance, the problems will get progressively worse. In spite of the increasing problems, however, we often blame our discomfort on something or someone else. "I would always get mad at my wife when things weren't working for me," says Daniel. "In my heart I knew she wasn't to blame, but I sure took it out on her." For Carlos, it was the people at work who got the brunt of his anger. "I was a holy terror to my employees. As my addiction progressed, I looked for someone to blame. If I wasn't yelling at them, I was blaming the economy. I'd do anything but face myself."

I call this avoidance approach the "ostrich formula," since our inclination is to put our head in the sand and hope the problem will disappear. Men also employ a "search-and-destroy" technique. At the first sign of addictive problems, we ruthlessly attack the addiction on all fronts and refrain from any activity that is fun. We are sure the problem can be removed quickly and easily, even if force must be used.

The approach I prefer is one that neither allows us to do nothing, hoping against hope that things will improve, nor violates our being, or those we love, by trying to wipe out a part of ourselves. Rather it assumes that we are all addictive to a degree. Many of us can live with a low level of addictiveness. The time and energy it might take to change it is not worth the effort. For others, even a low level may be intolerable, they'll want to change.

"It really helped me to work at my own pace," recalls Joseph, "to think about how much risk I was willing to take with my life."

Joseph was able to decide, for instance, that his sexual preoccupation was causing enough problems to threaten his health and well-being. He recognized that the level of danger had reached a point where he had to get help.

Evaluating the Pros and Cons of Addiction

Unlike many who work in the field, I don't assume that everyone who has an addiction should immediately get into treatment. I think there are both advantages and disadvantages to whatever addictions we have, and there are advantages and disadvantages to giving them up.

To every person I work with who wishes to explore his or her addictions, I address four simple questions. Though the questions are simple, coming up with the answers can provide my clients with some of their most powerful therapeutic experiences. Almost all people who go through this process find that, afterwards, they are much better able to decide on the next steps they wish to take.

The questions are:

1. What are the specific problems you're having as a result of your relationship to _____? (The blank may be alcohol, cocaine, work, gambling, heroin, food, or some combination.)

2. If you stopped using these substances or practices, how would your life be better?

3. In what ways do your relationships with _____ serve you (i.e., what are the advantages to overeating, using marijuana, tranquilizers, and so on?)

4. In what ways would your life be worse if you gave up _____? (i.e., what would be the disadvantages of giving up cocaine, working less, ending your extramarital relationship?)

The first two questions are generally easier to answer than the last two. I usually have people write their answers on four sheets of paper so that they can be put side by side and compared. Label the four sheets A, B, C, and D. Carlos's responses looked like this:

A. Problems With My Alcohol and Drug Use

- Costs me money.
- I'm scared of being arrested.
- Makes my wife angry with me.
- Keeps me from being with my kids.
- Customers sometimes notice my condition, and I'm afraid of losing business.

B. Advantages of Giving Up Alcohol and Drugs

- I would feel better about myself.
- My marriage would improve.
- I wouldn't feel so hyped and frantic at work all the time.
- I would be a better father and a better boss.
- I could save money.

C. Positive Things About Using Alcohol and Drugs

- I love the excitement I get from taking risks.
- I like winding down in the male atmosphere of bars.
- When I use cocaine, I have more energy and can get more done.
- I can take on more business when I'm high.
- Alcohol calms me down when I'm feeling too hyper, and cocaine inflates me when I'm feeling depressed.

D. Negative Things About Giving Up Drugs and Alcohol

- I'm afraid I couldn't do it.
- I'd be lonely—most of my buddies drink and use.
- I'd feel like I'd been tamed, like a wimp.
- I'd be clean, but life would be dull and boring.
- I wouldn't be as successful at work. I'd lose the killer instinct.

I think of these answers as being balanced on a scale, with A and B on one side (the problems with our addictions and the benefits of stopping) and C and D on the other (the benefits of our addictions and the negative things about stopping).

When we deny that there are any advantages to our addictions, or no negatives about stopping, we are in effect continuing to say, "I want to stop," while our actions keep saying the opposite. Only by looking honestly at both sides of the scale can we begin to form an effective plan of action.

According to Ron, this evaluation was one of the most profound and helpful aspects of his recovery. "For years people kept telling me about the problems my work and relationship patterns were causing, and how much better things would be for me if I changed. I agreed, but deep down I felt there was another side that I couldn't talk about. I knew there were positive things my addictions were doing for me, and that quitting wouldn't necessarily make my life better. This process gave me permission to be honest with myself, to see the whole picture. It was the key to my recovery."

Trying the Simple Solution

Everyone who has an addiction of any kind first wants to try the simple solution. People don't want to make major changes in their lives. This goes back to our early family experiences when our basic desire was to find safety and security. The most visible manifestation of this secure state of mind is a steady state, a regular pattern; what is known. As my friend, psychologist John Enright, says, "Be it ever so shitty, there's no place like home."

This is why so many of us can and do continue in situations that are so obviously painful. We might ask ourselves why we just don't leave or make a major change. The answer is that no matter how bad a situation is, at least we know what it's like. There are no surprises in our addictive patterns. Although each situation gives a new rush as we convince ourselves that this time things will be different, each new situation within our addictive pattern is strangely familiar. And, in fact, it is this familiarity that we crave. The saying that the more things change, the more they stay the same reflects this notion.[2]

When we do conclude that we need to change our behavior, we search for the change that will be the least disruptive to our old pattern. If we had a drinking problem, we would change our brand of booze, or switch from whiskey to beer, or from vodka to wine. We would decide to drink only on weekends or never before five o'clock.

What is surprising is that sometimes the simple solution works.

It obviously doesn't make all our problems go away, but sometimes we are at a point in our lives where one action can tip the balance. We still must make other changes to keep ourselves healthy and reverse the addictive ways we have been living. But sometimes small changes can work wonders. Don't discount them.

On the other hand, we need to guard against deluding ourselves that the real answer is just a different "simple solution," while we continue trying one after the next and our addiction continues to get worse. If the simple solution *doesn't* work, it's time to take a serious look at the addictive process and how it's affecting your life. This is one of the major advantages of having a guide work with you as you move through the process of recovery.

Tony sought the simple solution of stopping his cocaine use while believing that he could still drink and use marijuana. "Looking back now, I'm glad I tried the simple solution while I was in therapy. I needed to see if it would work without someone telling me I would fail, but I'm glad I didn't try it on my own. Even though alcohol wasn't a problem for me then, every time I drank I went back to my cocaine use, and cocaine *was* a problem."

Acknowledging Where You Are in the Addictive Process

It's part of human nature to avoid what we are afraid of in our lives. Most people are afraid they might get a cavity and have to have their teeth drilled. Lots of folks avoid dentists. Everyone is afraid of getting cancer. We avoid health checkups. Everyone is afraid their kid might get hooked on drugs. We avoid talking about drug use.

Our addictions go to the core of our being. They touch the most basic needs we have. It is never an easy task to look honestly at ourselves and our addictions. As men, we are trained from childhood to ignore internal signals such as pain; to push harder if something isn't working. I saw a sign in the window of a car recently that offers typically manly advice about how to operate in the world. "If it sticks, force it. If it breaks, throw it away." In our fear of appearing weak, we often ignore our problems, or force solutions that only make things worse.

I would go so far as to say that no one can honestly see by themselves where they are in the addictive process. The best a man can do is to put himself in the way of other people who have the courage to be honest and tell him what they see. This is why a guide is absolutely essential. Only someone close to you, or close to the addictive process, can see the behaviors that you unconsciously deny. Even with guidance, it may be a long time before you are ready to accept the truth about your situation.

You *are* ready to accept the truth when you've taken a serious look at your addictive behavior. At this stage, you've gathered a good deal of information about yourself and the degree to which your addictive behavior is both helping you and causing problems in your life. "This was the toughest stage for me," Carlos recalls. "I couldn't ignore the problems I was having with drugs or that I was having more problems with food. I kept coming across articles on bulimia, and though I kept telling myself this was a problem that only women could get, the light was beginning to shine through the chinks in my armor. I knew I was getting close to a decision that would change my life, and I was terrified."

Admitting the Need for Help

You may have acknowledged the possibility that you need help when you first picked up this book. Somewhere deep inside there was a voice that said, "My life isn't right. Something is wrong somewhere." If you're like me, the closer you've gotten to asking for help, the more terrified you've become.

As you examine your relationship to alcohol, cocaine, work, food, gambling, and the other "manly" pursuits that seem to help you cope, you may have begun to recognize that you're getting farther and farther away from who you really feel yourself to be. Perhaps you have come to see that the addictive path will lead to destruction. But, on the other hand, admitting your need for help is terrifying. "I felt like my whole world was coming apart, and I needed to hold it together at any cost," Kevin recalls. "I thought if I asked for help, I'd be admitting that I couldn't handle things, that on some deep level I wasn't really a man. There were times when I felt I would rather die than admit I needed help. At least, I thought, I'd die like a man."

You may be aware that the old way doesn't work. But it's familiar, and familiarity counts for a lot in everyone's life. Admitting that you have a problem requires an act of total surrender. Some have described this as "being sick and tired of being sick and tired." But to surrender to the unknown also feels like death: our fear tells us that surrender will be the end of us. Only trust in something greater than yourself will help you realize that the death is of an old way of life that no longer serves your best interests.

As we get up to the edge of making the decision, the terror increases. Once you have taken that leap and say, "Yes, I do have a problem. My addictions are out of control. I can't do it myself. Please help me," you are free.

"It was like dying and being reborn," Kevin remembers. "Once I stopped trying to hold it all together and reached out for help, life became so much simpler. I felt like I could finally take the world off my shoulders and set it down. Damn, that felt good!"

Finding an Approach Appropriate to Your Type of Addiction

Traditionally, the decision about what kind of a program to enter involved the choice of outpatient or residential programs. Yet a more fundamental question is whether the primary addiction being treated is an arousal or a satiation addiction.

One reason why 12-step programs have been so successful is that they accommodate all sorts of people, in various stages of recovery, and help them feel safe and accepted. For instance, arousal types—such as cocaine addicts, sex and romance addicts, compulsive gamblers, workaholics, and so on—are often extroverted, "Type A" personalities. They are competitive, fast-living, and excitement-oriented. To be effective for such people, recovery programs must take into consideration the arousal type's prejudices and needs. For instance, whereas a satiation type would benefit from getting information by watching a video program or hearing a lecture, arousal types might feel restless or bored. They probably need to get the information in a more stimulating way. I often do my therapy with arousal types while we are walking or even jogging.

Satiation types often enjoy meetings that are small and intimate. Arousal types would rather go to large meetings where there is a lot of action and high-energy people abound.

An appropriate sponsor for a satiation type might be quiet, supportive, and passive. Arousal types may need a more talkative, directive, and active person to work with them.

The ways in which people in recovery interact with their families is quite different for the two types of addictions. Satiation types may be best reached through quiet activities—reading, talking, listening to music. Arousal types may need something more kinetic and exciting. Such family activities as bowling, jogging, or bicycle riding can afford the arousal addict an avenue to reconnect with family members in relative comfort and an atmosphere that feels supportive.

We often teach people to pray or meditate as part of the recovery process. For satiation types, quiet meditation is right up their alley. For arousal types, sitting still and keeping the mind quiet can seem like an impossibility.

I remember my own early recovery. I was told to close my eyes and let my body relax. I couldn't keep my eyes closed for more than three seconds. My body was restless and I wanted to get up and move around. I found running to be a much better way for me to begin to learn to meditate.

Once a person has been in recovery for some time, and begins to acquire some emotional balance, he can learn more generalized therapeutic skills and behaviors. But initially, it is vital—especially for the arousal type—to offer activities and provide supports that take the needs of the two different types of addicts into consideration. The high incidence of relapse we see with people hooked on cocaine and other arousal drugs and experiences is due to using a treatment philosophy and approach that do not fully take into account these differences.

Involvment in the Right Support Group

Alcoholics Anonymous and the many 12-step programs that evolved from it have become the major support for people in recovery. We are now, however, on the verge of a recovery revolution. In the next few years we will see support groups expand and develop to accommodate our insights into arousal addictions. There will be new programs which will focus on such '90s issues as wealth addiction, compulsive spending, and unemployment; we will perhaps even see groups that focus on societal issues, on poverty, homelessness, war, and violence. This revolution is reflected in the recent formation of Adrenalin Addicts Anonymous, designed to deal with *all* problems that are arousal based.

Never before have there been more options available to people in recovery. There are many new group supports that are not based on the 12 steps of A.A. In all probability, it is now possible to find just the right support group for your particular need—and if not, to find something closely related. I recommend that you try a number of different groups to learn which ones will best suit your needs. I have found it helpful to attend at least six meetings of each group you're considering before deciding if it's right for you.

Developing Safety, Support, and a Personal Definition of Abstinence

Many of us grew up in an unsafe world. We were abused by those whose job it was to protect us. We refused to die and learned to be survivors. Yet we went through life as wounded children of wounded parents. We built walls around ourselves. Our addictions became our way of dealing with our wounds.

The key to feeling safety and support is to be accepted, unconditionally, for who we are. One of the other reasons why 12-step programs work so well is that they offer people a place where their security is honored. The tradition of anonymity allows us to be on an equal footing with all others in the group, and to know that we need not fear the betrayal of our confidences.

"I had to sit through a lot of A.A. meetings before I felt safe enough to share my personal story," says Daniel, remembering how frightened he was. "I was sure someone might know me, and my professional reputation would be ruined. But gradually I listened and realized that we were all in this together and people really listened without judgment or blame."

We need to be able to tell our own story to people who will listen and accept us just the way we are. Yet feeling safe also requires us to recognize that people are fallible and we can't ever expect to find 100 percent security. "It was a shock," says Tony, "when I realized that my sponsor had his own problems and wasn't always going to be there for me. At first I wanted to drop out of the program. I told myself it was all a sham—I couldn't really trust anyone but me. Only gradually I accepted that I could feel safe even though I knew that no one, not even my therapist or sponsor, is perfect."

The key to developing safety and security is to find a support network that contains a number of good people, so that when one falters, as all humans will, someone else can fill in.

As we learn to define abstinence for ourselves, we can begin to live our lives without the addictive substances or behaviors that seemed absolutely necessary to our survival. For some of us, what we must abstain from is obvious. For others, abstinence is a more complicated issue.

Tony remembers the process taking much longer than he expected, and that the focus of his abstinence expanded over time. "I knew, once I was committed to treatment, that I had to stop using cocaine; but it took me a year before I recognized I needed to stop drinking, and another six months before I decided to add marijuana to my list of drugs I had to give up." As people grow in recovery, they often find that they want to give up other habits and substances which once seemed perfectly acceptable. "I never thought I'd give up smoking cigarettes or drinking coffee; but two years into recovery, I realized that they were restricting my freedom and limiting my ability to be totally healthy. I finally gave them up, too."

Dealing With Grief, Defenses, and the Meaning of Being an Addict

When you examine the pros and cons of addiction after entering a recovery program, it usually becomes clear that your addictions were causing you more pain than pleasure. For me, they were like an old lover I knew I needed to withdraw from.

Even though you may initially feel relieved to get rid of these old toxic connections, a feeling of loss may follow. "I was glad to get rid of my drugging and compulsive work habits," says Carlos, "but periodically I missed them terribly. I felt like I had lost a piece of myself." It's common to feel as if someone had died when you've given up your addictive behavior, and you must actually go through a process of mourning.

At first you may feel tremendous joy when you and your addiction part company. Later you may experience a period of bargaining as you try to hold on to the positive parts of your addiction and let the negative parts go. "Maybe I could use just a little," you say to yourself, "or switch from hard liquor to beer."

Gradually you realize that you can never go back to your addictive relationship, and a period of anger ensues, followed by feelings of loneliness and depression. These feelings may recur, often over a period of years. It's during these times that you are at the highest risk of relapse.

However, if you recognize that this is part of the healing process and not a sign that you should return to your addictive patterns, you will finally experience a deep feeling of acceptance: "I know I've got to let you go now and move on with my life." This is the basis for true serenity. We cannot avoid the grief process. We can only understand it and go through it to the other side.

You may come to see that many of the defenses you used to survive the past are now interfering with your continued recovery. Blaming is a big defense for many addicts. At first, many people blame others for their misfortunes. It seems the only way to avoid utter despair and suicide. As people progress in their recovery, they may begin to see that blame is a defense against taking responsibility for ourselves and letting others get close to us.

It's also common to take the opposite tack to survive. You assumed that if there's a problem, it must be your fault. "You're right and I'm wrong" is also a defense against anger. Both extremes are equally unhelpful. Eventually you need to assert your own strength and tell others when you think they're wrong, while assuming an appropriate amount of responsibility for your own actions.

Whatever defenses you employ, at this stage you can begin to examine them with some objectivity, and to get rid of the defenses that are out of keeping with your new-found strength.

Finally, you have to come to terms with what it means to be an addict. For most of us, our early beliefs about addiction merged with our early beliefs about ourselves. We felt that we were born bad, and that nothing we did could make us good; yet we had to keep on trying. It seemed that to be an addict was to be a hopeless loser.

Stage 1 of recovery entails coming to see that to be an addict is to be human. Accepting our addiction and developing a program of recovery for ourselves can take us beyond just being "normal," to the point where we can lead a life of real value and worth. We come to see that our gold, as Robert Bly would have it, is acquired only as we accept our wound.

Addiction is not just an affliction which we reluctantly come to accept, but something to be truly thankful for. Being an addict in recovery means that we must continue on a path that brings peace and love to ourselves and others.

As you move through this stage of recovery, you will see that you've completed the first task of mature masculinity. You will have found more balance in your life as you accept your own unique way of being in the world. You will then be ready to move on to the next stage of recovery and begin dealing with your love life.

Notes

1. A portion of the data collected was reported by Barbara Yoder in her excellent book *The Recovery Resource Book*, Simon & Schuster, New York, 1990.

2. In their book, *Change: Principles of Problem Formation and Problem Resolution*, (W.W. Norton, 1974) Paul Watzlawick, John Weakland, and Richard Fisch use a systems approach that describes change in terms of different levels or "orders" of change. They help us understand why some changes make a difference, while others just bring us back to the place where we began.

4

Healing Our Codependency, Sex, and Love Addictions

 One of the characters in Steven Soderbergh's film, *sex, lies, and videotape*, says that "a woman is more and more attracted to a man she loves, while a man learns to love a woman he's attracted to."

Task 2: Understand and Heal Our Confusion About Sex and Love

After treating thousands of people for their "outer-ring" addictions to alcohol, cocaine, food, money, and power, I began to recognize that something was missing. Many clients had relapses even though they seemed to be following an excellent program of recovery. Others couldn't seem to get started in a program, dropping out after only a few months.

I came to the conclusion that unrecognized issues concerning sexuality were operating beneath the surface of these addictions, and needed to be treated if recovery was going to progress. Many clients used sex and love just as they had once used cocaine and food. The task of the second stage of recovery is to help men clear up their confusions about sex and love. To do that they need permission to talk freely about some of the most sensitive areas of their lives.

Kevin voiced the confusion that many men feel. "My intellect tells me that sex should be a normal part of life, like eating and sleeping," said the 53-year-old psychologist. "Yet, for me it's so charged with excitement, desire, fear, and longing, I'm never really comfortable. I think about sex constantly. Some women turn me on, just with a look—even women I know I shouldn't be having these thoughts about. My cock has a will of its own."

Jamie had this to say: "Sex has never felt comfortable or natural for me. Somehow sex is associated in my mind with the manly strength of doing battle. A warrior would never use his sword to chop wood! Swords are used to defend the kingdom. For me, sex is all wrapped up with aggression. Is this confusion enough, or what?"

Ron admitted, "Sex has been my reward for being good. Before I was married, that meant being smart, talking fast, and being willing to take the risk of initiating all my sexual encounters. In marriage, being good means working at jobs I hate so I can be counted on to pay the bills. I often feel like I lose myself in my relationship, like I can't let go, and will do anything to get my wife's approval."

Codependency, Sex, and Love: The Hidden Addictions

Stanton Peele, an expert on addictions, says "'Love' and 'addiction': the juxtaposition seems strange. Yet it shouldn't, for addiction has as much to do with love as it does with drugs. Many of us are addicts, only we don't know it. We turn to each other out of the same needs that drive some people to drink and others to heroin .... Interpersonal addiction—love addiction—is just about the most common, yet least recognized, form of addiction."

"I grew up on *Playboy* magazine," Kevin told me. "For me, normal, healthy sex meant fantasizing about making love to beautiful women and making every attempt to bring my fantasy into reality. It was only when I got into recovery that I really came to see that, for me, pornography was as addictive as cocaine. I'd get high with each turn of the page, frantically looking for a greater and greater rush. But like a drug, I'd built up a tolerance to the pictures and wanted something more exciting. I knew I was in trouble when I got involved with a wonderful woman who I really loved, yet I couldn't get sexually aroused because she wasn't as perfect as the pictures in the magazines."

Codependency, sex, and love addictions have been hidden from men because they are so much a part of the accepted male role that we don't recognize them when we see them. Questioning whether having more and more attractive partners, either through fantasy or reality, might be addictive, is like questioning the very roots of masculinity. Kevin said it well. "If I'm not constantly on the prowl, constantly looking to connect with attractive women, I'm not sure who I'd be. I'm just beginning to learn that I can still feel like a man without trying to make every woman I see. In fact, I'm learning that the compulsive need to get women takes me farther and farther away from feeling truly manly. Sexual stimulation is like a drug: I can never get enough of it, and it never really turns off the quiet little voice inside that tells me 'you're just a stupid little boy—you'll never be a man.'"

Typical Characteristics of Codependent, Sex-, and Love-Addicted Men

1. We assume responsibility for others' feelings and/or behavior.

2. We have difficulty identifying, accepting, and expressing our own feelings.

3. We have difficulty in forming and maintaining close relationships.

4. We are perfectionistic, and place too many expectations on ourselves and others.

5. We tend to put others' wants and needs first.

6. Our self-esteem rises and falls depending on how others respond to us. We value others' opinions more than our own.

7. We judge ourselves and others quite harshly. Nothing we do is quite good enough.

Addictive and codependent personalities come into full bloom in adult relationships, but are rooted in early childhood experiences in the family and the culture. As children we all experienced feelings of powerlessness. Dependency is a natural part of childhood. That's why the use and abuse of power in families has such a profound effect on children.

Boys (and girls) who grow up in dysfunctional families spend all their energy dancing to the tune of the parents in the hope of being loved or avoiding shame and abuse. As a result, they don't learn to know themselves.

Codependents can't tell you how they *want* something to be, but they can tell you the rule for how it *should* be. Kevin recalls the early days with his wife. "When our dog died, Linda was in tears and wanted me to hold her. She asked me how I felt. I knew that I was supposed to feel sad, but I didn't have any idea how I really felt."

Codependency: What Is It?

Codependency has become a much used and abused term in the recovery field. I like the simple definition of Charles Whitfield, M.D. "Co-dependency is any suffering and/or dysfunction that is associated with or results from focusing on the needs and behaviors of others." It is addiction to looking elsewhere.

"Sometimes I feel so hungry for affection," says Ron, "I'd do anything just to get a kind word. I feel I need Jane to respond or I'll die. Jane says I get a hang-dog look on my face that makes her furious. She says it just distracts her from her work and makes me seem like one of the kids. I tell myself to just let it alone. In my mind I want to tell her to fuck off, but I don't say anything. I smile forlornly and keep coming back for more. I can see why she doesn't respect me. I don't respect myself. All I want is to be held and cared for, and yet all I seem to get is anger and abuse."

It isn't just gentle men who tend to be codependent. So-called macho men are also out of touch with their own feelings as they strive to achieve material and sexual success. They also suffer as their personal relationships fall short of meeting their emotional needs. As Robert Bly once observed of these types, "John Wayne is Woody Allen turned inside out." The reverse, of course, is also true.

Not having a center to resonate from, we take our cues from the outside. Our greatest fear is that if we lose or let go of external forms (my friend Sally Dennett calls it our scaffolding)—the house, the spouse, the rules, the status—we will fall into a terrifying emptiness. I call this emptiness the Black Hole and will discuss it in more depth in Chapter 8. Developmentally, we are like tiny children who have not left our mothers' arms; we cling to structure, to people and things representing safety, believing that without this illusion of security we would perish.

Codependency, at its core, is addiction to security.

Codependency: Really Four Different Addictions

People who might otherwise be put off by the thought of seeing themselves as an addict can sometimes ease their way into recovery by identifying with the term "codependency" instead. It is similar to the use of the term "neurotic" in the '50s. That term allowed many people who needed help to get involved in counseling without being stigmatized as "crazy." Though calling yourself codependent can help you get into the doorway of recovery, you need a more specific focus to get any further.

In my booklet, *Fatal Attractions: Understanding Codependency, Sex, Romance, and Relationship Addictions*, I first suggested that codependency could best be understood as including four different, but interrelated, addictions that need to be understood and treated separately: sex addiction, romance addiction, relationship attachment addiction, and relationship attraction addiction.

I agree with Anne Wilson Schaef that there is a difference between sexual addiction, romantic addiction, and relationship addictions. She says in *Escape From Intimacy: Untangling the "Love" Addictions*, "Sexual addicts 'come on,' romance addicts 'move on,' and relationship addicts 'hang on.'" I summarize the addictions slightly differently: sex addicts "turn on," romance addicts "shine on," relationship attraction addicts "move on," and relationship attachment addicts "cling on."

Sex Addiction: Hooked on the Turn-On

Sex addicts are constantly seeking the rush of the sexual turn-on.

Daniel recalled the period when he began to recognize that his sexual behavior was addictive. "I had an affair or major flirtation going on all the time. It was a major preoccupation each day. I thought it was the spice that made my life worthwhile. But it was more than a spice—it was my drug." He admitted the terror he felt when he first thought of making changes. "I truly couldn't imagine a life without constant sex. Even more important than the physical act was the thrill of the chase, the excitement of seeing who I would be with the next weekend, and the rush of making all the pieces fit together without getting caught."

Many addicts use sex, like drugs, to deal with uncomfortable feelings. Carlos recalls, "Whenever there was conflict, I ran for a fix. I would look for sex to make me feel good when I was depressed or to calm me down when I'd get too wired at work."

Romance Addiction: Hooked on the Shine

Romance addicts love to fall in love. They have a certain starry-eyed look and are attracted to the shine and glitter of romantic illusion.

Romance addicts believe that love is blind and accept that it's often painful. When they feel an intense attraction to someone they don't know, and become obsessed with meeting and wooing her, this is their cue that they're "in love." Romance addicts literally fall in love—for them it's like stepping off a cliff.

Psychologist Sarah Cirese describes the "True Romance Package" in *Quest: A Search for Self*:

> [Two people] young and beautiful, are drawn to-
> gether by a strong physical attraction that tells
> them that they are meant to satisfy one another's
> erotic and affectional needs. They are tossed
> about by the fury of passion and excitement and
> pain and fear, the two of them alone against the
> world and others who will intrude, forever and
> everlasting. Obsessed with one another to addic-

tion, they are willing to risk all to retain the feeling of being in love. They are scornful of reason or harsh realities—the two of them, in love with love.

The blindness that romance addicts experience is not always one-sided. Couples can also lose themselves in an obsessive love relationship. Tony described the rush of falling in love. "It was so powerful it would make all my pain go away. When I was in love, everything in the world seemed right. I felt like my life had direction and meaning." Many romance addicts don't get sexually involved, and sometimes don't get involved at all. Tony told me. "I was really terrified of relationships. It was so much easier and safer to fantasize about being involved with a beautiful woman than to risk rejection by actually getting involved. Long-distance love affairs were perfect for me. The more distant, the more I felt love's longing—a feeling that I craved."

Relationship Attraction Addicts: Hooked on Moving On

Attraction addicts are always out looking for their ideal partner. Their ideal is often so rigid though, and so impossible to achieve, that every new relationship falls short. These people like the *idea* of a relationship, but are often afraid of getting too close; so their relationships don't last. Only the first part of the cliche about a man's attitude toward women—"I can't live with them and I can't live without them"—is true for attraction addicts. The everyday realities of living with another person take away all that person's attractiveness and charm. And so the search continues. Underneath this pattern, there's often a man who doesn't know how to be close to a woman without having his personal boundaries violated.

Joseph talked about the conflict between his desire to be in a relationship and his need to maintain a protective distance. "The possibility that no long-lasting happiness or fulfillment could ever come from living out these brief love affairs did not occur to me at all. The promise of the 'next one' being the perfect person who at last was going to make me whole was the carrot that seemed to be forever dangling in front of my nose, drawing me onward. I wanted to be close and free at the same time, but mostly I was afraid of getting tied down."

Kevin also had a series of very intense but brief relationships. "I felt like I had to be in a relationship, but was always terrified to get too close. I would be extremely focused and persuasive at first. But once I'd get a woman hooked on me, I'd find reasons to run away. I would tell myself that there was something about her I didn't like, usually something about her being too clingy. But the reality was, I was terrified of losing myself."

Relationship Attachment Addicts: Hooked on Clinging On

Whereas relationship attraction addicts are afraid to get too close and tend to be "dance-away lovers," relationship attachment addicts suffer the opposite problem. Once they make a commitment to their mate, they want to hold on tight and never let go. No matter how bad or destructive things get, they stay, rationalizing that they're still in love, after all, or "it's for the kids." "In chemical addiction," says psychologist Linda Leonard in *Witness to the Fire*, "the preferred substance always becomes the end to which all else is sacrificed. [In addictive relationships,] the corresponding 'substance' is the passion to merge." Attachment addicts fear abandonment and solitude: they are terrified of the prospect of finding an identity outside the context of a relationship.

Although women are more often conditioned to become attachment addicts, and men are conditioned to become attraction addicts, I believe that both sexes are susceptible to either pattern. In the age of liberation, many men have given up their macho conditioning, which would have them always on the prowl, only to get hooked on destructive relationships.

Many of us thought we were becoming more liberated when, in fact, we were just trading one kind of relationship addiction for the other. As Anne Wilson Schaef so aptly put it, "Relationship [attachment] addicts do not have relationships, they take hostages." I might add that they also become hostages.

"When I met my wife," Jamie confided, "it was love at first sight. After being together for a while, it became obvious that we were very different, and that our differences were serious. But I kept hoping she'd change, if I could only show her how much I cared for her. As time went on she seemed to become more and more unhappy. All I could think about was, 'What did I do wrong? What can I do to be a better husband?' My needs always seemed less important to me than hers. My job in life was to make her happy. I felt like a miserable failure, but I kept on trying."

Ron, too, always felt like a failure when his wife didn't respond to his attempts to make her world right. "Whenever Joyce would get angry, I would shrivel up inside. It was like being a little boy again, trying to please Mommy; afraid if I couldn't make her happy, she'd leave me and I would die. It didn't matter if I had to sacrifice myself. Her needs counted, because without her I was nothing."

All four types of codependency addicts confuse intensity with intimacy. If excitement and danger are present, they are attracted like magnets. Certain underlying needs and fears further distinguish the different types of codependency. Sex addicts and relationship attraction addicts often have an overdeveloped need for space, and a fear of being engulfed and trapped. By contrast, romance addicts and relationship attachment addicts have an overdeveloped need for connection and a fear of being alone and abandoned.

Healing Our Love Addictions

I have found the following rules to be useful in healing all varieties of love addiction:

- Recognize that love addictions do exist.
- Remember that addiction needs to be self-defined: no one has the right to call anyone else an addict.
- Acknowledge that love addictions, like all addictions, are progressive and fatal if not treated.
- Realize that any sexual/romantic behavior can become addictive, but none—no matter how unusual—is necessarily addictive.
- Understand that sex, love, and relationship addictions are not about sex, love, or relationships.
- Remember that it is important to name our addictions and name them correctly.
- Recognize the value of support groups that deal specifically with sex and love addictions.

- Know that counseling is helpful for most addicts.
- Accept that residential support programs are essential for some.

Recognize That Love Addictions Do Exist

If you've dealt with addictions to alcohol, cocaine, food, or gambling, the idea of becoming addicted to love seems far-fetched. Perhaps you were in denial for a long time, but you came to recognize that being on a binge and missing your son's big game, or spending money on cocaine you had planned to spend fixing the kitchen, were signs that your life was becoming un-manageable. It's more difficult to recognize the effects of addictive patterns of love.

When we can't sleep at night because our beloved is away, when we have obsessive fears of being left alone, when we fly into a rage when we think our lover isn't paying enough attention to us, when our desire for sex never seems to be satisfied, when we feel like dying when a relationship ends, or feel like killing to hold on to a relationship that's slipping away, we don't often recognize these experiences as signs of addiction. Rather, we tell ourselves that we are "in love."

It's been suggested that love addiction is just some modern mumbo jumbo designed to sell books and take the fun out of people's lives. Yet those of us who have worked with love addicts, and have been witness to the compulsion, the lack of control, and the repetitive patterns of pain and destruction, have no doubt that love addiction is real.

Remember That Addiction Needs To Be Self-Defined: No One Has the Right To Call Anyone Else an Addict

I am often called by media people, particularly at election time, and asked to comment on someone in the public eye. "Is so–and–so a sex addict?" they often want to know. I try to explain to them that not only do I not diagnose someone I haven't seen, but I don't believe in diagnosis at all.

Even in my role as a professional therapist, I refuse to di-agnose people. I have found that the benefits of giving someone an appropriate label are far outweighed by the drawbacks. Once we put a label on someone, it has a tendency to stick for life. For some, the label "addict" becomes the core of their identity. They no longer see themselves as a beautiful, complex human beings who may be behaving in compulsive ways, but as an addict who will always be subject to someone else's will.

Labeling people as addicts, even for their own good, has elements of social control. Names and diagnoses go into computers. Decisions are often made that are not based on the needs of the person, but on the needs of a repressive system which thinks it knows us because it has our name and number in its data banks.

Clients will say to me, "You're the expert. Tell me if you think I'm an addict." I always reply that a decision to use that name must come from them. I help them examine their behavior and answer the question for themselves. I always encourage them to use the name if it helps them to heal, knowing that "addict" is not a statement of their identity. If the name addict is no longer useful, I encourage them to drop it.

Acknowledge That Love Addictions, Like All Addictions, Are Progressive and Fatal If Not Treated

Many people I know have seen the movie *Fatal Attraction*, and those who were willing to talk about it freely said that it frightened them. It struck a chord of truth for many. We don't think of love addictions as having the same potential for destruction as heroin or cocaine addiction. Yet we need only open our eyes and see through our denial to recognize the danger in addictive relationships. Here are some news summaries from my local newspapers which illustrate the point. The stories behind the headlines are tragic enough, but the real tragedy is our failure to recognize the seriousness of these addictive relationships. Many of these fatalities could have been prevented:

> A Little League coach who shot his star female pitcher before killing himself was determined to break up her friendship with another girl, a friend says.

> Spurned love, bloody murder—Mark Hudson is suspected of fatally shooting his ex-girlfriend, Theresa Ann Freitas, as she left work.

> The 26-year-old woman, who apparently was shot to death by her ex-boyfriend Thursday night, had been threatened by the man before.
>
> Fantasy fueled fatal attraction—in a series of increasingly frightening letters to the woman he longed for, mass-murder suspect Richard Farley hinted at violence if she didn't return his affections.[1]

These headlines reflect only the most sensational cases—and the most violent aspects of love addiction. I see a great deal of physical illness including ulcers, cancer, and heart disease—as being directly related to sex, romance, or relationship addictions.

To say that addictions are fatal may seem like an overstatement. Obviously we will all die sometime: in that respect, life itself is a fatal disease. When I categorize addictions as fatal, what I mean is that they limit our lives and cut them short. This is true in the physical sense, that people who are addicted to sex, romance, and relationships die sooner than people who have a healthier approach to these issues. It's also true that love addicts may not be physically dead, but they can be dead in spirit.

We all know people who remain in addictive, destructive relationships, who have just given up on living. We think of them as the walking wounded and, in extreme cases, as zombies. They have the external appearance of being alive, but inside they are dead. Love addictions are even more dangerous than drug addictions because they so effectively lull us into accepting a life of nonliving in exchange for the sweet taste of sex, romance, or relationship. Roberta Flack's song "Killing Me Softly" gives a chilling sense of the hidden dagger beneath love's cloak.

Realize That Any Sexual/Romantic Behavior Can Become Addictive, But None—No Matter How Unusual—Is Necessarily Addictive

The more we learn about addictions, the more we recognize that addiction doesn't reside in the substance or the activity, but in the way an individual relates to these. Falling in love, having sex, being in a relationship can be healthy, or it can be addictive. No particular form of activity is automatically "healthy," no matter how socially acceptable; and none is automatically addictive, no matter how socially unacceptable. Intercourse in the missionary position with one's wife can be addictive. So can masturbation with pornography.

The use of pornography is so common among men in the U.S. that we view it as normal and even healthy. Author Steven Hill says, "In the U.S., 22 million men spend $2 billion a year on a range of 105 pornographic magazines. Porn films gross $5 million per day and the porn industry earns over-the-counter profits of $8 billion per year."

Hill goes on to discuss the ways in which pornography has affected him. I believe he speaks for many men:

> I fantasized and masturbated to the images in *Playboy*, *Penthouse*, and other magazines countless times. I would spread them out on my bed, or wherever, and flip from page to page, searching, searching, for the *perfect* picture, the perfect image . . .
>
> This pornographic fantasy behavior has affected, and to a lesser degree still does affect, my relationships with women, even the most casual ones. I learned to continually sift women who I knew or met through my pornographic, media-conscious, beauty image "eyes," and judge them first and foremost by whether or not they physically "attracted" me. There was a tape loop going round and round my head that said: "beautiful" woman, if I possess her, *I* must be successful.

Just as any sexual or romantic behavior can become addictive, there is none that is automatically addictive, no matter how negatively it's perceived by society. Dr. Eli Coleman, an expert in treating love addictions, points out in a journal article cited at the back that no particular behavior (for example, prostitution, sadomasochism, cross-dressing, fetishes, anonymous sex) is automatically addictive. The distinguishing marks of addiction are "the pattern of excesses, the lack of control, the amount of preoccupation, and the disruption of their lives." He feels that this understanding of sexual compulsivity avoids the necessity of making value judgments about any type of sexual behavior.

Understand That Sex, Love, and Relationship
Addictions Are Not About Sex, Love, or Relationships

It would seem that people who are compulsively involved with sex, love, and relationship are really just taking a good thing too far. Robin Norwood captures this belief in the title of her book, *Women Who Love Too Much*. Love addicts seem to be saying, "We really *are* seeking love—we just go overboard." Actually, nothing could be farther from the truth. Love addicts don't love too much. Sex addicts don't enjoy sex too much. And relationship addicts don't overdo intimacy. In fact, addiction and intimacy are mutually exclusive. So, too, are love and addiction.

Often when I write about the love addictions, I put "love" in quotes to indicate that addictive love is quite different from healthy love. We are so well trained by our families, peer groups, and society to confuse addiction and love that we fail to see the two as being completely distinct from each other.

People who seek out sex, romance, and relationships and become addicted are really seeking a "fix" to cover their pain. In this context, sex, romance, and relationships are about self-protection rather than about connection. We are not really relating to another person, but to our own projected need for security.

Many of us believe that we are seeking love, but in fact we are hooked on pain. We often measure the degree of our love by the depth of our torment. As Kevin once put it, "I feel like I'm living an impossible dream out of some crazy music video, like I'm walking the wire of pain and desire, looking for love in between. No matter how hard I look, I never seem to find it."

Remember That It's Important To Name Our
Addictions and Name Them Correctly

The naming process is extremely important. Once we have named something, we are able to mobilize our energy to deal with it. All addictions thrive in the dark. Naming our addiction shines light on our situation and allows for growth to begin.

Naming, however, is not the same as labeling. Naming is done by the person involved. "I am a sex addict" is naming. "You are a sex addict" is labeling. When I name my addiction, I can also love it: it is part of me, and all of me is lovable. Labeling an addiction is always an act of violence. My wife, Carlin Diamond, wrote a book titled *Love It, Don't Label It* which reminds us that labeling and loving can never go together. Labeling always ingrains in us the mistaken belief that there is something essentially wrong with us. The label "addict" increases self-hatred. The name "addict" can increase self-love.

It is important to give things their proper name. When I wrote *Looking for Love in All the Wrong Places*, in 1988, I used such names as "sex addict," "love addict," "romance addict," and "relationship addict" interchangeably. I felt that we weren't clear enough about the different addictions to be able to separate them. It was more important at that time to offer people support in the area of general issues. Now it is important to become more precise.

Sexual addiction, romance addiction, relationship attraction addiction, and relationship attachment addiction are related but separate addictions and must each be understood and treated if full recovery is to occur.

We know that for all addictions there is a high rate of relapse. I've come to believe that the primary cause for this is our failure to name addictions or to name them correctly. Many clients I've seen reported that they had been in various 12-step programs such as A.A., Al-Anon, Cocaine Anonymous, and so on. A number felt they had a sexual or romantic addiction in addition to their drug addiction, but were told to "just keep coming to meetings and working the steps, and your sexual problems will take care of themselves."

This type of denial is reminiscent of the past, when we told alcoholics not to worry about their drinking: "As soon as we solve your family, psychiatric, or emotional problems, your drinking will take care of itself."

Many people have an addiction to alcohol, and act out sexually as part of their alcoholism. Once their alcoholism is treated, the sexual acting-out goes away. The reverse is also true, and is almost always neglected. There are some people who have a sexual addiction and drink excessively to cover their pain. When their sexual addiction is dealt with, their excessive drinking stops. Finally, there are people who are alcoholic *and* sexually addicted. If this is the case, both addictions must be treated together. Addictions must be understood, named, and dealt with correctly for recovery to progress.

Recognize the Value of Support Groups That Deal Specifically With Sex and Love Addictions

It took almost 50 years from the founding of A.A. in 1935 for 12-step programs to be developed that focused on sex and love addictions. The reason why it took so long for us to deal with the various love addictions is that cultural denial has been so prevalent in our society. Even 12-step programs, which focus on addiction and recovery, are not always able to recognize the destructive sexual behaviors in their midst. Many people I see for counseling have commented on the difficulty of attending traditional 12-step meetings once they have become aware of sex and love addictions.

"I couldn't believe the amount of sexual acting-out that goes on at A.A. meetings," said Tony. "Before I began to understand the love addictions, I thought of it as normal behavior. But now I see that it's the same kind of compulsive attempt to deal with anxiety and fear—only using sex and romance instead of alcohol and cocaine."

In fact, issues of sex and love addiction may go back to the earliest days of the cofounding of Alcoholics Anonymous by Bill Wilson. According to Pulitzer Prize-winning author Nan Robertson,

> Bill Wilson's marriage to Lois Burnham in 1918 lasted until his death at the age of 75 in 1971. She believed in him fiercely and tended his flame. Yet, particularly during his sober decades in A.A. in the forties, fifties, and sixties, Bill Wilson was a compulsive womanizer. His flirtations and his adulterous behavior filled him with guilt, according to old-timers close to him, but he continued to stray off the reservation. His last and most serious love affair, with a woman at A.A. headquarters in New York, began when he was in his sixties. She was important to him until the end of his life, and was remembered in a financial agreement with A.A. ...
>
> "Dr. Bob," is a more shadowy figure than Bill Wilson, partly because he died when A.A. was only fifteen years old, in 1950. He was a dig-

nified man, gallant to women, yet had a slangy
way of speaking about them. He called women
"frails," or "skirts," or, if he really liked one, simply "Woman." He relished a dirty joke in the company of men.... Conventional and sometimes dog-
matic, Dr. Bob opposed the admission of women
alcoholics into the initially all-male A.A. In those
days, "nice" women were not supposed to be
drunks.

Dr. Bob's" attitude toward women is typical of men who
are conflicted over their desire for and their fear of women. There
may or may not be any truth to the notion that the early A.A.
founders had unresolved issues concerning women and sexuality;
but many people believe that 12-step programs tend to ignore and
sometimes perpetuate sex and love addictions.

Kevin told me that before he began dealing with his sexual
and romantic addictions, A.A. became just another hunting
ground for his sexual acting-out. "In A.A., just as in all other areas
of my life, I collected 'rainchecks' with vulnerable, attractive
women. I didn't really want them, or even want to know them,
but I needed to know I always had a few phone numbers available if I needed them. I came to see that I was a junkie with his
stash, always afraid to be without his precious supply of dope—
only my drug was the promise of sexual and romantic intrigue."

Kevin needed a program that dealt specifically with love
addictions. "The addict in me wanted to believe that just working
the steps of A.A. would solve my relationship problems," he told
me. "But the healthy side knew that just as marital counseling
wouldn't take care of my alcoholism, neither would A.A. take care
of my sex and love addiction. I needed something more."

It was in response to such needs that specific 12-step programs—such as Sex and Love Addicts Anonymous (SLAA) and
Co-Dependents Anonymous (CODA)—were founded.

"I finally felt like I had come home," Daniel recalled after
attending his first meeting. "I had been to A.A. and other 12-step
meetings, but I never felt I could really talk about my compulsion
to buy pornography, or my visits to prostitutes, or the fact that I
had spent god knows how much money on 976 numbers. In
SLAA, I felt like I wouldn't be judged as some pervert."[2]

Know That Counseling Is Helpful for Most People

Twelve-step recovery programs are a core aspect of recovery, but I've also found good counseling to be very helpful as well. Many clients I see begin counseling with me, and then get involved in 12-step programs. Others get settled in 12-step programs first, and then come in for additional counseling. Either way, the two approaches complement each other.

Whereas 12-step programs offer a fellowship of many, counseling offers a fellowship of two. In the safe, supportive, and accepting environment of an intimate two-person relationship, healing can occur on a deeper level. There are things we would never say in a group that we can develop the courage to say to a skilled counselor. A healthy relationship with a counselor can help heal some of the damage done long ago within the intimate confines of our families.

Counseling services for sex and love addicts are few and far between. There are literally thousands of therapists who are trained to deal with the various "outer ring" addictions—to alcohol, cocaine, gambling, food, and so on. But there are relatively few counselors with the training and competence to deal with sex and love addiction.

An even more difficult problem is that many therapists themselves have unresolved issues involving sex and love. Some therapists are sex, romance, or relationship addicts who have not yet dealt with their problems. Such people can cause great harm to clients. Peter Rutter, M.D., talks about these issues in his fine book, *Sex in the Forbidden Zone: When Men in Power—Therapists, Doctors, Clergy, Teachers, and Others—Betray Women's Trust.* Although he focuses on men violating the trust of women, men are also violated by male counselors and by female counselors as well.

Yet a good therapist can be absolutely crucial in helping you deal with sex and love addictions. One of the best ways to find someone good is to talk to others. Often within the 12-step programs there is a very accurate grapevine about which therapists are helpful, and which talk a good line but haven't done their own healing work. There is also an organization, the American Academy of Health Care Providers in the Addictive Disorders, that keeps a directory of trained professionals. Their listing of therapists who treat sex and love addictions is particularly valuable.[3]

Accept That Residential Programs Are Essential for Some People

Far fewer sex and love addicts than substance abusers need residential support. But even though residential programs are often quite expensive, finding the right one if you need it may be a matter of life and death. There are some men who continue dangerous acting-out behavior in spite of 12-step support or counseling. Others may have so much stress in their lives that they need a quiet, supportive atmosphere to begin their recovery. For such people, residential support is essential.

Since relatively few people have been through these programs, finding one through the grapevine may be difficult. But therapists trained in dealing with sex and love addictions will be familiar with the most effective residential programs available. Seeking a professional referral in this case is your best bet.

As you work through the issues related to sex and love and deal with your addictions, you will complete the second stage of recovery and the second task of mature masculinity. You are now ready to move deeper to deal with the issues that underlie our addictions.

Notes

1. Quotes from the following newspapers: *Marin Independent Journal*, August 14, 1989; *San Francisco Examiner*, June 16, 1989; *Marin Independent Journal*, May 20, 1989; *San Francisco Examiner*, February 18, 1988.

2. The National Council on Sexual Addiction Problems of Colorado, P.O. Box 3097, Boulder, CO 80307; (303) 499-7969, has developed a very useful booklet titled *Twelve Step Resources For Sexual Addicts & Co-Addicts*. The booklet describes and contrasts seven nationwide fellowships, including the following: Sex Addicts Anonymous (SAA), The Augustine Fellowship, Sex and Love Addicts Anonymous (SLAA), Sexaholics Anonymous (SA), Sexual Compulsives Anonymous (SCA), Codependents of Sex Addicts (COSA), Co-Sex & Love Addicts Anonymous (CO-SLAA), and S-Anon Family Groups (S-Anon).

3. The American Academy of Health Care Providers in the Addictive Disorders, 260 Beacon St., Somerville, MA 02143; (617) 661-6148.

5

Healing the Addictive Core

 Masculinity is not something
given to you, something
you're born with, but
something you gain.... And you gain it
by winning small battles with honor.
— Norman Mailer,
Cannibals and Christians

She called to me from across her beauty. It stretched between us like a maze. I disappeared inside it, never to be seen again.

—Sy Safransky,
Editor, *The Sun*

Task 3: Transform Our Ambivalent Feelings Toward Women and Children

Having journeyed through the outer two rings of addiction, it is now time for us to descend into the realm of the feminine. We have called addiction the disease of lost selfhood. In the broadest sense, we can say that addiction is the loss of our male identity to the power of the archetypal feminine. When we stopped being hunter-gatherers and became estranged from mother earth—from the stones, plants, and animals—we developed an addictive longing for what we had lost.

Addiction as Enmeshment in the Feminine

The addict is not simply looking for an escape from life's problems, but is on an endless journey to find the feminine connection he feels he is missing. "What the Addict is seeking (though he doesn't know it)," say Robert Moore and Douglas Gillette in *King, Warrior, Magician, Lover,*

> is the ultimate and continuous "orgasm," the ultimate and continuous "high." This is why he rides from village to village and from adventure to adventure. This is why he goes from one woman to another. Each time his woman confronts him with her mortality, her finitude, her weakness and limitations, hence shattering his dream of *this time* finding the orgasm without end—in other words, when the excitement of the illusion of perfect union with her (with the world, with GOD) becomes tarnished—he saddles his horse and rides

out looking for renewal of his ecstasy. He needs
his "fix" of masculine joy. He really does. He just
doesn't know where to look for it. He ends by
looking for his "spirituality" in a line of cocaine.[1]

The association of cocaine and the feminine is obvious from
the common names given the drug on the street: "Lady," "Girl,"
"Her," "La Dama Blanca," "The White Lady." Cocaine is also seen
by many users as the premiere enhancer of sensuality and sexual
pleasure.

However, it isn't only a particular drug like cocaine, or even
drugs in general, that are associated with the feminine, but the
entire addictive process that hooks so many men. In *Witness to
the Fire: Creativity & the Veil of Addiction*, author Linda Schierse
Leonard, a Jungian analyst and recovering alcoholic, makes explicit the connection between addiction and the desire to merge
with the cosmic other. "In my experience," she says, "it is the archetypal figure of the Demon Lover to whom one gives oneself
in addiction. For the Demon Lover seduces and can possess the
soul as a slave."[2]

When we fall in love, and when we use drugs, we create
an altered state of consciousness. There is blurring of boundaries,
a feeling of giving ourselves over to an overwhelming cosmic
force. Both altered states are often described in similar terms.
Those who take stimulants or narcotics often describe the initial
"rush" when the drug hits their system as being like a "full body
orgasm." Poets for hundreds of years have compared falling in
love to overwhelming natural and unnatural phenomena: being
struck by lightening; falling under the spell of a sorceress, the
moon, or a witch; feeling drunk with love; being madly in love.

The connection between the drug rush and the rush of love
may actually have biochemical roots. According to Michael Liebowitz, author of *The Chemistry of Love*, a substance known to bio-
chemists as phenylethylamine, or PEA, is released in the brain
when we fall in love. It certainly is more than a coincidence that
the PEA molecule, which is considered an excitatory amine, bears
a striking structural similarity to the pharmaceutically manufac-
tured stimulant amphetamine.

I believe that our addictions—whether to drugs, work, or
women—are in some way connected to our addiction to the "eternally feminine," as Goethe would have it: to Woman. Having

moved this far, we are now ready to confront both the dominance of the feminine principle in our relationships, and our denial of its power. As we do that, we will see that fear and discomfort with the feminine is directly related to the absence of a strong, nurturing, masculine presence in our lives. This is the third stage of the recovery process: tackling the twin tasks of understanding and healing our confused feelings toward women and children, and dealing with the absence of our father and our fear of getting close to other men.

To complete these tasks, we must work through the following issues:

- Acknowledge our love/hate relationship with women and children.
- Separate from the feminine, our mothers and other women.
- Feel the hunger for our absent fathers.
- Uncover the core beliefs that emerge from our loss.
- Receive validation from a male ally.
- Reconnect with the mature masculine, our fathers and other men.
- Balance the male/female within us.

 If a person continues to see only giants, it means he is still looking at the world through the eyes of a child. I have a feeling that man's fear of woman comes from having first seen her as the mother, creator of men.

—Anais Nin

Acknowledge Our Love/Hate Relationship With Women and Children

"Most of the time I feel like all I want to do is make Lisa happy." Kevin looked pained as he sorted out his ambivalent feelings. "But there are times when a rage comes over me, and it's overwhelming. I feel like I want to hurt her, rip her apart. I don't know where these feelings come from, and they scare the shit out of me. The only way I know how to deal with them is by turning off my feelings completely."

The reasons why a man loves a woman are usually clearer to him than the reasons for his rage. What I've found in my personal experience, and my work with men over the years, is that the anger and hate are connected with the deep-seated fear men have of women.

I remember when I was a preadolescent, 11 or 12 years old, talking with an older buddy about what it was like to "do it" with a girl. As a worldly 14-year-old, he seemed to know everything about the mysterious opposite sex. He told me that the best sex was when the woman was underneath you, with her legs spread wide apart. I nodded with understanding I hoped I would gain some day. Then he leaned forward and beckoned me closer. As I turned my head to listen I knew I was about to receive an important and deeply held truth about girls and sex. "Don't ever let a girl cross her legs while your dick is inside. If she does, you can't get it out and she can hold you there forever if she wants. It happened to a friend of mine in a drive-in movie. They finally had to call the fire department and have them sprayed with water to get them apart." I remembered just such a thing happening to my pet dog, Spotty. My eyes got wide and I gulped. Though I acted calm, I was terrified, but glad to know *the truth.*

This fear of women, though often repressed, is widespread and pervasive. Psychiatrist Wolfgang Lederer, in his important book *The Fear of Women: An Inquiry into the Engima of Woman and Why Men Through the Ages Have Both Loved and Dreaded Her*, offers the following examples drawn from his clinical practice: "A lawyer races his sports-car home, lest his wife accuse him of dawdling. A full-size man has nightmares that his wife, in bed, will roll on him and crush him. A car salesman, single, is afraid to be roped in, and a wine merchant, married, is afraid of being kicked out by their respective women."

"So it goes," Dr. Lederer concludes. "So, and in a thousand other ways, Man, confronted by Women, does seem to feel, variously, frightened, revolted, dominated, bewildered and even, at times, superfluous."[3]

In my own life, I have loved a number of women deeply, and have been loved deeply in return. We cherished each other, supported each other, cared for each other. Yet there was always an element of fear in me which I had difficulty understanding. With the fear came anger and resentment.

I began to get a glimpse of the root of this fear when I was sick for a month with pneumonia. I never had been a very good patient, but this time I was worse than ever. I wanted to be reassured that everything would be okay, but when my wife offered words of support, I told her that she didn't know what she was talking about. I demanded constant attention and care, but when I got it I flew into a rage. I wanted to be held and cuddled, but when my wife reached out to me, I pushed her away.

In a moment of insight, I realized that what I really wanted was to return to childhood, to be an infant that was loved unconditionally by its mommy. But on an even deeper level, I wanted to return to the womb, to fuse back into my mother's body, to reexperience the oneness of total merger. I was also overwhelmed with terror. If I allowed myself to be nurtured, I was sure I wouldn't ever want to go back to the real world. I was afraid I would just crawl up inside the woman's body and cease to exist.

I came to recognize that my demands on women were expressions of an unrealistic need to be mothered. My rage and anger expressed my childish belief that I was entitled to such care and would die without it. They also represented my adult need to push the woman I loved away to ward off my fear that I would give up my separate identity in order to fuse my identity with hers.

In her book *Man's World, Woman's Place*, Elizabeth Janeway gives us a broader understanding of the dynamics underlying men's desire for women and our simultaneous anger toward them.

> In this relationship, we can see, it is a demand
> for the renewal of past happiness, which might
> be stated badly this way: "I want a woman of my

own, to comfort me in my lack and loneliness and frustration as my mother did long ago."

With such a plea we can surely sympathize. This is the internal, remembered reality which corresponds with the external social reality, the emotion imprinted by the fact that children need mothering and get it most often and most easily from their mothers. Out of need, however, grows the demanding mythic imperative, for our statement goes on to assert that a man does not just need a woman, he has a right to her and that right is a part of the order of the world.

Along with my feelings of entitlement for endless expressions of love from my wife, I realized that I also felt jealous and angry at my infant son, Jemal. I told myself that I was being stupid, that I had no reason to be angry at him or resentful toward my wife. He was just being a baby, and she was just being a good mother. Yet over time I came to realize that I resented the care he was getting, and the very fact of his infancy.

There were so many times I wanted to give up being an adult, to let go of my struggles for success. I railed inside my own mind: "Why does *he* get so much love and care? Why is *he* allowed to just lay back and enjoy life, while *I* must be forever on the run, fighting the battles of the world? Why can't *I* be taken care of for a while? I hate you, Jemal!"

I felt like some kind of monster. How could a man hate a little baby, his own son?

It took me years to admit my feelings to myself, many more to have the courage to tell another human being. I finally learned that it was okay to be weak and vulnerable, and to need support from a woman. I still remember the first time I was able to crawl up in my wife's arms, let out my sobs of frustration and pain, and know I wouldn't cease to exist.

Separate From the Feminine, Our Mothers and Other Women

In the first crosscultural study of manhood, anthropologist David Gilmore found that becoming a man is a process that must be achieved through some sort of stressful series of tests that begin with boys being separated, sometimes forcefully, from the women of the tribe. In cultures as diverse as those of Japan, India, China, the Mediterranean lands, aboriginal South America, Oceania, East Africa, ancient Greece, and modern North America, the patterns are similar. Gilmore notes that although the pattern is widespread, it is not universal. The Tahitians of Polynesia and the Semai of Malaysia, for example, do not place a great deal of emphasis on sex roles or initiation rites for young men. Yet in most cultures throughout the world, boys cannot become men except through a rite of passage.

Although there are rites for initiating girls into womanhood, there is no parallel crosscultural belief that girls have to be *made* into women. In all cultures Gilmore studied, womanhood is seen as developing naturally, needing no cultural intervention, its predestined arrival at menarche commemorated rather than forced by ritual. Why is there a forced need for males and not females to pass a test before becoming an adult?

The answer lies in a phenomenon so universal and accepted that, like the air we breathe, it is invisible to us: "It *is* a fact," says social scientist Lillian Rubin, "that a woman, even if not the mother, is almost always the primary caregiver of infancy. *And no fact of our early life has greater consequences for how girls and boys develop into women and men, therefore for how we relate to each other in our adult years.*"

We see the effect of this deep connection in boys around the age of three or four. "When I grow up I'm going to have a baby," a toddler proudly proclaims. Mother quickly intervenes and says, "No, only girls can have babies." The small boy bursts into tears of rage and disappointment. He can't understand why, since he has learned to identify with mother at the core of his being, he can't do what she has done. For girls the same statement has no traumatic consequences, but rather is a source of pleasure and reassurance. A girl learns early that her identification with mother is consistent with her identity as a female. She will naturally grow up to be like Mother and be able to do the things that Mother does. A boy must give up this identification: the reality of this limitation shapes his future.

For a boy to establish a male identity requires a profound upheaval in his internal world. Despite the fact that other connections are made during the early months of life—with father, siblings, grandparents, babysitters, friends—if mother has been the main caregiver, the attachment and identification with her remains the primary one. "Thus," says psychologist Robert Stroller, "the whole process of becoming masculine is a risk in the little boy from the day of birth on; his still-to-be-created masculinity is endangered by the primary, profound, primeval oneness with mother, a blissful experience that serves as a focus which, throughout life, can attract one to regress back to the primitive oneness."[4]

It is against this backdrop that we see the importance of male initiation. We need help in separating from the force field of the Woman or we will never make it to manhood. Her gravitational pull is too strong to resist on our own. Older males must be there to exert an even greater pull or we will always be afraid of being sucked back in to our mother's orbit. If we do not experience the male counterinfluence, we grow up feeling like adult children: we may grow physically, and do all the "manly" things, but inside we still feel like mama's boy.

It is only after we've been able to separate from the archetypal mother that we can truly have a loving, intimate, adult relationship with a woman.

Task 4: Express the Grief Over the Absence of Our Fathers and Risk Getting Close to Other Men

Feel the Hunger for Our Absent Fathers

In traditional societies, our confusion over the desire to merge with Woman and our need to be separate from her is resolved through rites of passage in which boys are removed from their mothers and connected with the adult men of the tribe. In the modern world, with fathers off working, often at jobs that are stressful and dehumanizing, boys are often left without adult male love or support. The result is that we have ambivalent feelings toward our fathers, just as we do toward our mothers. Mothers, at least, were present for most of us. Fathers were generally emotionally if not physically absent; hence we long for the presence we never felt and we share a deep hunger for what is missing.

In saying that we "hunger" for our absent fathers, I mean that we are, metaphorically, missing some basic nutrient that only fathers can provide. Robert Bly suggests this magical transmission: "When a father and son do spend long hours together ... we could say that a substance almost like food passes from the older body to the younger body." This was the natural order of things for all hunter-gatherer peoples, and something we have let slip away. As we have become less physically attuned, living more in our minds, we have lost the male substance of life. With fathers often absent, we get the appearance of love and support without the substance. We eat the white bread of refined male energy, but have lost the rough male grit of the whole grain.

Our bodies and souls starve. "The son's body—not his mind—receives and the father gives this food at a level far below consciousness," says Bly. "The son does not receive a hands-on healing, but a body-on healing. His cells receive some knowledge of what an adult masculine body is."

What would we give to know our fathers so well that our cells vibrated in unison? How many lifetimes have we been searching for the nutrients that would nourish us and validate our manhood as sons of our fathers? I shiver when I say these words out loud. It's no wonder that so many of us feel a grief beyond imagining and a rage that knows no bounds.

Uncover the Core Beliefs That Emerge From Our Loss

Many of us feel as though we have gotten too much mothering and too little fathering. I believe the truth is that we never got enough of either. We are starved for both, yet we are missing fathering more. As a result, we live our lives out of balance: the need for fathering rules our psyches. While our feelings toward our mothers (and hence other women) alternate between love and hate, our feelings toward our fathers (and other men) alternate between longing and grief.

To satisfy this lifelong hunger, men must first recognize that our experiences have been ground down into beliefs that are so deeply ingrained that they have become part of the fabric of our lives, and are accepted by most of us as givens.

These core beliefs include the following: [5]

- *I am damaged and therefore bad inside.*
    Men with this belief feel a great deal of shame.
- *To know me is to abuse or abandon me.*
    Men with this belief are always afraid.
- *If I have to rely on people to meet my needs, I will die.*
    Men with this belief distrust intimate relationships.
- *I must fill up the emptiness inside me. I need more*
    (i.e. sex, money, power, drugs).
    Men with this belief alternate between feeling
    intense excitement and extreme depression.

When we aren't loved unconditionally by our parents, we blame ourselves. As children we aren't able to see that our parents are themselves damaged. If they aren't available to us in a caring way, we come to believe that it is because there is something wrong with us. We feel like damaged goods, and are sure the damage is inherent.

Feeling damaged at our core, we believe that to reveal ourselves as such will cause us even more damage: "If I really let you see me as I am, I'm afraid you will abandon me or abuse me." As a result, we live in constant fear of being found out and rejected.

Having been damaged by the people closest to us—our fathers and mothers—we assume that all people are dangerous. We hunger for intimate human contact, but we are also wary. We don't want to get hurt again. We believe, deep inside, that people cannot be trusted. We are sure that if we have to rely on people to meet our needs, we will die. We go through life distrusting others and distrusting ourselves.

Cut off from others and cut off from ourselves, we attempt to fill the void within. Some of us try to fill it with food; others try alcohol, sex, drugs, power, or money. Yet the hole inside never fills. In fact, the more we try and fill it, the larger it gets. And the larger the hole becomes, the more desperate we become to fill the void. It isn't surprising that this cycle runs out of control. It becomes like a deranged thermostat. Instead of turning off when the heat in the room reaches the desired temperature, it turns on. The hotter it gets, the more heat is turned on. One addict I know described the situation by saying, "My drug of choice is 'more.'"

As we attempt to fill ourselves up with more of the same, our emotions fluctuate wildly. We feel intense excitement as we hope against hope that this time we will fix the pain. Then when the inevitable crash occurs—when the drug wears off, the love affair ends, the market crashes, our bodies fail—we go into a deep depression. It's the reason addicts, in the later stages of their addiction, look and act so crazy.

Receive Validation From a Male Ally

However we manage to get ourselves separated from the Woman, we are left in an exhausted state. If we are to survive and prosper, we need the ongoing support of a few good men. You might think of these men as allies. I like the word ally. For me it suggests someone who is compassionate, friendly, and helpful. There is a gentleness and kindness implied. But ally also brings to mind the warrior energy of men who support each other under fire. Ally has the additional connotation, from Carlos Castaneda's stories of the shaman Don Juan, of a spiritual helper. This ally is in touch with powerful forces that transcend the physical realm. There is some danger in asking to be supported by an ally and tapping into this kind of power. We learn that he will help us only if our lives are lived impeccably, with truth, honor, and total commitment. If we are unwilling to live fully and with integrity, our ally can harm us.

Chuck Dederich was the founder and director of Synanon, an organization set up to treat drug addicts, and a man who wanted to change the world. Dederich started Synanon in 1958 in Ocean Park, California, with a $33 unemployment check. By the time I had joined in 1965, Synanon had grown to become a multimillion dollar corporation helping thousands of addicts.

Dederich was a controversial figure when I met him. He was called by various people a madman, a saint, an opportunist, a brilliant executive, a latter-day Socrates, an earthquake, a herd of one elephant. Chuck was my first ally.

I had been involved with Synanon for nearly a year, and had taken a lot of flack in the groups for my job at Napa State Hospital, where I directed the program for addicts. Many group members felt that only Synanon could get people to break their addiction to drugs: to them I was just a 22-year-old kid pretending to function in the adult world. One day Chuck came into my group, and I felt my blood turn to ice. I was terrified of what he would say to me. When it was my turn to come under his scrutiny, he fixed me with a stare that allowed no possibility of escape. "I heard of you. You're the youngster who thinks he's going to help addicts. Is that right?" I wanted to run. "Yeah, Chuck," I finally blurted out. "Nobody around here thinks I can help those people, but I think I'm doing the right thing."

Chuck's gaze was intense and I shivered. Then he cracked a smile, shaking his head. "I do believe you just might do it. Keep up the good work, son. Someday you're going to be running that hospital." I never ran the hospital, but I always felt that Chuck believed I could.

"A young man who is not being admired by an older man is being hurt," says psychologist Robert Moore in *King, Warrior, Magician, Lover*. "If an older man is not empowering other men by blessing them, then he is cursing them." The blessing I received from Chuck in those few moments has lasted for decades.

Reconnect With the Mature Masculine, Our Fathers and Other Men

My father left when I was six years old. For most of my life, I had seen him only through my mother's eyes. Even when I met him as an adult, I still maintained my mother's view of him as a man. It was not a very flattering portrait.

As long as we are unwilling to love and accept our fathers just the way they are, we cannot totally accept ourselves. We have to go through the earlier stages where we recognize our wound and the hurt, pain, fear, guilt, and shame that goes with it. But then it becomes time to move beyond that wound and reintegrate our father into our psyche, if not into our lives.

In the popular film *Star Wars*, the viewer hates and fears "Darth Vader," a pun on dark father. But George Lucas's message is also that we cannot banish our dark father from our lives, nor destroy the feelings for him we carry in our heart.

Many of us who haven't come to peace with our own father seek out older men in an attempt to fill the void our father's absence left inside us. But we can't replace our father; we can only come to peace with him.

It took me many years, but I could finally forgive my father for not being around when I needed him as a child. Without the veil of my own resentments, and those of my mother, I could see him more clearly. What I saw I came to admire.

I invited my men's group to come to my house, where my father was going to be putting on one of his puppet shows especially for us. The group had been meeting together for a long while, and we had learned to move beyond our barriers and share with each other on the deepest levels of our experience. We'd been through the births of our children, marriages and divorces, job changes and retirements. We also spent time honoring the male elders in our lives.

My father talked a little about his life, and answered questions, but mainly he spoke through his art as a puppeteer. As my friends interacted with me and my father, a bonding occurred. The group's presence helped me accept my father for who he was as a man. My father's presence in the company of my men's group helped me reconnect with my male soul.

As my father performed for the group, I remembered watching one of his first spontaneous shows in San Francisco. His performances had always embarrassed my mother. It was a joy to watch him now without the overlay of my mother's judgment.

He didn't even need his puppets with him to get a crowd laughing and cheering. On the day I remembered, he'd approached a somewhat bored group of people waiting for the ferry.

Pulling off his coat and waving it in front of the people, he shouted, "What is this?"

"A coat," someone answered back a bit tentatively, unsure about what they were getting into.

"No, this can't be a coat. This is the world of make-believe!"

He put the coat over his head with the sleeves hanging down in front. As he swung one sleeve he called out, "One elephant," moving the elephant's trunk from side to side. "Two elephants!" he shouted as the other sleeve joined in the back-and-forth sway. Then the sleeves crossed each other, interlacing. "Two elephants in love," he crooned to the delight of his audience. Then removing the coat from his head, he asked the crowd, "Isn't it crazy that elephants have to show humans how to love one another?" In many other shows I saw, his puppets talked about racial equality, healing, peace and love, and ending war.

My dad came to visit yesterday. As usual, he brought flowers for my wife and a little gas money for me. We went out to eat at an inexpensive chain restaurant. Living alone in the Tenderloin area of San Francisco on his Social Security income, he doesn't eat out often. He couldn't get over the salad bar piled high with food. At 87 he walks slowly now. It took him 10 minutes to make three trips around the food bar. He didn't put anything on his plate; said he just wanted to marvel at the beauty. How wonderful, I thought. Most of us can't wait to fill our plates and feed our faces. Here's a man who takes time to admire beauty wherever he finds it, even under the bright lights and in the false plastic elegance of a fast-food restaurant.

I can't forget the past and all the disappointments I experienced as a child. They are part of the fabric of my life. Yet I can stop blaming my father for what I never received. He loved me as well as he was able. Life is too short to allow past hurts to ruin the beauty of the present. My father is precious to me, and through him I am linked forever to all men back to the beginning of human history.

Balance the Male/Female Within Us

I always believed in the ideal of balancing male and female qualities in the individual. But it was a wholeness I never seemed able to achieve. Never having had much fathering growing up, I was always confused about the male side of things; and women seemed even a greater mystery. When I was able to look at my mother and father with more objectivity, I found they didn't play the usual male/female roles.

My father exemplified more of the traditional feminine qualities. He was emotional to the point of melodrama. His poetry was of sunsets and beauty. He was more interested in quoting Shakespeare than in making money—much to my mother's exasperation. My mother, on the other hand, spent her life making money and focusing on job security. She was a social activist who was still marching at age 75—this time for the rights of senior citizens. Her walls were covered with awards from various community groups and political leaders. Over her bed was a large poster with words in red against a black background, "Seniors! On your feet and off your rockers."

If I wrote poetry and wept, was I being manly, I wondered? Or nose to the grindstone, 9 to 5 until I die: is that an expression of the woman in me? I finally gave up trying to figure it out, and in the process of giving up came to a few realizations.

Carl Jung suggested that all people have a contrasexual element within their psyches. Men have a feminine element, which Jung called the *anima*. Women have a masculine *animus*. Psychological maturity depends on finding a harmony between these two principles within ourselves. This is the sacred marriage at the core of many religions and philosophical beliefs throughout the world.

Many of us, hungry for balance in our lives, want to go directly to the chase. We want to taste the sweetness of merging before we have completed the necessary elements of the journey. Men, as we have seen, must first separate from the energy of the feminine, from Woman. We must then get support from male mentors so that we can reconnect with our absent fathers and develop healthy relationships with men in our lives. Only then can we experience a true merging of the inner masculine and inner feminine.

This balance has deepened for me over the years. Some time ago during one of my meditations, I asked for guidance from my "higher power." In the meditation I am in a place I love. It's the place that seems to be with me whenever I want a sense of peace and tranquility. I am sitting along a beautiful stream in the countryside in southern Germany, in the Black Forest region—I spent part of a summer there after my junior year in college. The day is warm and I feel a connection to the water, the small insects dancing on the shimmer. Across the stream is a bicycle path with people riding between the towns of Emmendingen and Freiburg. Rows of corn swish in the breeze.

In the meditation two figures appear—one male, one female. The woman has dark hair and wears robes of white. She is infinitely warm and caring, nurturing in the way I dreamed my mother would be, and also very sensual without any sense of shame or fear. When I ask her name, she replies, "Rebecca." Her voice is as light as the air, but strong.

The male guide is big and tall, with a full beard and warm blue eyes that twinkle when he smiles. He wears the clothing of a Viking—a fur vest over layers of skins. He's strong but not violent. In some ways he is even gentler than Rebecca. His name is Guntar.

They say they were sent to guide me and teach me the ways of becoming a spiritual warrior.

Sometimes I consider my spirit guides to be real. At other times I think they are just in my imagination. Yet at some very deep level, they represent the male/female within me. Neither is traditionally male or female, but each seems to comprise a mixture of both. When I feel out of balance, I meditate on the place I love, and talk to Guntar and Rebecca. Their counsel is always helpful. Often they just put their arms around me and hug me. Just being in their presence is healing.

Guntar and Rebecca are like portable parents who are available anytime to love me, unconditionally, just the way I am; they also make me feel connected to God. But God now seems less to me like a bearded man in the sky than an energy source which is loving, which balances male and female qualities.

When I've been with Guntar and Rebecca, I often think of a friend, Shirley Luthman. Shirley's view of the male/female balance seems to fit with my experiences. She says our first task in life is to be committed to ourselves. This commitment to self is not being selfish, but rather involves a commitment to aliveness and therefore to a passionate life.

She goes on to say in her book, *Collection, 1979*, "Such a commitment then requires an understanding of the male and female (yin-yang, receptive-aggressive) energies within each individual." Her way of describing the relationship between the Yin and the Yang has been very helpful to me. "The nature of commitment to self," she says, "is the ownership of the intuitive-feminine as director and the use of the masculine energy to back up your intuitive with words, behavior, logic, and aggression."

In my meditations, it is the feminine principle, Rebecca, who usually has the intuitive understanding of a situation. But it is the masculine, Guntar, whom I call on to put my intuition into action. Without the feminine, we have action without purpose: we are loose cannons shooting off in all directions. Without the force of the masculine, we know what is right, but we never put our knowledge into action.

As we integrate and balance the male-female, yang-yin, sun-moon, dynamic-magnetic aspects of our lives, we complete the twin tasks of healing our relationships with women and children, and healing our relationships with men. We are now ready to move on to the fourth stage of recovery and deal with the false masks we have learned to wear.

Notes

1. Moore, Robert, and Douglas Gillete (1990) *King, Warrior, Magician, Lover: Rediscovering the Archetypes of the Mature Masculine.* San Francisco: Harper-San Francisco.

2. Leonard, Linda Schierse (1990) *Witness to the Fire: Creativity and the Veil of Addiction.* Boston: Shambhala.

3. Lederer, Wolfgang, M. D. (1968) *The Fear of Women: An Inquiry into the Enigma of Woman and Why Men Through the Ages Have Both Loved and Dreaded Her.* New York: Harcourt Brace Jovanovich, Inc..

4. Stroller, Robert (1974) "Facts and fancies: An examination of Freud's concept of bisexuality." In *Women and Analysis,* edited by Jean Strouse. New York: Dell Publishing Co.

5. These core beliefs were adapted from Patrick Carnes, *Out of the Shadows: Understanding Sexual Addiction.* Carnes describes the following core beliefs of the sexual addict:

   1. Self-image: I am basically a bad, unworthy person.
   2. Relationships: No one would love me as I am.
   3. Needs: My needs are never going to be met if I have to depend on others.
   4. Sexuality: Sex is my most important need.

   Although Carnes connects these beliefs to sexual addicts, I believe that similar beliefs underlie all addictions.

6

Healing the False Self

 "When I get to heaven," said the Hasidic rabbi Susya shortly before his death, "they will not ask me, 'Why were you not Moses?' but 'Why were you not Susya? Why did you not become what only you could become?'"

It was a great mistake, my being born a man. I would have been much more successful as a sea gull or a fish. As it is, I will always be a stranger who never feels at home, who does not really want and is not really wanted, who can never belong, who must always be a little in love with death!
—Eugene O'Neill,
Long Day's Journey into Night

Task 5: Change Our Self-Hatred to Self-Actualization

In November 1965, I had just dropped out of medical school and enrolled at U.C. Berkeley. On the inside I was terrified and confused, but I kept up the appearance of a self-assured young graduate student who knew exactly what he wanted and where he was going.

Though I wasn't aware of it at the time, I think I joined Synanon because I hoped they might look below the surface and see the lost child I was hiding. Maybe they would force me to do what I didn't feel I could do myself—help me drop my mask and develop the courage to let others know me. As I signed up for my first Synanon game, I thought of the words my mother had written in my fourth-grade autograph book. Quoting Shakespeare's Hamlet, she told me: "This above all: To thine own self be true, And it must follow, as the night the day, Thou canst not then be false to any man." It was the only time in my life she ever quoted poetry, and so it had a particularly strong impact on me.

I always felt those words held the key to my life, but I had no idea how to put them into practice. How did I go about finding my true self? If I did find it, would people really want to know me? The few times I had let "the real me" out in front of my mother, it was all too plain that there were aspects of me that she found unacceptable. My anger, sexuality, and independence clearly made her uncomfortable.

It was in the small group sessions of the Synanon games that I began to learn the tools of self-knowledge and self-care. Before each session, someone in the group would read the Synanon philosophy out loud. Based on the writings of Ralph Waldo Emerson, the philosophy gave me a structure to guide my search for self. Twenty-eight years after I first heard it, I still remember the first lines:

"The Synanon philosophy is based on the belief that there comes a time in everyone's life when he arrives at the conviction that envy is ignorance; that imitation is suicide; that he must accept himself for better or for worse as is his portion ..."

Each time I heard the philosophy, I thought of the evening when I had first heard Chuck Dederich talk about the game, and how it was the core experience for helping addicts find their way back to themselves. I was mesmerized. It felt like he was talking just to me:[1]

"Some young guy will come to me and say, 'Chuck, what'll I do? I'm frantic, I'm desperate.' And I'll say, 'Lad, go find yourself!' And he'll say, 'Oh, gee, thanks. That's great ...' And he walks out of the office door and ... what in the hell does he do? Does he start looking around the stairway or over his shoulder or what? What in the name of God does it mean: 'Lad, go find yourself'?"

As I listened, I felt certain that I was finally going to gain the self-knowledge that Shakespeare couldn't give me, but I'd always longed for; and it was going to come from an ex-drunk from Toledo, Ohio (the same place where my mother was born).

"Synanon," Dederich went on, "provides an opportunity to open the door. It's a key to the room where you are, the room that life has locked you into; where you can't find yourself. You stand outside the door, or outside the room—sometimes you don't even know where the door is—and there you are ... in there. You can't find yourself."

I felt that Dederich understood my confusion and fear. He seemed to know what it was like to go through life trying to be someone else—I didn't have a clue about how to find my true self.

"In Synanon we have found the key. We know that if you take this key in your hot little hand and insert it into the lock and twist hard enough, that door will open. The door will open a little at a time and you'll begin to find yourself. You'll get a glimpse, at first. Then more will be revealed as time goes on."

I was ready to take the key and open the door. I wanted to know how playing the Synanon game would help me open the door to my true self. Dederich had an answer that was so simple and direct, I had trouble believing it would really work.

"Here's the key: If you're a tantrum-thrower, a guy who loves being the center of attention, then by all means make every effort you can to do it well ... for a while. But then, for heaven's sake, start doing yourself a favor. Sit back and listen to others. Just sit there. Keep your mouth shut. I'll tell you something ... you're not going to believe it because you won't believe it until you've had the experience. You won't die. You really won't, you know. And you might just begin to find out about who you are under all of that bluster.

"And you people on the other end of the stick. You know who you are." When Dederich's gaze fell on me, I swallowed hard. "You people who tend to be somewhat passive and seek the dark corners of the room, you know who I'm talking to. You'll do anything to melt into the background and keep from calling attention to yourselves. Well by all means be a good wallflower, for a while. But then learn to get into the fray, roll up your sleeves and learn to spit out some real good invective at a tyrant. What the hell's the difference who. We're all tyrants sometimes, and we all need to stand up against the bullies of the world."

I was beginning to understand how to use the key. I had to practice doing something which at first seemed like a violation of my very being. To be the center of attention, to yell and scream, to stand up and fight for what I believed in was terrifying. In my family you just didn't do that. But I found out that I needed to allow the hidden to emerge if I was going to learn who I was and what it meant to find myself.

The Synanon game was the situation in which I began to learn how to tell the truth and speak from my heart. I remember the first time I could raise my voice and scream at a woman who was trying to make me feel guilty for not being a good enough son to my parents. I remember the first time I could say "fuck you" out loud and not feel ashamed. I remember refusing to go along with Synanon and sell fight tickets, because I didn't believe in violence. For months I was attacked in the games and learned how to stand up for my convictions.

It didn't occur to me at the time, but these attacks were actually offered with love. They weren't meant to beat me into submission, but rather to force me to own my own strength. Once I defended my position long enough to be convinced I was right, the attacks stopped. Even Dederich slapped me on the back and gave me his support, but only after I had stood up to my own fears.

Memories of the Synanon game were vivid in my mind during the first meeting of our men's group in 1979. I was listening to Jamie. He was out, but not down. I had the image of some futuristic prize-fighter who took all the blows on the inside. He was obviously a man in terrible pain, but afraid to let us know, and too proud to fall down.

Jamie was telling us what it was like for him growing up. The story was agonizing to hear, but Jamie seemed unflappable, almost buoyant. The incongruity was frightening. His words described a man who was dying inside, but his exterior was charming and chipper—he looked like someone all ready for a job interview. His hair was wavy, fashionably groomed, with just the right amount of gray to make him look distinguished. His voice was strong, his manner assured. I wanted to shake him until his teeth rattled and he looked as messed up on the outside as he was on the inside; but I just sat like the others and listened.

"I never had a personal relationship with my father," Jamie said with detachment and a touch of compassion. It sounded like he was talking about someone else. "I don't recall him ever asking me how I felt. He seemed to think his job was just to approve or disapprove of me. I was dying for him to show he cared about my feelings: and in the meantime, I lived for his approval." The seven other men in the group leaned forward as Jamie talked. The story was familiar to us.

"My father acted strong, but I came to realize that his strength was only on the surface. In most matters, he deferred to my mother. I hated that." Many of us nodded as we thought about our own fathers and the masks they wore and still wear. Our nods also were a sad acknowledgment of the ways in which we had carried on the tradition of the strong man, secretly ruled by women.

"Dad had those amazing forearms—he seemed like a giant to me. He was a professional wrestler when he was younger, and played semi-pro football. He was a steelworker while I was growing up—about as macho as you can get. I remember the big tools he carried in his truck." Jamie's face lit up with pride as he remembered his dad's tools. "It was the first thing he taught me growing up, how to respect and take care of tools." Jamie's pride dissolved into hurt and sadness. "I wish he would have taught me how to take care of myself instead of the fucking tools.

"I learned early that a man's duty is to others, and that men have to make sacrifices for their women and children." As Jamie continued remembering the things he learned from his father, he became more animated and his voice grew more strident. His anger, just below the surface, began to emerge. But you could see Jamie trying to hold his feelings in: his voice was constricted, his jaw clenched. "Strong men like my dad do what the women say," he told us. "Strong men like my dad stay behind on the sinking ship while the women and children take to the lifeboats. Strong men like my dad stand tall with stiff upper lips and clenched fists as the dark waters of the sea close over them, pulling them down."

More than one man in the group had tears in his eyes. But Jamie wouldn't allow himself to cry. He still seemed to be in his childhood, walking alongside his father, only allowing himself a very limited range of emotions. His look was focused somewhere in the distant past. "Mom told him that he would have to stop wrestling before she'd marry him.... Of course, he did what she told him."

One of the other men in the group asked Jamie how the past affected him now. "It's really hard for me to get in touch with my own needs and desires when I'm in a relationship. When I try to figure out what my needs are, I run up against this image—this large, angry woman who looms up whenever I try to think about myself. She says something like, 'okay, fucker—go ahead, do what you like. But you know you can't get along without me, and you know I'll leave the moment you do what you want to do.' She's kind of like the worst aspects of my mother, but seen from the points of view of, like, a little kid. I don't have a chance against her. I see her, and I just shrivel up inside."

Other men in the group talked about the ways in which they, too, would lose themselves in relationships. We all had difficulty being alone; but it was even harder being ourselves when we entered a woman's force field.

Jamie finally broke down when he started talking again. "I try to hide it, but I really feel worthless. I feel like a child who doesn't know how to take care of himself. Who needs to be extra nice to other people, so they'll like me and approve of me. The slightest nuance of a spoken word—if someone just looks at me critically, it can just send me into a tailspin.

"I feel like I'll die without a relationship, but when I'm in a relationship it feels like the death of my self." Jamie showed the first real signs of anger as his voice rose. "Punishment and death by relationship!" he shouted. "Death and punishment if I'm alone!"

Jamie's words belied the image he tried to project of the carefree bachelor who enjoyed exploring relationships.

From the outset, our men's group forced us to confront, and finally drop, the false masks we wore.

Ten years later, I was still working on my search for self. I was listening to a PBS program that featured Robert Bly, another ally who reminds me a lot of Chuck Dederich. Robert Bly is also a big man, charismatic, honest, and irreverent. "I'll begin with a poem by Antonio Machado, the Spanish poet," he said during his broadcast with Bill Moyers. "There's a lot of pain and grief around men these days and he touches on it here." After finishing the poem to responsive "Ahs," Bly asked, "Would you like to hear it again?" The audience yelled back a "yes" in unison.

> The wind one brilliant day called
> to my soul with an odor of jasmine.
> The wind said, "In return for the odor
> of my jasmine,
> I'd like all the odor of your roses."
> [Machado said,] "I have no roses; all the flowers
> in my garden are dead ..."
> The wind said, "Then, I'll take
> the withered petals, and the yellow leaves,"
> and the wind left. And I wept. And I said
> to myself,

"What have you done with the garden that was
entrusted to you?"

"Good poem, hmm?" asks Bly. "I think this feeling of the
garden being blown apart doesn't happen much to you until
you're 35 or so."[2]

When I was 9 and my mother told me, "This above all else,
to thine own self be true," it sounded so simple. By the time I
was 22 and Chuck Dederich said, "Lad, go find yourself," I realized that the task was in fact quite difficult. As I approach 50,
I've experienced many barriers to being truly myself. I have confronted the decay of my own garden, and know firsthand the fear
of trying to find my true self among the rotting leaves of my relationships. Now I know that to approach our true self, we have
to be willing to experience grief, to acknowledge and feel our
losses—the marriage that didn't turn out the way I'd hoped, the
career that went flat, the kids who took on many of my dysfunctional qualities despite my best efforts, the father who got old,
and the mother who died too soon.

In this stage of recovery it's necessary to recognize that we
create a false self that allows us to hide from our self-hatred. In
order to heal, men need to work through the following issues:

- Recognize and let go of the two false masks—Macho and
  Nebbish—we have learned to wear.

- Accept our weakness and accept our strength.

- Honor ourselves and our feelings.

- Confront the new sexism of male battering.

- Move from self-sacrifice to self-actualization.

Recognize and Let Go of the Two False Masks We Have Learned To Wear: The Macho and the Nebbish

When I was growing up, the heroes I sought to emulate
were the strong, silent cowboys I saw on my seven-inch black-
and-white T.V. and on the big screen on Saturday afternoons. Gary
Cooper and John Wayne were the dominant models of the time:
tall, silent, fast on the draw, strong, hard, and emotionally controlled. I remember looking in the mirror and trying to get that
look—hard, fast, silent, cold.

Though I didn't know it at the time, the mask of the macho gunfighter kept me from having to deal with my fears—fear of girls, fear of violence, fear of sex, fear of failure, fear of success, fear of homosexuality, fear of the unknown. It never occurred to me that I was learning to wear a mask (actually a whole body suit of armor with the mask the crowning glory), or that there was anything against which I needed to protect myself. I thought I was just being male. All my buddies acted the same, and the girls in my life seemed to be learning the complementary role.

And then the Vietnam War showed me that cowboys grow up to be soldiers, and soldiers grow up to kill and to die. I decided I didn't like what I had learned about being a man, and many young women seemed to agree.

I was certainly having my own doubts about the war, and about the way men were conditioned to sacrifice themselves on the altar of honor.

When the cowboy/soldier image paled, I looked for another to take its place. Since I couldn't abide war, I decided I would be a war protester. I took my cues for manhood not from an inner sense of who I was or what I wanted, but from who I didn't want to be and what I wanted to rebel against. The clearest image I had of manhood involved what I wanted to get away from. I traded hard for soft, fast for slow, cold for warm, heartless certainty for soulful hand-wringing. I traded the macho for the nice guy.

John Wayne was my mythic hero growing up in the 50s; without making a conscious decision about it in the '60s I modeled myself on Woody Allen. The characters Allen played were gentle and caring, intellectual and thoughtful. They listened to women and were responsive to women's needs, and as a result had the likes of Mia Farrow and Diane Keaton madly in love with them (things ultimately turned out differently, of course). The fact that Allen's persona was always anxious, and had lost his joy for life, seemed, at the time, a small price to pay to break out of the old mold of destructive masculinity.

I thought I was a new man. I thought I was my own man. I thought I had found my true path. Yet I began to feel that something was wrong when I increasingly found the "new me" sitting alone in front of Wheeler Hall on the U.C. Berkeley campus, trying to decide whether to kill myself or forget my unhappiness in a hamburger, fries, and a double-chocolate milkshake. If this was liberated, enlightened, new-age manhood, I was in trouble. I knew I couldn't go back to John Wayne. Maybe I had gone too far with Woody Allen, I thought.

Finding manhood and recovery by doing the opposite of what doesn't work, isn't really an answer. In my case, I simply took on the opposite set of addictions and the opposite set of protective gear, complete with appropriate mask. Truly, Woody Allen is just John Wayne turned inside out.

So many of the men I've worked with over the years, including myself, have spent a great deal of time alternating between hard and soft, invincible strength and unhealable weakness. We need to recognize the pattern, stop our compulsive search for manhood at either extreme of the spectrum, and begin to look inside ourselves for our identity rather than relying on cultural stereotypes.

Accept Our Weakness/Accept Our Strength

When we are under the influence of the hard male stereotype, we deny our weakness and run away from our grief and pain. Under the influence of the soft male, we deny our strength and run from our anger and creative passion.

Healing requires that we go inward and feel and accept both sides of ourselves.

In order to begin this phase of our journey, we need to recognize and accept our limitations as men. To be truly strong, we must accept our own weakness. The invulnerable hero, the gung-ho soldier, is really trying to deny the reality of his own frailty. As social scientist Andrew Bard Schmooker says in *Out of Weakness: Healing the Wounds That Drive Us to War*, "We posture to display our power and purity and certainty; but in Hamlet's phrase, we do protest too much. We pretend to be godlike because our inner torment has rendered us the sickest of animals. It is not because we are free of fear that we charge the enemy, but because we are fleeing inner demons."

My fear was that if I didn't keep myself hard and strong, I would slide the other way and be soft and weak. The fear I carried, although it was most often unconscious, was that if I didn't keep my male engine revved up and running at high speed all the time, I would run out of power and be dead in the water.

To complete the image, I would see myself being carried by the current over the falls to my death. As I get closer and closer, I work with frenzied attention to get my engine started, but it is too late. I go over the falls and die.

Being a man always felt to me like going against the current. Any lapse in attention would result in my demise. It wouldn't be a hero's death, going out in a blaze of glory, to be remembered in song and legend—but an invisible death, one in which I would fade away, swallowed up by the dark sea, my life erased, as though I had never existed at all. Those were the demons that drove me onward and outward.

The fear seemed to be most potent when I was around a woman I loved. It seemed that if I acknowledged any weakness and need, I would be overwhelmed by weakness and need. They didn't seem to be qualities that could coexist with a sense of my independence and strength.

Acknowledging our strength is also frightening to many of us. The only strong male energy many of us have ever experienced is the strength of the tyrant. We have all experienced fathers who dominate with fear, or older brothers who torment us with threats, bosses who pull the rug out from under us, presidents who send us off to war. We may recognize that dominance is not really strength, but we still have trouble finding our real power.

For me, I have found my strength in small acts of self-assertion: standing up to a boss who was constantly undermining me, saying "no" to the draft, allowing myself to cry at work and risk being seen as unmanly, confronting a man in my men's group whose hostility was wounding me, recognizing that my wife's constant criticism was not for my own good and being willing to say "no" to her—an act even more difficult for me than standing up against the draft.

The acceptance of weakness and strength is a crucial part of the warrior's journey home. In his book *Fire in the Belly*, Sam Keen gives a magnificent description of this phase of the journey:

> This isn't the fun part of the trip. It's spelunking
> in Plato's cave, feeling our way through the illu-
> sions we have mistaken for reality, crawling
> through the drain sewers where the forbidden
> "unmanly" feelings dwell, confronting the de-
> mons and dark shadows that have held us cap-

tive from their underground haunts.

In this stage of the journey we must make use of the warrior's fierceness, courage, and aggression to break through the rigidities of old structures of manhood, and explore the dark and taboo negative emotions that make up the shadow of modern manhood. The journey involves a series of passages: from sunny pragmatism to the dark wisdom of dream time; from having the answers to living the questions; from emotional numbness to manly grief; from cocksureness to potent doubt; from artificial toughness to virile fear; from infantile guilt to mature responsibility; from isolation to loneliness; from false optimism to honest despair; from compulsive action to relaxed waiting, fallowness, and renewal.

Honor Ourselves and Our Feelings

If we reexamine the stereotypes of the macho and the Nebbish, John Wayne and Woody Allen, we can say that both types are cut off from their full range of feelings. The John Wayne type is strong and silent. The Woody Allen type is vulnerable and intellectual. If either of these types express feelings, they are like an instrument played without a full set of strings. Mr. Strong-and-Silent sounds the notes of anger and outrage; Mr. Vunerable-and-Intellectual is a virtuoso in expressing his feelings of being hurt. But each repertoire is strictly limited, and the result is only a maimed version of what, in healthier circumstances, might have been music.

If we tend to identify with one type, we are often cut off from the feelings of the other. That is, men who are taught that it's okay to express anger are often cut off from their ability to express hurt and sadness. Those who are allowed to express their hurt and sadness are often not allowed to be angry. It's as though the same inner switch that turns on anger turns off sadness and vice versa.

The task that men must tackle in this step of their recovery is to reconnect with their feelings. When we are caught in the role of the macho or the perpetual nice guy, we live like robots or zombies. We go through the motions of living, but there is no real life: a real life can only come from allowing our feelings to be expressed. Cutting ourselves off from our feelings is the ultimate expression of self-hatred. To love ourselves entails allowing ourselves to feel fully.

The Feeling Tree

I think of this process as getting in touch with and moving down a *feeling tree*. Underneath every hard man is a hurting man, and underneath every soft man is an angry man. Depending on which end of the spectrum you've been most conditioned to express, the feelings you need to learn about are on the opposite end. I was raised to be soft, gentle, and intellectual, and crying came easily to me. It isn't surprising that I was terrified of anger, and spent my first year in Synanon insisting that I wasn't angry. Learning to yell "fuck you" and feel it was a real achievement.

Once we get in touch with our anger and hurt, we are able to move down the tree to the next level. Underneath every angry man and hurting man is a fearful man. Our fears are most often of two types. Either we are afraid of being abandoned and fear we'll be left all alone to die; or we're afraid of our violence, that we will kill those we love and be left all alone to die. Loving ourselves means being able to feel our fear.

Once we do that, we can go deeper still into the tree of love and life. Underneath every fearful man is a guilty man. We feel guilty for things we have done that we wish we hadn't, and we feel guilty for our omissions. It was an act of self-love when I could admit that I had hit my children when they were young—something so out of character for the nice Jewish man I tried to be. I had repressed all memories of the events. But I carried the guilt with me anyway. Acknowledging my actions allowed me to feel the guilt, express it, and move through it to the next level.

Underneath every guilty man is a shameful man. Once I had acknowledged and felt the wrenching guilt over the things I had done or failed to do, I got in touch with my feelings of shame. Shame, for me, feels like standing naked in front of a crowd that laughs and jeers because I am so ugly and dirty.

Loving ourselves at this level means recognizing the shame that is at the core of our emotional selves, the ultimate feeling we are afraid to feel. I came to believe that if I felt the shame, the thing I feared most would come true and I would be removed from the list of the living, blotted out and erased. In truth, cutting myself off from my shame kept me trapped and living the life of a zombie—not dead but not alive.

Rather than killing us, expressing our shame allows us to heal it and move to the base of the tree where we experience love and acceptance. When I had felt my anger and rage, my hurt and sadness, my fear and insecurity, my guilt and shame, I could truly feel my love for myself.

It's not surprising that most of us would like to take the shortcut to love and acceptance. We want instant cures for everything, the short course on enlightenment. After all, who wants to feel anger and blame, hurt and sadness, fear and insecurity, guilt and shame? Yet I see now that all these emotions are expressions of love. Each one is trying to take us deeper down the tree until we return to the roots. If people were raised in totally healthy families within healthy communities, within a healthy country, and a healthy world, we probably wouldn't need to go through this process of feeling and healing our emotions in order to experience such a simple pleasure as love.

Self-love begins with seeing the truth and accepting things the way they are. I came to see that my family was dysfunctional, as were many aspects of my community, my country, and the world I live in. Learning to love myself has meant that I have been able to find love for my family, community, country, and world. I can love them all just the way they are, in all their magnificence.

I can finally begin to feel the words I had once heard at a lecture given by a wise healer, Dr. Elisabeth Kubler-Ross: "Life becomes richer when we realize that each of us is like a snowflake, absolutely beautiful and unique, and each one here for a very short time."

Confront the New Sexism of Male Battering

Men's self-hatred is often reinforced by women and society at large. A 1990 Roper Organization survey found that American women increasingly believe most men to be mean, manipulative, oversexed, self-centered and lazy."

There are some who blame the women's movement for the new wave of male-bashing. But I don't believe feminism to be the cause. Most feminists I know recognize that women's liberation and men's liberation are both necessary and complementary. They love and honor the men in their lives, and fight to change the things in society that damage both women and men.

There is, however, a vocal minority of women who would have us believe that all the problems in society are caused by men, and that women are only innocent victims. These are often women who are still living with unhealed wounds from childhood. Since they play out their pain unconsciously, they often believe that liberation involves putting men in the same one-down position that women have lived in for so long. These women aren't feminists. They don't want liberation. They want revenge.

It is women like these who rage at men for being sexist, yet make jokes that dehumanize men. In her book, *Picking on Men: The First Honest Collection of Quotations About Men*, Judy Allen gives us a sampling of this kind of humor:

> Men are like eggs—they're fresh, rotten or hard-boiled.

> Men are those creatures with two legs and eight hands.

> The male genus has two varieties: good providers and bad providers.

> There are only two kinds of men, the dead and the deadly.

In his book, *Why Men Are the Way They Are*, Warren Farrell takes another look at "male humor" and shows how it expresses a new sexism. "In the past quarter century," writes Farrell, "we exposed biases against other races and called it racism, and we exposed biases against women and called it sexism. Biases against men we call humor."

We may laugh at the jokes, squirm with discomfort, or react with rage, but they tell us something important about the social attitudes about men and what we must confront if we are to change them. As Farrell reminds us, "Objectification of a group is a prerequisite to not caring if the members of that group are hurt or killed. Objectification of women is a prerequisite for the rapist; objectification of Vietnamese as 'gooks' was a prerequisite for dropping bombs on them. *Until recently, we have objectified men more subtly—by bribing them. We told men that if they killed them-selves, we'd call them heroes."*

Learning to move beyond our self-hatred means that we are called upon to confront the ways in which women, in the guise of liberation, objectify us. It means confronting the ways in which other men put us down by calling our manhood into question if we don't follow the prescribed male role. And it means confronting the way in which society tries to convince us that we're not men unless we are willing to destroy ourselves in the name of manhood.

Move From Self-Sacrifice to Self-Actualization

Men have seen themselves as the expendable sex for 10,000 years. Sports has been the training ground where men learn the rules of self-sacrifice. Exploring the manly world of football can help expose the truth behind the pomp and ceremony.

In his book *Knights Without Armor*, psychologist Aaron Kipnis says, "Thirty-six percent of all high school and college football players receive serious injuries. This translates to approximately 331,000 boys injured every year, with about 14,000 actually requiring surgery. At least twelve boys *died* from injuries in 1989 alone."

A recent survey reveals that 78 percent of retired professional football players suffer physical disabilities. The average life expectancy of a former professional player is about 56 years.[3]

Dave Meggessey played football for Syracuse University and the St. Louis Cardinals. For many years he was director of the West Coast Office of the National Football Players Association. In his autobiography, *Out of Their League*, he points out that "one of the justifications for college football is that it is not only a char-acter-builder, but a body-builder as well." Meggessey sees this as one of the many lies we tell our young men. "This is nonsense," he says. "Young men are having their bodies destroyed, not de-veloped. As a matter of fact, few players can escape from college football without some form of permanent disability. During my four years I accumulated a broken wrist, separations of both shoulders, an ankle that was torn up so badly it broke the arch of my foot, three major brain concussions, and an arm that almost had to be amputated because of improper treatment. And I was one of the lucky ones."

Since we know that men are not born masochists, how do we get them to engage in sports that will leave them injured for life? The answer is that we convince our young men that to be manly means to endure pain and injury. If a man begins to connect with his life-saving humanity, and questions this culture of violence, we ridicule him and question his manhood.

Meggessey describes how on one occasion his coach accused him of being afraid, and told him that he had looked "almost feminine" in making a tackle. "This sort of attack on a player's manhood is a coach's doomsday weapon," he writes. "And it almost always works, for the players have wrapped up their identity in their masculinity, which is eternally precarious for it not only depends on not exhibiting fear of any kind on the playing field, but is also something that can be given and withdrawn by a coach at his pleasure."

Indiana University basketball coach Bobby Knight was known to have put a box of sanitary napkins in the locker of one of his players so that the player would get the point that Knight considered him to be less than masculine. When I played ball I remember the locker-room wisdom that was pounded into our heads: "A man who won't fuck, won't fight. A man that won't fight, ain't worth a fuck." Acceptable manly behavior entailed joking about what we would do to women sexually, or how we would bash in the heads of our opponents.

Having learned the rules as boys, we are ready to sacrifice ourselves in the work world. Men men take 98 percent of the jobs working with dangerous equipment, yet we rarely hear about the 10 to 20 men who are killed on the job each day.[4] Even if we're lucky enough to have white-collar jobs in which we seem to have more control over our lives, we're still not safe. The destruction just takes longer to notice.

Psychologist Robert Pasick quotes one of his clients who, like so many men today, is trying to make it on his own. "When I decided to start my business, I threw myself into it wholeheartedly. I got up at three every morning and would be at work by four-thirty. I worked every night until ten or eleven. To build up the business I worked seven days straight for five years. No days off at all. I kept up this routine until I had my heart attack shortly after my 48th birthday."[5]

It's difficult to maintain our view of America as the land of the brave and the home of the free if we open our eyes to the daily sacrifice of our young men. To change self-sacrifice to self-actualization, we need to expand the options available to all men, and recognize the ways in which our social roles severely restrict who we can become.

It was through my involvement in the women's movement that I recognized that the roles which women are forced by society into taking are the very ones which men are restricted from playing. If the neighbor girl had to be "sugar and spice and everything nice," I learned that I could not be those things. If she could not be aggressive and play soldier, I knew I had to be the one to go off to war.

Psychologist Ann Neitlich makes this relationship explicit. "Women's and men's conditioning, while different," she writes in *Building Bridges: Women's and Men's Liberation*, "are opposite sides of the same coin. The qualities men are taught they *must* be are the exact qualities women are taught they cannot be and vice versa."

Neitlich offers the following two lists:

- Men *cannot* be and women *must* be: loving, nurturing, tender, feeling, domestic, beautiful, soft, curvy, thin, passive, receptive, nice, sweet, hairless, quiet, giving, apologetic.

- Men *must* be and women *cannot* be: economically powerful, physically strong, courageous, cool, stoic, protective, responsible, logical, active, aggressive, hairy, athletic, muscular, outspoken, rugged, tough.

We could all pick out those qualities from Dr. Neitlich's list which we were most often forced into assuming, and those which we were forced to deny. We could also add many "musts" and "cannots" of our own. Dr. Neitlich concludes, "One must fulfill these societally determined requirements or pay the price of not being considered a 'real' man or woman."

We must learn to reject those aspects of the male role which are destructive, and embrace the life-enhancing qualities that we have rejected because we were told they were "feminine."

The Hero Is Really Just a Big Boy

One of the most seductive, yet most destructive, roles men have been taught to embrace is that of the hero. We grow up with heroic images of manhood: Soldiers taking the beachhead in the face of enemy fire, cowboys saving the town from outlaws, adventurers overcoming obstacles to return the beautiful woman to her home.

Many of us are still trying to be heroes. Like Tom Cruise, we want to be Top Gun, beat out the other men we can only see as competition, and claim the beautiful woman who is the ultimate reward. We begin to think we are invulnerable, that only the "impossible dream" is for us, that we can "fight the unbeatable foe" and win. It's easy to become addicted to the adrenalin rush we get from these doomed battles with life.

What is not obvious, though, is that the Hero archetype is *not* the pinnacle of mature masculinity. "The Hero is, in fact, only an advanced form of Boy psychology," say psychologist Robert Moore and mythologist Douglas Gillette. Heroes are often boys pretending to be men.

It is often only apparent in retrospect, but when we are under the influence of the Hero archetype, we are really cut off from ourselves. We are driven to achieve. We can't back down, slow down, or rest. And we can't ask ourselves: "What do I really want? Is this really an expression of who I am?" The intoxicating ambrosia of the hero's journey often blinds us to the fact that it is a journey away from self, a pseudo-journey, often addictive, which is still dominated by the power of Woman.

I have often thought of Anthony Quinn in *Zorba the Greek* as a real hero, a real man. He lives life fully, drinks and dances and dreams his impossible dreams. Yet, for all his wisdom and joy for life, he constantly loses himself. "When a woman calls, you must go," Zorba tells his young friend.

The hero is not his own man, but only seems so. The hero's journey is tragic, not because of his trials and tribulations, but because the hero never really leaves home. He is still unconsciously tied to his mother.

The tragedy of the Hero is not that he must face death in order to save the sweet damsel, but that once having saved her, he doesn't have a clue about what to do with her. He hasn't yet separated from the archetypal Woman and hasn't developed the mature sense of self that would allow him to have a healthy, intimate relationship.

It is not the Hero, but the Warrior who is the archetype of mature masculinity that we seek. At this stage of our journey, we need to let go of the hero's willingness to sacrifice himself. Self-actualization begins on the other side of that decision. As we slow down and quit pushing to "be all that we can be," a small quiet voice of our actualized self begins to break through. As we listen to it, we also feel the tentacles of shame that pull us down. We are now ready to heal our body and soul.

Notes

1. This quote is from a talk I heard Dederich give. The speech was reprinted as "Lad, Go Find Yourself," by Charles E. Dederich, *Synanon Literary Journal,* Vol. II, No. 1, Spring 1966, Issue No. 3.

2. From "A Gathering of Men" with Bill Moyers and Robert Bly, Public Affairs Television, New York, 1990.

3. Messner, Michael "When Bodies Are Weapons: Masculinity and Violence in Sport," *International Review of Sociology of Sport,* August 1990.

4. Farrell, Warren (1993) *The Myth of Male Power.* New York: Simon & Schuster. These statistics are from the chapter called "The Death Professions: Men's Biggest 'Glass Cellar.'"

5. Pasick, Robert S. (1990) "Raised to Work," in *Men in Therapy: The Challenge of Change* by Richard L. Meth and Robert S. Pasick et al. New York: Guilford Press.

7

Healing Men's Shame

 Freedom is what you do
with what's been done to
you.
　　　　　—Jean-Paul Sartre

Task 6: Acknowledge Our Wounds and
Heal Our Bodies and Souls

"Shame," says author Merle Fossum, "is feeling alone in the pit of unworthiness." He describes shame as being much more deeply rooted than most people believe. "Shame is not just a low reading on the thermometer of self-esteem. "Shame is something like cancer—it grows on its own momentum."

Both shame and guilt are ways in which people experience feeling bad. Yet the two are quite different. Guilt involves feeling bad about what we do or fail to do. Shame is feeling bad about who we are, about our very being. The shame that men experience is a kind of soul murder, undermining the foundations of our masculine selves.

If we want to understand the roots of men's shame and begin to heal, we must begin by directing our attention to the male body and the way it has been treated. We often think of women as having trouble with body image. Yet we men also feel uncomfortable about our physical selves, but often deny the discomfort and rarely talk about it.

I asked a number of my clients to tell me about their experiences of shame. Their responses may help break the silence within you and let others you care about know what men really feel like inside.

Joseph. "I'm too, too, too short! Girls would never like me because I didn't measure up. I was terrified to even walk up to a girl I liked if she was even an inch taller than I was. At five feet, five inches tall, I always felt below average and I always felt I had to make up for it by proving myself in other areas of my life."

Carlos. "I always felt bad about my body. As a kid, I was pudgy, and learned early the shame of being called 'Fatso' or 'Piggy.' I was always too big around. But in the genital area, I was always too short. I hated to get undressed in the locker room in junior high. Some guy would yell, 'Squirrel!' and then grab my nuts. I felt invaded. Worse than that was when they'd yell, 'Shit, I can't even find your little wienie. Are you a girl, or what?'

Daniel. "My father was a star football player in college, and only an injury in his senior year prevented him from becoming a pro. As far back as I can remember, I knew my father was disappointed that I wasn't big like him. I was tall, but thin. I never felt like I was okay in his eyes."

Tony. "I felt like a freak growing up. I towered over all the kids in my class, stood out in all our class pictures, and had to suffer all the jokes about nose bleeds and 'how's the air up there?'

When I was alone, I never felt strange; but whenever I went out in public, I always felt ashamed."

Though each man identified a different aspect of his body image which had been a source of shame, there was one that all of the men shared, but no one mentioned. All had been circumcised.

The Silent Knife: Why Isn't Circumcision a Men's Issue?

As I began to gather information for this chapter, I would regularly break into tears for no apparent reason. Gradually, the tears began to form themselves into unspoken, long-hidden questions which bubbled to the surface. What is it like for an infant boy—a boy born perfect, whole and complete—to have part of his body removed? What is the effect of having a large person, most often a man, spread the baby's little legs and cut away the end of his penis? Could the trauma of this event have anything to do with men's later feelings of shame about their bodies, their concern about the size of their penis, their anguish over sexual performance, their frozen feelings, or the male ability—which is really a liability—to ignore pain?

These questions are unavoidably personal. How had circumcision affected me? Was my own sexual confusion and anger related to this event? What had I really done to my son when I had him circumcised with so little inquiry? Would I be stirring up old wounds if I looked more deeply? Would people ridicule me if I talked and wrote about circumcision as an important men's issue?

Despite my fears, I decided to move ahead. Surely, I thought, with all the focus on men these days, there must be a lot of discussion on circumcision in the literature on men. Just because I had avoided this issue, surely others must be talking about it. As a writer, I have accumulated a fairly good-sized collection of books on men. I was sure I would find a lot of information right here.

Out of the 58 books I had on my shelf which were specifically focused on men, only 8 mentioned circumcision at all. Of those, 5 of the references were so brief that I had trouble finding them when I looked up the page number. In only 3 of the books was circumcision discussed in any depth, and from none of my books did I feel I had gotten a clear understanding of the effects of circumcision on men's psyches and men's lives.

In Search of the Truth About Circumcision

What I learned in the months since I began asking questions has shocked and upset me. The foreskin, I learned, was not some useless appendage that could be discarded without harm. Actually, the foreskin provides protection for the glans, and is abundantly supplied with nerve endings. These afford unique sensual stimulation. During masturbation and intercourse, the foreskin stimulates the glans and acts as a natural gliding mechanism which provides a great deal of pleasure. Like the clitoris, the glans is naturally an internal organ and should be treated as such.

The reasons usually given for circumcising baby boys—the intact penis is difficult to keep clean; circumcision prevents future medical problems, such as urinary tract infections, venereal disease, penile and prostate cancer, and cervical cancer in partners—are based on faulty medical data.

Jews have traditionally circumcised their infant boys in fulfillment of a covenant with God. The original practice involved a symbolic removal of the tip of the foreskin. The more radical surgery practiced by modern Jews and the medical establishment, in which the entire foreskin is removed, is not in keeping with the original practice.

The surgery itself, far from being benign, causes extreme pain and trauma. It is not as risk-free as we have been told, and instances of mutilation and death have been reported.

The United States is the only country in the world that still practices routine medical circumcision for infants. Three thousand three hundred boys each day—that's 1.2 million per year—undergo this so-called elective surgery that's done without the patient's permission. Though the rate of circumcision declined from a high of 85 percent in 1980, it has remained constant around 60 percent since 1988.

Some of you may feel that I'm devoting too much space to this topic. Before I learned the facts, I would have agreed with you. Consider the following:

- The facts about circumcision are still unknown to most people: it's only misinformation that allows the wide practice of this surgery to be continued.

- The effects of circumcision on the male infant are traumatic and long-lasting.

- Since the trauma occurs before language development, it is difficult for men to remember what happened, and hence difficult for them to heal their emotional scars.

- The act of circumcision itself is abusive, contributing to later problems with addiction and violence.

- Ending this practice is one of the most important things we can do to ensure that the next generation of boys has a chance to grow up healthy and free.

Words From Those Who Were There

Most of the men reading this book have been circumcised. Many of us had our sons circumcised when they were born. Learning the truth about circumcision is difficult. It's easy to feel angry, guilty, and shameful. Yet, I know that we each did the best we could, and our parents did the best they could, given the knowledge available at the time. Hearing from those who have had the courage to remember can help us get back in touch with the feelings we have so long suppressed. What we feel we can heal.

I began by asking my wife what she felt about circumcision. Her three sons from a previous marriage were all circumcised routinely as infants. I was surprised by the strength of her feelings.

> I thought it was done for health reasons. I knew it was done for boys, because I had two younger brothers and assumed they were circumcised to protect them—like getting an immunization shot.
>
> With Dane, my first-born, it wasn't until we left the hospital and I changed him at home that I saw what had been done. I had been given instructions in the hospital about keeping his penis clean, but I was shocked when I saw how red and swollen it was. Every time he peed, it seemed to irritate him. The wound would begin

to heal then become irritated again and break
open.

It didn't seem right. A baby should cry
when he is hungry or cold, not because his penis
is hurt.

With each child, I had more and more
doubts, though the social pressure kept me agree-
ing. All the many guilts I have felt about not being a good enough mother pale in comparison to
the guilt I feel for not being strong enough to do
my own investigating. If I had, my boys would
still be whole and complete. Any discomfort they
might feel in the locker room because they look
different is nothing compared to what I let them
go through as babies.

By the time she finished talking, we were both crying. The
tears continue to flow as my body, if not my mind, remembers
what was done to me as an infant. Listen to the experiences of
others.

Unfortunately, I'm another son of another new
mother who fell into the automatic circumcision
trap. It makes me wonder where the hell my father was, or if he ever knew what was going on.
I want it back!

They strapped him down, which we hated. We
massaged his head, stroked him, and talked to
him the whole time.... My husband said it was
the most awful thing he'd ever seen or done.

I stood outside the door while they were doing it
to him and listened to him scream and cry. That's
the first time I really began to wonder what the
hell I had let them do to my baby! Since then I
have asked myself that a million times.

I am a 17-year-old male who is circumcised. I got
to thinking, what am I missing? Most likely, I'll
never know. It makes me sad because I'm not
whole, as I was intended to be. I try not to be bit-
ter about it. I try not to blame my parents, but

who can I blame? I had no say in the matter, and after all, it is my penis. It's a part of me that I'll never know.

I'm a victim of infant circumcision, and even though I'm 55 years old, I'm forcefully and painfully reminded of this atrocity, perpetrated upon me deliberately by my mother, who ordered it done, every time I take a shower, dress and undress, look at myself in a full-length mirror, or masturbate. And my studies indicate this atrocity even takes all the fun out of the last item above. I am still dealing with deep anger and rage over this.

I was deprived of my foreskin when I was 26. I had ample experience in the sexual area, and I was quite happy—delirious, in fact—with what pleasure I could experience, beginning with foreplay and continuing, as an intact male. After my circumcision, that pleasure was utterly gone.

Let me put it this way. On a scale of 10, the uncircumcised penis experiences pleasure that is at least 11 or 12; the circumcised penis is lucky to get to 3. Really—and I mean this in all seriousness—if American men who were circumcised at birth could know the deprivation of pleasure that they would experience, they would storm the hospitals and not permit their sons to undergo this unnecessary loss. But how can they know this? You have to be circumcised as an adult, as I was, to realize what a terrible loss of pleasure results from this cruel operation.[1]

Marilyn Milos is the mother of three circumcised boys. She was a student nurse in 1979 the day she first saw the operation performed. "It was a day that changed the course of my life," she says now.

We students filed in the newborn nursery to find a baby strapped spread-eagle to a plastic board on a counter top across the room. He was struggling against his restraints—tugging, whimpering, and then crying helplessly. No one was tending the infant, but when I asked my instructor if I could comfort him, she said, "Wait til the doctor gets here." I wondered how a teacher of the healing arts could watch someone suffer and not offer assistance. I wondered about the doctor's power which could intimidate others from following protective instincts. When he did arrive, I immediately asked the doctor if I could help the baby. He told me to put my finger into the baby's mouth; I did, and the baby sucked. I stroked his little head and spoke softly to him. He began to relax, and was momentarily quiet.

The silence was soon broken by a piercing scream—the baby's reaction to having his foreskin pinched and crushed as the doctor attached the clamp to his penis. The shriek intensified when the doctor inserted an instrument between the foreskin and the glans (head of the penis), tearing the two structures apart. (They are normally attached to each other during infancy so the foreskin can protect the sensitive glans from urine and feces.) The baby started shaking his head back and forth—the only part of his body free to move—as the doctor used another clamp to crush the foreskin length-wise, where he then cut. This made the opening of the foreskin large enough to insert a circumcision instrument, the device used to protect the glans from being severed during the surgery.

The baby began to gasp and choke, breathless from his shrill, continuous screams. How could anyone say circumcision is painless when the suffering is so obvious? My bottom lip began to quiver, tears filled my eyes and spilled over, I found my own sobs difficult to contain. How much longer could this go on?

During the next stage of the surgery, the doctor crushed the foreskin against the circumcision instrument and then, finally, amputated it. The baby was limp, exhausted, spent.

I had not been prepared, nothing could have prepared me, for this experience. To see a part of this baby's penis being cut off—without an anesthetic—was devastating. But even more shocking was the doctor's comment, barely audible several octaves below the piercing screams of the baby: "There's no medical reason for doing this." I couldn't believe my ears, my knees became weak, and I felt sick to my stomach. I couldn't believe that medical professionals, dedicated to helping and healing, could inflict such unnecessary pain and anguish on innocent babies.[2]

Since that day, Marilyn has dedicated herself to providing information to parents and medical professionals so they can have all the facts available *before* they decide whether circumcision should be performed. She is the Director of the National Organization of Circumcision Information Resource Centers. Among their various activities, they have put together two international conferences on circumcision.

What The Health Professionals Say Now

The most authoritative book on the subject, *Say No to Circumcision! 40 compelling reasons why you should respect his birthright and keep your son whole,* was written by Thomas J. Ritter, M.D., in 1992. "I am a general surgeon," he writes. "The prime dictum in medicine is 'Thou shalt do no harm.' The intent of this book is to explode the myth that routine newborn circumcision does no harm." After years of having gathered information, he draws the following conclusion:

> The operation of routine, infant circumcision of males involves a paradox of absurdities completely at variance with sound medical–surgical–legal practice; a normal structure is operated upon; no anesthesia is used; the patient does not give his consent; he is forcibly restrained while a normal segment of his body is removed; the parental consent is of quasi-legality since the part removed is a healthy, non-diseased appendage; there are no

legitimate surgical-medical indications for the operation; the patient and the part operated upon are subject to a host of possible complications, including death; the genitalia are now irrevocably diminished in appearance, function and sensitivity.

Dr. Ritter is not alone in his opinion. Here are the words of a few experts who are calling for an end to the cruelty we are inflicting on our baby boys:[3]

> My own preference, if I had the good fortune to have another son, would be to leave his little penis alone.
>
> —Benjamin Spock, M.D., author,
> *Baby and Child Care*

> Circumcision is a very cruel, very painful practice with no benefit whatsoever.
>
> —Ashley Montagu, Ph.D., anthropologist,
> author of *The Concept of the Primitive*

> In addition to the obvious discomfort involved, there is now serious concern this routine procedure may actually deprive adult men of a vital part of their sexual sensitivity.
>
> —Dean Edell, M.D., National
> radio and television personality

> All of the Western world raises its children uncircumcised and it seems logical that, with the extent of health knowledge in those countries, such a practice must be safe.
>
> —C. Everett Koop, M.D.,
> former U.S. Surgeon General

> In this case, the old dictum that "if it ain't broke, don't fix it" seems to make good sense. Minor surgery is one that is performed on someone else. Using the surgical treatment of circumcision to prevent phimosis is a little like preventing headaches by decapitation. It works but it is hardly a prudent form of treatment.
>
> —Eugene Robin, M.D., Stanford
> University Medical School

Even if you found that there were absolutely no harmful psychological effects, it would still not justify doing an unnecessary procedure. You just should not be cruel to babies.
> —Paul Fleiss, M.D., University of
> Southern California Medical School

No one seriously advocates removing the breasts of female infants to prevent the more common malignancy of breast cancer. Circumcision must be recognized as an equally serious mutilation of men with equally insubstantial justification for continuing the practice.
> —James Snyder, M.D., past president,
> Virginia Urologic Society

We cannot but wonder why such a torture has been inflicted on the child. How could a being who has been aggressed in this way, while totally helpless, develop into a relaxed, loving, trusting person? Indeed, he will never to able to trust anyone in life, he will always be on the defensive, unable to open up to others and to life.
> —Dr. Frederick Leboyer, author,
> *Birth Without Violence*[4]

There is a relationship between the later experiences men have with shame—*I'm too short, too fat, too tall, too hairy, not hairy enough, not a real man*—and the first experience that gave us the message that our penis was wrong.

Stage 5 Recovery: Healing Men's Shame

To accomplish the task of healing our body and soul, we must work with the following issues:

- Recognize the hidden purpose in circumcision and other forms of male shaming.

- Learn to accept and love our bodies.

- Begin moving toward a healthy, shame-free diet.

- Discover how to earn a shame-free living.

Recognize the Hidden Purpose in Circumcision and Other Forms of Male Shaming

Male genital mutilation is the first way in which men are shamed. It is also the most damaging, and lays the foundation for later assaults on our body and soul. In order to heal, we must understand why we continue to condone such behavior in the United States.

"Circumcision," says Dr. Nicholas Cunningham of the Departments of Pediatrics and Public Health at the Columbia College of Physicians and Surgeons, "is probably an idea whose time has gone."[5] Yet the practice continues, and the majority of baby boys in America are still subjected to this cruel and unusual punishment. We must ask why.

"Male babies need to be circumcised" is a mythic statement, not a statement of fact. Mythic statements are not just untrue and superstitious, but connect with our deepest desires and fears. Social Psychologist Elizabeth Janeway says that it is characteristic of mythic statements generally to be *prescriptions* more than *descriptions* reflecting reality. "For it is the nature of myth," she asserts, "to be both true and false, false in fact, but true to human yearnings and human fears and thus, at all times, a powerful shaping force."[6]

To change behavior based on social myth, we need to uncover the roots and understand the real reasons why a given behavior is valued in a culture. This is explored in greater detail below.

The Tame-and-Shame Syndrome: Hidden Reasons for Cutting Boy's Genitals

We can get clues about the hidden agenda supporting circumcision if we understand why the practice began to spread in the U.S. in the late 1800s. Circumcision gained importance only after the medical profession, playing upon prevailing sexual anxieties, urged it as a "cure" for a long list of childhood diseases and disorders, including polio, tuberculosis, bedwetting, and a new syndrome which appeared widely in the medical literature of the time, "masturbatory insanity." Circumcision was then advocated along with a host of exceedingly harsh, pain-inducing devices and practices designed to thwart any vestige of genital pleasure in children, and to ensure that they remained under parental control.

I found the religious roots and reasoning for circumcision by looking to my Jewish heritage. The thirteenth-century Rabbi Moses Maimonides was more honest than almost anyone since in his reasons for supporting circumcision:

> The bodily injury caused to that organ is exactly that which is desired, it does not interrupt any vital function, nor does it destroy the power of regeneration. Circumcision simply counteracts excessive lust; for there is no doubt that circumcision weakens the power of sexual excitement, and sometimes lessens the natural enjoyment.[7]

We need to recognize that decreasing sexual pleasure and increasing sexual pain has a very useful purpose in a dominator culture. It produces men who are numb, cut off from their feelings, with a great deal of repressed rage. The real purpose of circumcising baby boys is to begin a process of taking the "wild" out of them.

This has been the goal of all the dominator cultures that have arisen over the last 10,000 years. As we have tried to wipe out the indigenous wild cultures of the world, kill the wild animals, and destroy the naturally occurring plant life, so too have we tried to tame men's "wild sexuality." What better way to destroy the hunter-warrior in us all than to attack the basis of our manhood, our genitals? What better way to make us docile enough to be willing to go off to desert wars, or fight in the jungles of Wall Street to keep the overconsumptive, addictive, American dream alive?

Shame of all kinds serves the same purpose. If men can be convinced that they are inherently bad, that there is something wrong with us at our core, then we are more easily controlled.

The final step in the shaming process calls for us to forget the source of our shame. The first step in healing is to remember what was done to us, feel the feelings we have so long repressed, and allow ourselves to grieve for what we have lost.

Accept and Love Our Bodies, Begin To Heal

To begin to love ourselves, we must love our bodies. Loving our bodies begins with accepting our wound, which for many of us means accepting that our penises have been cut. For most of my life, I didn't think about my wound. I didn't even know I was wounded. Healing begins when we confront what happened to us, and consider whether we feel bad about our basic selves because of the physical and psychological wounds we have received.

Men hide from themselves and others their true feelings about their most vulnerable body parts. To hide and protect our wound, we armor our bodies, and in the process lose touch with our feelings and ourselves. Some of us grew up feeling ashamed of being too heavy, or that we walked with a limp, wore glasses, had a big nose, were too thin, or too short. Whatever the wound, men often deny how deeply they have been affected.

One of the most prevalent hidden wounds for men is how we feel about our length, whether the length of our penises or the length of our bodies. Being 5' 5" tall, I thought it was just us short guys who felt ashamed of our height. After talking with thousands of men, I've come to believe that height for men is what weight is for women. Most women feel that they cannot be attractive unless they match the current culture's ideal for body type and weight. Men feel the same way about height. Many women feel ashamed of their weight, while men tend to be ashamed of their height or the length of their penises. Women spend a king's ransom and a lifetime trying to diet themselves to the proper size. Because height and penises cannot be changed— at least not yet, and not with demonstrably good results—men simply take what they've got and lie about the rest.

Few would guess that Bill Moyers is uncomfortable with his god-given height. "I'm prone to add an inch to 6' 0", Moyers is quoted as saying in The Height of Your Life by Ralph Keyes. Why? "Sounds ... sounds better. More like a man." Moyers seems to reflect the consensus in America about how tall you have to be to be a real man. 6' 1" seems to be the magic number. How many of us don't qualify? The reality is that 70,113,000 men in this country, almost 85 percent of us, will never make it to the big 6' 1". Those who go beyond that, unless they are named

"Michael," "Larry," or "Magic," feel like they, too, are built wrong. Most all of us suffer the shame of being the wrong height.

Healing involves going through a process of grief, no different than if someone close to us had died. There are identifiable steps to the process of healing our grief about our bodies:

- Recognizing our denial and ways in which our feelings have frozen
- Accepting that our feelings about our bodies are crucial to the way we feel about ourselves
- Allowing our repressed anger to surface
- Letting ourselves feel the hurt and sadness that follows
- Accepting ourselves just the way we are in all our magnificence

One of the most powerful and healing experiences I have ever had took place in our men's group about three years after we first began to meet. We decided on an exercise in which each man would take off his clothes and stand naked before the whole group.

Each of us commented on the body of the man standing before us, letting him know the things that each of us liked. I remember waiting for my turn and feeling unbearably nervous. I was sweating like crazy, and I wasn't even sure why. These were men I had gotten to know well over a period of three years. We had soaked in Jamie's hot tub every Thursday after the group, and had talked about our homophobia. So why was I so nervous?

As I took my turn and stood before the seven other men, I realized that my fears had to do with adolescent memories of being ridiculed by other boys. I was teased because I was short, laughed at because I had pubic hair before the other boys; I was threatened in the locker room.

I realized that I was much more terrified about being ridiculed by guys than I was about being put down by women. Yet, as I stood before the men and was able to hear and feel their tenderness, care, and support, something vital in me was released. I was appreciated for my body—not in a sexual way, but in a way a father or older brother who had a healthy love for his own body might respond. They told me they liked the pattern of the hair on my chest, the way I stood, the set of my shoulders.

For the first time in my life, I truly appreciated my body. I no longer felt it as an instrument for killing or fucking, but as a natural expression of beauty, male beauty. I learned, as Robert Bly says in *Iron John*, "at what frequency the masculine body vibrates." I began to grasp "the song that adult male cells sing, and how the charming, elegant, lonely, courageous, half-shamed male molecules dance."

Begin Moving Toward a Healthy, Shame-free Diet

How we feel about our body has a lot to do with what we put into it. The Modern American Diet, with its emphasis on meat and dairy consumption, is unhealthy. In fact, next to cigarettes, diet is the number one killer of Americans, according to Dr. Michael McGinnis, director of the Office of Disease Prevention and Health Promotion at the U.S. Department of Health and Human Services. Dietary excess is one of the chief reasons why men die seven years sooner than do women.[8]

There is a greatly increased risk of fatal prostate cancer for men who consume large quantities of meats, dairy products, and eggs: 360 percent higher than for men who use these products sparingly.[9] The risk of death from heart attack for the average American man is 50 percent.[10] On the other hand, the risk of death from heart attack for American men who consume no meat is 15 percent and for men who consume no meat, dairy products, or eggs it is 4 percent.[11]

Not only would a change away from meat and dairy products toward a more vegetarian diet improve men's health, but it would also decrease the shame we feel about how we treat animals.

For most of human history, the relationship between men and the animals they killed was one of respect and reverence. We killed only what we needed, and we maintained a loving connection with the prey. Now we eat the meat of animals that were raised on factory farms with little care for their suffering.

In doing research for his landmark book, *Diet for a New America*, John Robbins interviewed many people, including the owner of a stockyard. He asked him how he felt about the charges from animal rights groups that what was done to the animals was cruel. "It doesn't bother me. We're no different from any other business. These animal rights people like to accuse us of mistreating our stock, but we believe we can be most efficient by not being emotional. We are a business, not a humane society, and our job is to sell merchandise at a profit. It's no different from selling paper-clips, or refrigerators."

We certainly have gone from an I-thou relationship to an I-it relationship. And although we may not be conscious of it, the shameful way we have come to treat the animals we eat adds to our own feelings of shame as men.

I now recognize that my shame over how we have treated the animals is related to the shame I feel about the effect of our meat-centered diet on the rest of the world. Each year, 20,000,000 people in the world die of malnutrition. If Americans reduced their intake of meat by 10 percent, the freed-up land, water, and energy could be used to provide an adequate diet for 60,000,000 people.[12]

Changing the way we eat would not only save the lives of millions, it would help save the planet as a whole. "If you're a meat eater, you are contributing to the destruction of the environment, whether you know it or not," says Neal Bernard, President of the 30,000 member Physicians Committee for Responsible Medicine. "Clearly the best thing you can do for the Earth is to not support animal agriculture." He cites statistics to make his point:

- Producing enough food to feed a meat-eater requires 4,200 gallons of water a day; to feed a vegetarian requires 300 gallons.

- Nearly 4 billion tons of topsoil are lost each year in the United States, chiefly because of overgrazing by livestock and unsustainable methods of growing feed.

- It takes 39 times more energy to produce beef than soybeans having the same caloric value.

- Tropical rain forest is being cleared in Latin America to raise cattle; a pound of hamburger represents 55 square feet of burned-off forest.[13]

More than any single person, John Robbins, who wrote *Diet for a New America* and *May All Be Fed*, has helped raise my consciousness about the effect of our food choices on our personal and planetary health. Recently I talked with John about these issues.

Manhood and the American Diet: A Conversation
With John Robbins

Groomed from childhood to succeed his father as head of
Baskin-Robbins, it wasn't easy for John to leave and eventually
oppose both the meat and dairy industry's dominance in directing
our food choices. I began by asking him the reasons he tried so
hard to fit in with his father's dream.

"Well, the reason was very simple. That's what my father
wanted me to do. He was a master at what he did. He was focused. He was clear. He was friendly. His energy was positive. It
was a pleasure to be around that kind of person.

"I was quite into it, but ..." John paused to think. "I began
to feel my own conscience. As the years went along I felt pulled
in another direction, and it was very frightening. It was the only
sense of love and support that I had, and I *knew* that my father
couldn't understand my need to individuate and separate from
him and from his dream for me and for him."

"Do you remember what some of those key realizations
were for you?"

"Yeah, there were some key moments. I think they were
triggers. Baskin-Robbins was developing an advertising campaign
and had come up with the slogan, 'We make people happy.' Everyone else was pleased, but I felt uncomfortable with that slogan.
It was so clear to me that ice cream doesn't make people happy.
It would, perhaps, be true to say we offered a product that gives
people momentary pleasure. But happiness? No! Human happiness seemed too important a thing to trivialize that way.

"I tried to say something like that, but my father didn't understand at all."

John and I both laughed.

"But my father was right. The advertising business is not
about conveying existential truths, or about people being authentic. It's about selling products and using whatever hooks you can
get into people's psyches."

"There are many things that people can get hooked on," I
said. "Do you feel ice cream can become an addiction?"

"Absolutely! I have a lot of willpower. There was a time I
chose not to drink or smoke, and these presented no problem to
me. But the place where I had the most trouble was ice cream.
Ice cream was more difficult for me than anything.

"I tried to notice just when it was that I was most compulsively driven to eat ice cream. It turned out that it was when I was feeling hollow and empty. It was a particular kind of void. I went into it and I knew there was grief there and I knew there was loneliness and I knew there was anger." Listening to John, a man who appears genuinely caring and gentle, I began to see that it wasn't that he was born that way, but he had worked through a lot of his demons.

"I went into those feelings," John continued, "but for a long long time all I found was darkness. I beat pillows and yelled. I went for long runs until I was exhausted. I did yoga and bioenergetics. But I'd get back and still have to have ice cream.

"Nothing worked until one day it finally became clear to me. I found that what I was really trying to do was to find my father." The relief on John's face was apparent.

"He'd come home at night and I was missing him terribly. He'd bring home these brown tubs of ice cream with his name all over them. That was my dad." I could see the mixture of pride and pain as John talked.

"Once I saw that my ice cream addiction—and addiction is exactly what it was—stemmed from really missing my dad, something freed up in me. Ice cream lost the compulsive charge it once had in my life."

"How about meat?" I asked. "I know that's an addiction I've had."

"We *are* taught to associate meat with masculinity," John began. "When I was growing up I wanted to play baseball. I had a lot of childhood illnesses and I wasn't very good, but they accepted everyone on the team. But I quickly found out that they only *played* the kids that were good. My father would drive me to the games sometimes, but he didn't have time to stay. He was always busy with work. I was kind of glad he didn't stay so he wouldn't know that I didn't play.

"On days of the big games, he'd make me a steak for breakfast. I loved the attention and I loved the approval. I associated all that—Dad's attention, steak, athletics, being strong. When he would do that, it was like he was investing in me with his own manhood in some way. He was transferring something of his own energy to me." John's voice picked up speed and I recalled Robert Bly saying that boys are hungry for the nutrients of manhood.

Do we give our boys meat as a substitute for the real nutrients we don't know how to give, I wondered?

"He wanted me to be strong," John said. "He wanted to be proud of me, and this was the way he thought he could make that happen. He himself was big and strong, and I assumed that eating meat was part of what gave him that strength."

"Just as we seem to be hungering for father energy, we also seem to be hungering for a kind of warrior spirit that was present in our hunter-gatherer heritage," I said. "Are there men you have met who seem to you to exemplify the modern warrior spirit?"

"Yes, I've met a number of them. They're not the typical stereotype of the modern hero. They haven't won medals of honor in wars, or Heisman trophies. They are men who heard the call of their own spirits, and answered with their lives. I think of a fellow I met in Iowa while doing research for *Diet for a New America*. He ran a pork production facility and treated the hogs he owned—as is the standard in the factory farms of America—abominably. I had gone to the ranch to learn what really goes on, and though I didn't voice any judgments about what he was doing, he became more and more agitated in defense of his methods.

"When his wife invited me to stay to dinner, he was not pleased. Though I hadn't presented myself as an animal rights advocate, at one point he burst out in anger. "Sometimes I wish you animal lovers would just drop dead! Just go and fall off a cliff or something. It's hard enough to make a living these days without having to be concerned about all this stuff!' I just listened.

"Later in the evening the anger drained away and he began to open up. 'I'm sorry I got so mad at you before,' he said. 'It's not your fault. You are just showing me what I already know but try not to think about. It just tears me up, some of the things we are doing to these animals. These pigs never hurt anybody, but we treat them, like, like … like I don't know what. Nothing in the world deserves this kind of treatment. It's a shame. It's a crying shame. I just don't know what else to do.'

"As he began to open up to his feelings, he remembered an incident from his childhood that had been long repressed, of a time as a little boy that he got a pet pig, a pig he came to love dearly. As he told the story, he began to weep as he remembered when his father had forced him to kill his pig. When at first he refused, his father had given him a choice. 'You can either kill that pig or you're no longer my son.'

"That experience had been so traumatic to him, so violating, that he must have resolved somewhere in his young psyche never to be that vulnerable again. The pain had occurred right at the point where he had felt affection. He grew up to become a very guarded and defensive man who ran this pig Auschwitz."

"Treating animals this way, or eating animals that have been treated this way," I said, "does something horrible to the male spirit."

"Yes, it does," John said. "Here was a guy who in his heart and soul loved animals, yet who was living in complete contradiction to his feelings, trying over and over to become his father's son, still trying to get his father's approval."

John continued with the story. "After the book came out, I sent him a copy, with a letter telling him that I had mentioned him in the book. I didn't hear from him for a long time until a letter arrived unexpectedly. When I read it I smiled from ear to ear. After much soul searching, he and his wife had sold the whole operation and moved to Missouri. He's still raising pigs, but he doesn't do it the same way. He doesn't keep them cooped up, like in factory situations. He doesn't slaughter them. He doesn't sell them to a slaughter house. He doesn't kill them at all. He has a 'pet-a-pig' program with the local schools. He also raises miniature Southeast Asian potbelly pigs that he sells as companion animals."

This man is a sterling example of a warrior who confronted his own demons, went through the wound, and transformed his work life from one of exploitation and hatred to one of cooperation and love.

"Every time I meet a man," John continued emphasizing each idea with pauses, "who has managed to make a living ... doing something ... that they feel good about, I feel grateful.

"That's always been a goal of mine. That's why I left Baskin-Robbins. I didn't feel that developing a thirty-second flavor was a meaningful or valid response to the suffering of the world. I didn't know at the time whether I could make a living and could also do something that fed my spirit and my soul.

"But I saw the way men, so often, become trapped by the paycheck into work that is boring and meaningless and doesn't contribute to the well-being of the planet. I saw it with so many of the men I knew growing up. There's a man who is a friend of my father. If he's not the richest man in the United States, he's got to be in the top ten. His income after taxes is probably over a million dollars a day. And yet he weighs in the neighborhood of four hundred pounds. When you see him, you can see his pain, the disconnection from life, the lack of openness to spirit. He is cut off from the joys of life and is only driven by the desire to make more and more money. He's the ultimate winner of the monopoly game, but the loser of life."

"There are a lot of men like that," I said, "who are harming themselves while they harm others and the planet. If you could whisper in these men's ears and have a direct line to their hearts, what would you say to them?"

"I'd ask about them as little boys. I'd ask them what they enjoyed, what did they like, what was beautiful, and what made them smile? I'd want to know about their pain, how they were abused, neglected, abandoned. I'd want to know what made them decide that it wasn't safe to be vulnerable, it wasn't safe to be really human. I'd tell them I understood the belief we develop that if people aren't going to ever freely love us, and we're sure of that, maybe we try to buy love or buy obedience. We seek power that creates fear in others when we have given up on a life that is based on respect and love."

"I've seen so many men in my practice," I told John, "men who appear cold and heartless, men who cause pain to others, who may even sexually molest their own infant children. Our first reaction is to feel outrage and revulsion. Yet I haven't found one man who abuses others—humans, animals, or the natural environment—who wasn't himself abused as a child. When we open our hearts to these men and listen to them without judgment, the story has a chance to come out and the healing can occur."

"It's true," John went on, a look of compassion on his face. "The changes that can occur when we listen with love are nothing short of miraculous."

"I've found my own children have been wonderful teachers for me in understanding manhood," I said. "Have you experienced that?"

"Yes, absolutely," John said. "I remember an incident some years ago when I was planning to leave for a 10-day meditation retreat. I thought that I was being spiritual, learning to become a better person. I was packed, I had paid for the thing and was ready to go, when suddenly I realized I didn't want to go. What I *really* wanted to do was stay home and play with my son Ocean, who was four or five at the time. I wanted to build blocks with him. I wanted to sleep with him and I wanted to take him for a ride, go somewhere, just the two of us.

"And this time I acted on that. I canceled the retreat and I had the most fun in my life. He loved it. I loved it. We just spent all that time together.

"He taught me so much, and continues to teach me, about what male energy is about. The innocence and spontaneity of children can teach us about life, about ourselves, about God. My own love for my son has taught me more wisdom than the words of any guru."

"What has your son taught you about what it means to be a man?" I wanted to know.

"That I don't have to prove I'm a man," John said with the warmest, most contented smile on his face I'd ever seen. "I don't have to be special or better than anybody. I don't have to compete. I don't have to succeed." John laughed and I nodded.[14]

Discover How To Earn a Shame-free Living

Many men feel a sense of shame about how we make our living. During this phase of recovery, we begin to question what we do. It isn't enough to just survive. We want our work to mean something. Joseph's experience is typical of many men.

> After spending the better part of 10 years becoming a successful consultant, I began to examine what I was doing. Was I happy? Was my work worthwhile? Could I say it was contributing to making the world a better place? Was I working addictively or with healthy passion? These were questions that had never occurred to me before. I was too busy trying to actualize the American dream to slow down enough to wonder if it was worth achieving.

There was a lot of focus in the '60s and '70s on "right livelihood." We wanted to find work that was fulfilling and also worthwhile. In the '80s, economic pressures and fear forced many people to give up that vision and "go for the gold." As the Michael Douglas character says in the movie *Wall Street*, "Greed is good." Many felt the idea of doing what you love to be naive, that ultimately you had to make a choice between making a living and doing work that was worthwhile. But as we enter the '90s, more and more men are recognizing the need to heal their shame about doing work that is personally degrading, and doesn't make a positive contribution to the world.

Early in the post-World War II age of affluence, a U.S. retailing analyst named Victor Lebow proclaimed, "Our enormously productive economy ... demands that we make consumption our way of life, that we convert the buying and use of goods into rituals, that we seek our spiritual satisfaction, our ego satisfaction, in consumption.... We need things consumed, burned up, worn out, replaced, and discarded at an ever increasing rate."[15] Americans have risen to Mr. Lebow's call, and much of the world has followed.

We know that our addictive drive to consume more "stuff" is killing men and harming the planet. "The richest billion people in the world have created a form of civilization so acquisitive that the planet is in danger," says Alan Durning, senior researcher at Worldwatch Institute. "American children under the age of 13 have more spending money—$230 a year—than the 300 million poorest people in the world." Durning goes on to warn, "The lifestyle of this top echelon—the car drivers, beef eaters, soda drinkers, and throwaway consumers—constitutes an economical threat unmatched in severity by anything but perhaps population.... If environmental decline results when people have either too little or too much, we must ask ourselves: How much is enough?"

Is it really possible to get off the merry-go-round of our runaway consumer culture?

I saw an ad in one of the "new age" magazines that caught my eye: "Transforming Your Relationship With Money & Achieving Financial Independence: An Audio Cassette/Workbook Course by Joe Dominguez." Most programs of this kind promise the world, but only make money for the people selling the course. This one seemed different. It was sold with a money-back guarantee, and said that all the profits were distributed through a nonprofit organization to other nonprofit groups that are doing good work, such as Ecology Action, Tree People, the Seva Foundation, and the Planet Earth Foundation.

As I read about Joe Dominguez, he also seemed different from the get-rich-quick schemers who are so abundant in the world today. I learned that Dominguez was a former Wall Street whiz kid who made it from messenger boy to financial executive, and was on the brink of making it big time, when he began to have doubts. "Hey, there must be more to life than this," he thought. "Where's the fulfillment?" That's when he "retired"—in 1969 at the age of 30, feeling he'd learned the principles for transforming his relationship with money and achieving financial independence. He felt there was more to life than "9-to-5 'til 65."

"Using only the money from my modest salary," says Dominguez, "no speculations, no 'killings on the market,' nothing but paychecks, I had established a safe, steady income, adequate for my needs, for the rest of my life.... Since that time I have not accepted money for anything I do."[16]

The cassette course and workshop are designed to be done over a weekend. My wife and I set the time aside and found it transforming. We learned about our early education and assumptions about money, how our parents felt and how their beliefs influenced us today, what kind of work we'd do if we didn't have to worry about making a living, and most importantly we learned about the fulfillment curve. It showed graphically what most of us know intuitively, that having too little money is a source of stress, but more and more does not bring fulfillment. Helping us find out how much is enough, and teaching us how to get it, was spelled out in specific detail in the rest of the course.

Dominguez helped us recognize that the way we spend our money is a reflection of what we value. Recognizing that a great deal of what we bought did not add value to our lives enabled us to cut back on spending without giving up anything we really wanted. In fact, it allowed us to decrease our stress by not having a houseful of "stuff" that we rarely used, cluttered our space, and eventually needed to be repaired. It also freed up time that we had previously taken to earn the money to buy the stuff. Now we have more time available to do the things that mean something to us—more time for family and friends, more time to walk in the woods, more time to contribute our energies to the causes we believe in, more time to do work we love without worrying whether we'll have enough to make the next house payment.

Joe Dominguez and his colleague Vicki Robin have now written a book that makes the information in the course available to more people. In the introduction they ask questions that most of us need to answer: "Do you have enough money? Will you ever? Are you making a living or making a dying? If you lost your job tomorrow, would your world fall apart—or finally make sense?" The book tells us not just how to manage our finances, but how to integrate them with the rest of our lives. For example, in Chapter 4 of Dominguez's book we learn how to ask ourselves if we are truly getting fulfillment from the things we buy. Most of us spend money on things that don't really offer deep satisfaction. Once we become aware of this, we painlessly cut back on our spending. In Chapter 6 we learn how to live the American Dream on a shoestring, and are given 10 sure ways to save money.

As we heal our shame by healing our bodies and souls, we complete this stage of recovery. We learn to come home to ourselves. We are less susceptible to the propaganda of the addictive society that would have us believe that we must consume more and more if we are to feel better and better.

"In the final analysis," says Alan Durning, "accepting and living by sufficiency rather than excess offers a return to what is, culturally speaking, the human home: the ancient order of family, community, good work and good life; to a reverence for excellence of craftsmanship; to a true materialism that does not just care *about* things but cares *for* them; to communities worth spending a lifetime in."[17]

Our addictive culture has tried to convince men that "he who dies with the most toys, wins." Maybe Henry David Thoreau had a clearer vision for health when he scribbled in his notebook beside Walden Pond, "A man is rich in proportion to the things he can afford to let alone." What would it be like if men developed careers based on Dominguez's, Durning's, and Thoreau's values?

Notes

1. The above quotes from men are from, Ritter, Thomas J., M. D. (1992) *Say No to Circumcision: 40 Compelling reasons why you should respect his birthright and keep you son whole.* Aptos, CA: Hourglass Book Publishing.

2. Milos, Marilyn Fayre, R.N., quoted in *Circumcision: What It Does* by Billy Ray Boyd, Taterhill Press, San Francisco, 1990.

3. From Ritter, op. cit.

4. From Romberg, Rosemary (1985) *Circumcision: The Painful Dilemma*. South Hadley, MA: Bergin & Garvey Publishers.

5. From Ritter, *op. cit.*

6. Janeway, Elizabeth (1971) *Man's World, Woman's Place*. New York: Dell Publishing Co.

7. Maimonides, Moses (1956) *Guide for the Perplexed*. New York: Dover Publications.

8. Quoted form an article by Mary MacVean, Associated Press, "Eat Smart, Live Longer and Better," *Marin Independent Journal*, September 16, 1991.

9. Hill, P., "Environmental Factors of Breast and Prostatic Cancer," *Cancer Research*, 41:3817, 1981.

10. Gordon, T., "Premature Mortality from Coronary Heart Disease: The Framingham Study," *New England Journal of Clinical Nutrition*, 10:522, 1962; "Incidence and Prognosis of Unrecognized Myocardial Infarction—An Update on the Framingham Study," *New England Journal of Medicine*, 311:1144, 1984.

11. A number of studies support these findings, including:
    Hardinge, M., "Nutritional Studies of Vegetarians: Dietary Fatty Acids and Serum Cholesterol Levels," *American Journal of Clinical Nutrition*, 10:522, 1962.
    Phillips, R., "Coronary Heart Disease Mortality Among Seventh Day Adventist with Differing Dietary Habits," *Abstract Amer. Public Health Assoc. Meeting.*, Chicago, Nov. 16-20, 1975.

12. Statistics taken from *Realities 1990: Facts Excerpted From Diet For A New America* by John Robbins, Earthsave Foundation, Santa Cruz, California.

13. From Associated Press Article, "True Earth Lovers Are Vegetarians, Group Says," in *Marin Independent Journal*, April 25, 1990.

14. From a transcript of a personal conversation with John Robbins. Quoted with permission.

15. Quoted in article, "How Much is 'Enough?'" by Alan Durning, *World Watch*, Vol. 3 No. 6, November-December, 1990.

16. Dominguez, Joe (1986) *Transforming Your Relationship with Money and Achieving Financial Independence*. Produced and distributed by the New Road Map Foundation, Box 15981, Seattle, WA 98115.

17. Durning, Alan. "How Much is Enough," *World Watch*, Vol. 3 No. 6, November-December, 1990.

8

Moving Through
the Black Hole

 One does not become
enlightened by imagining
figures of light, but by
making the darkness conscious.

—C.G. Jung

Task 7: Uncover the Roots of Our
Basic Insecurity

"Why is this process so damn difficult, and why does it take so long?" Joseph's words reflected the frustration that was so obvious in his expression. I had frequently seen frustration in my clients at this stage of the healing process. In our quick-fix society, even recovery is supposed to move along rapidly. Joseph had been in recovery for three years. He had let go of his reliance on alcohol, dealt with his sex and love addictions, confronted the core beliefs he had learned as a child and reinforced as an adult, confronted his false self, and released a good deal of the shame he had lived with all his life. When I summarized all he had accomplished in *only* three years, he chuckled. "I guess I've done a lot. It just seems like I've wasted a lot of time and I need to catch up fast." Most addicts I've worked with have expressed this feeling in one way or another. For the first time in our lives, we're beginning to experience the joy of living, and we are frustrated at the years we spent hiding. We want to make up for lost time.

I know the feeling. After three years in recovery, I wanted to have done with it. Now, after 28 years, I can accept that recovery is a never-ending process. But what else are we here on the planet to do other than to heal ourselves and, in the process to heal each other and the fragile environment we all share? What amazes me is not how long healing takes, but how many people remain committed to the journey. Think about it. All you're being asked to do is to give up your outer-ring addictions—all the comfort and security of your booze, your drugs, your gambling, even your compulsive eating habits. Then you have the honor of delving into your confused and compulsive love life. Having sorted that out, you can deal with your addictive core and your false self. After all that work, can you rest? Not on your life. Now you get to reexperience all the shame that you've harbored inside of you. When you live to survive the shame game, you're supposed to continue your journey into "the black hole," with the vague promise that you'll find your "true self" on the other side.

What does it feel like to be at this stage of the journey? "Once I understood and moved beyond the shame I felt, there was a feeling of liberation," Ron told me. "For the first time in my life, I felt like I was okay, that there might be hope for me. But as I moved more deeply inside, I began to feel frightened, almost terrified. I'm not even sure what the fear was, but it felt cold and empty."

Carlos was even more aware of the terror. "When I was dealing with shame issues, it was as though I would look into the mirror and see a hideous, ugly reflection. But lately I've had a dream of looking in the mirror and not seeing any reflection at all. It's like I ceased to exist."

Kevin spoke to the issues underlying his fear. "When I began to confront the black hole, I realized I was dealing with some of the most basic insecurities we can experience. I felt I needed to confront death and annihilation, and it was terrifying."

My Experience of the Black Hole

I was elated. I had just spent a weekend with my men's group, and had gotten in touch with and released a lot of buried feelings. I had confronted my shame about my sexual acting out, shame over the way I had harmed my children, and my fears about being gay. I had risked revealing my darkest secrets, and I hadn't been rejected. I felt clean for the first time in my life.

That night I had a dream which I recognized as one I've had a number of times since childhood. I'm naked at the bottom of a huge amphitheater, looking up at thousands of people whose attention is focused on me. I don't know how I've gotten here, but I feel like a gladiator who must fight for his life. Suddenly a voice rings out that seems to be the voice of Everyone, of God. It fills the arena as it reverberates through my skull. "You've been put on this earth provisionally." The voice is loud and stern. "It is not likely that you will be allowed to stay." I scream, "Please, I'll do anything, just let me stay." The voice booms back at me, "Okay, then do it."

I feel I have been reprieved. I won't be destroyed: I will be allowed to live. I want to get right to work. I want to begin immediately. It's then that I realize I don't know what "it" is. I call back in desperation, "Do what? What do you want me to do?" "Just do it!" the voice screams back at me.

I woke up in a cold sweat, realizing that I had spent my life running faster and faster trying to "do it" so that I would be allowed to remain alive. I never knew what I was running toward, and was too terrified to slow down long enough to see what I was running from. I realized now that my addictions served to pull me away from something deep within. I knew that to return to my addictions would mean death. But I was afraid to confront what was waiting for me inside. To do so felt worse than death. There was a terrible feeling that things were not right with me.

Author Jean Liedloff says in *The Contiuum Concept: Allowing Human Nature To Work Successfully*, that a person who doesn't experience an inner sense of well-being "often feels there is an empty space where he ought to be." The morning after my dream was my first encounter with the "black hole."

I gave it the name "black hole" after hearing a guy on the radio from the Astronomical Society talking about stars. I didn't understand much about the astronomy, but the general description seemed to fit my experience. The black hole wasn't just a place where you entered and were lost. If that were the case, you could just stay away. No, the black hole, like a powerful magnet, had the ability to pull a person in. Once inside, nothing could get out, not even light. That was the dilemma I faced. Having gotten this far in my recovery, I was facing an inner force which at once terrified me and drew me inexorably inward.

Like so many other things in life, the black hole isn't a concept we can understand until we have experienced it. I've made the journey there and back many times, and have acted as a guide to others who give themselves over to the power of the black hole, assisting them in finding their way out again. And I firmly believe that going to the black hole, though frightening, is the key step to recovering our lost manhood.

There are two interrelated tasks that must be accomplished at this stage of recovery. You must get to the bottom of your insecurity, and you must confront the abuse from your childhood. There are a number of issues you must contend with in accomplishing these tasks:

- Understand your basic insecurity, and find the key to regaining basic trust.

- Uncover the traumatic events at the core of your addictions.

- Acknowledge your family secret, and accept the truth about your origins.

- Confront the social/cultural trauma that creates the background for your addictions.

- Return to where you got off track, and find the path back toward your true self.

Understand Your Basic Insecurity and Find the Key To Regaining Basic Trust

Prior to that morning when I understood my dream, I would never have recognized that my life had been run by my insecurity. I saw myself as a dynamic guy, a real go-getter. I knew what I wanted, and knew where I was going.

During my twenties and thirties I was moving too fast to feel the fear. Career and family took up all my time and all my energy. It wasn't until I began to approach 40, and wanted to slow down, that I began to feel the anxiety—very lightly at first, but very persistently. At first I responded by getting busy again. I thought that I must just need to take on a new project, or work out some problem with my wife. Gradually I began to recognize that the reason I was always on the run was that I was afraid something or someone might be gaining on me—and if it ever caught me, I would cease to exist.

It was a shock and a relief to have the dream again and to recognize that what I was running away from was an inner voice—something I had learned in childhood, but was part of me nonetheless. It wasn't something "out there" that was causing me to feel insecure, but was "in here." With that recognition, I knew, for the first time, that there was no place to run. As that great American philosopher Pogo once said, "We have met the enemy and he is us."

When I acknowledged that the insecurity was within, I could better understand how our security, or lack of it, affects our recovery.

The Importance of Security Needs

Abraham Maslow, the famous psychologist and authority on human development, tells us that there are certain needs that are shared by every human being. In the order in which they must be met, they are:

- Physiological needs
- Safety and security needs
- Belongingness and love needs
- Esteem needs
- The need for self-actualization

It is our unmet needs that motivate us. A person who is lacking food, shelter, self-esteem, and love will demand food first and, until this need is satisfied, will ignore all his other needs or push them into the background.

In our society, most addicts have managed to meet their physiological needs. What is lacking for them is the satisfaction of their safety and security needs. In recovery, we often focus on our needs for love and esteem, but ignore our safety and security needs. As a result, too many of us never fully recover. Those of us who have not had our safety and security needs met are forever anxious, forever on the run. "Such a person," says Maslow, "behaves as if a great catastrophe were almost always impending, i.e., he is usually responding as if to an emergency."[1]

Erik Erikson, one of the leading figures in the field of psychoanalysis, approaches the same issues from a slightly different perspective. He suggests in his classic work, *Childhood and Society*, that every person passes through eight stages. Each stage involves specific tasks that must be accomplished, and certain crises that must be confronted.

The issues in the first stage of life have to do with basic trust versus basic mistrust. For the infant to develop trust, his relationship with those who care for him must be based on consistency, continuity, and sameness of experience. As Erikson says, "Parents must not only have certain ways of guiding by prohibition and permission; they must also be able to represent to the child a deep, an almost somatic conviction that there is a meaning to what they are doing." This is exactly what is missing in many of our families of origin. Without the development of basic trust, safety, and security in childhood, a person continues to seek the fulfillment of these needs through all the later stages of his life.

Scott Peck, author of *The Road Less Traveled*, also makes the connection between the lack of our feelings of safety and security and our spiritual vulnerability. He calls addiction "the sacred disease," linking it to Adam and Eve's exile from the Garden of Eden.[2] We might see in the story of Adam and Eve the archetype for all addicts: the loss or absence of safety and security; the driving hunger to regain the lost paradise of abundance.

There is a regressive aspect to this longing: the addict longs to return to the safety, security, and abundance of the womb. Addictive drinking, gambling, sex, or romance can be seen as a misguided attempt to merge with our primal mother. But we can't go home again, not that way. Insecure at our core, we go through life feeling like orphans.

Psychologist Carol Pearson offers a clear description of this experience in *The Hero Within*. "The world is seen as dangerous; villains and pitfalls are everywhere.... It seems like a dog-eat-dog world, where people are either victims or victimizers. Even villainous behavior may be justified by the Orphan as simply realistic because you must 'do unto others before they do unto you.' The dominant emotion of this worldview is fear, and its basic motivation is survival."

It's no wonder that, feeling like insecure orphans, we become addicts always looking "out there" to find what we feel we need to make us whole. As each thing with which we try to fill the void fails us—drugs, sex, money, and so on—we desperately try another. There comes a time for us all—sometimes prompted by a crisis of health, sometimes by the loss of a relationship or a job—when we must stop the frantic search and confront the reality of our basic insecurity.

Task 8: Acknowledge and Heal Our Hidden Childhood Abuse

Uncover the Traumatic Events at the Core of Our Addictions

Once we've faced the reality of our basic insecurity, we can go deeper and confront the core. *All* addicts were abused children. Every one of us grew up in a family in which we experienced one or more of the following:

- Being battered—physically or emotionally

- Being sexually molested

- Being neglected when we needed support

- Being physically or emotionally abandoned, or feeling the fear of abandonment

- Feeling psychologically trapped or smothered

National estimates indicate that over one million American children are suffering from abuse and neglect at any given time, and that approximately one-quarter of these will be injured for life as a result.[3] A recent research study on child abuse called it "an American epidemic." Their findings: One in six adults across America were physically abused in childhood. One in seven were victims of sexual abuse as children.[4] Many experts believe that we are only seeing the tip of the iceberg—that abuse is even more widespread than these statistics would indicate. Though child abuse has come out of the closet, and there are an increasing number of excellent books written on the subject, a great deal of abuse toward boys remains hidden. It is to this hidden abuse that I'd like to draw your attention.

Sexual Abuse: The First Hidden Trauma

In the last chapter, I talked about the shame that men experience, and suggest that one of the roots of shame goes back to the experience men have when the ends of their penises are cut off during circumcision. I consider circumcision to be a form of sexual abuse, since it is a direct attack on a boy's genitals and his sexuality. It is the first form of abuse most boys experience. But there are other prevalent forms of sexual abuse as well.

In 1980, Florence Rush wrote *The Best Kept Secret: Sexual Abuse of Children*, which was hailed by many critics, including leading feminists of the time, such as Susan Brownmiller, Adrienne Rich, and Robin Morgan. In the first chapter, "A Look at the Problem," Rush offers the following anecdote: "More than one devoted parent has vowed, 'If anyone so much as lays a finger on my little girl, I'll kill him.' But when a mother or father, let us say, discovers that it was their good friend Jack (who just lent them money and took Mary to the hospital when the baby arrived two weeks ahead of schedule), who, their child reports, 'touched me all over' rather than some 'degenerate' stranger, they will have difficulty acting upon their anticipated rage.... At most, in the future they will not leave their daughter alone with Jack."

The previous paragraph reveals some truths about child sexual abuse, and one significant error. It is true that the abuser is most often someone the child knows well (most often a parent or stepparent), rather than a stranger. It is true that those involved have difficulty focusing on the needs of the child. And it is true that social denial often helps those involved to keep the family secret, and the abuse continues. However, the view—which was prevalent at the time and still continues to this day—that the victim is most often a young girl and the abuser an older man, is actually a distortion. The women's movement helped focus on the reality of child abuse, and forced a reluctant society to pay attention. With their feminist focus, it isn't surprising that sexual abuse among boys was often overlooked. Nor is it surprising that they neglected to recognize that many of the perpetrators were female.

All those who care about the welfare of children owe a debt to the women's movement of the '70s and '80s. By 1988, men were ready to speak out, and Mike Lew wrote *Victims No Longer: Men Recovering From Incest and Other Sexual Child Abuse.* "By the best estimates based on a compilation of government statistics and reports by professionals," says Lew, "there are over 40,000,000 American adults who as children were victims of sexual abuse. While if anything this figure is low, the incidence of widespread sexual abuse of children has only in the last few years come into public awareness. What the public is not aware of is the fact that males comprise a large percentage of the victims. The number is in the range of 15,000,000 male survivors."

Mark Matousek is a New York-based journalist who was doing research for an article on incest, "America's Darkest Secret." What started out as just another interesting assignment became, by his own admission, a journey into hell. He begins his article by asking us to imagine ourselves on a train. "Your bag is packed with a few belongings, enough for a short stay in the country. Your family is around you; a novel is tucked half-finished into your lap. You know that you are being transported, but you don't know where, and the soldiers laughing among themselves in the aisle do not speak your language. Because the landscape is familiar, because your family is there, because nothing in your experience could have prepared you for such a radical awakening, you do not see that you have crossed over an unmarked border. Even when the station stop—Dachau—appears outside the window and the lineups begin, the impact of what is happening does not jar you. It is not until you see the bodies and smell the smoke that the mask of unreality snaps off and the sleepwalk comes to an end."[5]

We recoil at such an image. The abuse that happens to children can't be compared to what happened in the concentration camps, can it? We did survive, after all; whatever happened to us is in the past. Can't we just forget it, and get on with our lives? Simone, a survivor of incest who was quoted in the article says, "The truth is that there are two kinds of people in the world, the ones who want to remember and the ones who want to forget."

Mark Matousek is clearly one of the ones who wants to remember. He says, "I began with such a painful image for two reasons. First, I know of no metaphor more appropriate to the tortures and helplessness of incest than that of the concentration camps. Second, what began for me as a press trip into the world of family sexual abuse became a kind of internment."

As I began my own research for this book, I had no idea it would lead me into the lessons of the black hole—that it would reveal truths long buried. When we are open to the pain of others, we often allow our own healing to occur. "The more people told me their stories," says Matousek, "the more kinship I felt. Symptoms, obsessions, half-forgotten scenes that had haunted me since childhood began to string themselves together, and I was shocked to realize that I was one of them."

This is a vivid description of that moment that most of us in recovery have experienced. We are listening to someone else's story and realize that it is our own. Mark's words reveal the wonder and terror of recalling instances of child sexual abuse. "Part of me was still floating in the water of the bathtub where my mother held me clutched between her legs, in the shower stall where my father flaunted himself in front of me, in the bed where I was molested by family friends at 13."

Matousek goes on to say that the recollections weren't new, but he could see them in a new light. As we do our healing work in the black hole, we often reclaim memories, one or two at a time, over a period of years. At first we may remember events, but be unable to recognize their significance, or to name what happened to us. "Still, it was difficult," the article continues, "to call these events by their proper name. Was this incest? Could the woman whose picture is on my desk actually be a sex offender? Did the men who took me to the beach that day deserve to be put in jail?"

Often we are afraid that if we reclaim our memories, what we learn will be so devastating as to overwhelm us. Maybe, we reason, it's better just to let the past alone. Unfortunately, the past often won't let us alone, and it certainly affects our present. Fortunately, remembering what happened, and naming our experience, can allow us to continue our healing. "These questions, rather than demoralizing me," writes Mark Matousek, "came as an opportunity. The more I investigated, the more certain I became that my hunches—long suspected as prurient fantasies—had been correct. Distasteful as it was, there was a name for what had happened to me, and a community with whose help I could begin to recover."

There are a number of reasons why we don't remember what happened to us. The first two are true for both males and females. The third and fourth are more often true for males. The first is that the physical, psychological, and spiritual trauma of being invaded by a parent who is supposed to nurture and protect us is just too painful to bear. We must separate our feelings from our body in order to survive the pain of betrayal. We must block out the memories in order to keep from killing ourselves. But we can't just cut off certain feelings. The result of the repression is that we are crippled in all areas of our emotional life, and most of us don't even know the cause. Our adult relationships suffer, and we carry the guilty certainly that somehow we are to blame.

The second reason is that if we are able to tell someone what happened to us, we are often not believed. Sometimes we are ridiculed and abused even more. Some of us tried to reach out when we were children, and were rejected. Most of us knew intuitively that telling someone would cause more harm, and so we kept quiet.

The third reason is that boys are brought up to believe that sex is part of what it means to be male, at any age. We suffer from the erroneous belief that men want sex all the time, and that boys are just little men. If we were abused by a woman, the attitude is often that "we just scored early." We don't even recognize the event as abuse. If we were abused by a man, we believe it must be because we are homosexual and must have communicated that to our abuser. Either way, the need to block out and forget what happened is strong.

The fourth reason why we repress the experience is that men are conditioned to be dynamic, active, and in charge. Being accused of being a baby is a mark of scorn. I remember the pride I felt in being called Mama's little man. Accepting our inherent weakness is difficult for males, because we were conditioned to deny it. With this general conditioning, it isn't difficult to imagine why we would quickly repress incidents of sexual abuse in which we were forced to be passive and receptive. This is so inconsistent with our view of masculinity that it's terribly difficult for us to allow the memories to return.

The whole journey into and through the black hole feels like a journey to death. We are forced to strip away all that we thought of as our former self. The fear is that nothing will remain. It takes a tremendous amount of courage, and consistent and supportive guidance, to stay with ourselves long enough to find our way home.

Poisonous Pedagogy: The Second Hidden Trauma

Several years ago, I worked with a program for battered women. It was heartbreaking to see women with small children come into the shelter who had been beaten by their husbands or lovers. My job was to work with the men involved. At first, it was difficult to feel much sympathy toward them, much less care for them. They didn't talk much, although they seemed to carry a great deal of pain. I remember the shock when one of the men finally opened up and told me about his childhood.

"My dad was a policeman, and I loved him with blind devotion," said William as we began one of our sessions. William was a big man, his hands callused from construction work. We had been working together for many months, but he had been unwilling to talk about his early family experiences except to say they were "okay."

William continued: "I didn't see my father a lot as a child, but when I did I would run to him and throw my arms around his neck. I remember a game we played when I was maybe two or three years old. I would climb up on a chair and yell "Catch me!" then jump into his arms.

"I remember the day it happened, as clear as something from yesterday," William said. His voice was flat, as if he were an unemotional observer. Only something in his eyes revealed a hint of what he felt. "I yelled out 'Daddy, Daddy,' as I jumped off the kitchen chair and flew through the air with my arms out-stretched. But just as I reached out to him, he looked right at me and folded his arms. I hit my head on the edge of the table as I fell to the floor. I don't remember much after that, except Dad yelling at me to be quiet as we drove to the hospital. Days later ..." William's gaze was steady as he remembered his father's words. I couldn't hold back the tears that ran down my own cheeks when he continued. "Dad took me on his lap and said 'Baby Boy, you have to learn. ... you can't trust anyone in this life, not even your own father."

William breathed a sigh. "I've never really remembered that scene until recently. I just know that I never again reached out for him. Something died in me that day, or got buried, I don't know." William paused for a long time. "There were other lessons along the way that were supposed to 'make me tough.' I never resented them at the time. I just thought that's what it was like to be a boy; and that's what I'd have to do to grow up and be a man. But I missed jumping into my father's arms."

It took William a long while to express his rage and the hurt and fear that went with it. It took him a long time to express the guilt he felt for not being a good enough son to his father, and to understand his experience growing up. For most of his life he had idealized his father, and felt ashamed that he himself had not done better. It was only since starting therapy that his anger and rage came out at all consciously. William had sworn he would never be like his father. And yet he found himself repeating many of his father's violent behaviors. Finally being able to let out all the feelings he felt toward his father, and finally to forgive him, began to free William to love himself and his family.

As I heard from more and more men like William, I began to see that many of us were abused by our parents as they mis-takenly tried to teach us about being "a good man." In a domi-nator society, to grow up male is to grow up with violence. Inside every cold, violent William—and there are a lot of Williams in this world—is a trusting little boy calling out "Daddy, Daddy, catch me, Daddy!" as he sees the floor instead of his father rush-ing up to meet him.

We can only speculate on what it must have been like for William's father to see the result of the lesson he thought he was administering: to see his son screaming, his face bloodied, to see the look of devastation in his eyes. What sort of upbringing gave William's father the twisted idea that this would be a valuable lesson for his son? Who had taught William's father such lessons of fear and mistrust? And will the cycle of violence end with William's sons, or will they perpetuate it?

In her extraordinary book, *For Your Own Good: Hidden Cruelty in Child-Rearing and the Roots of Violence*, psychoanalyst Alice Miller calls the child-rearing practices that most boys were subjected to "poisonous pedagogy." Whereas direct forms of violence toward children are devastating, what many of us experienced was even more subtle and in the long run potentially more damaging. Contrary to what is commonly believed, not all the poison came from men. A great deal came from the women in our lives.

I still remember my experiences as a boy of three lying naked on the cold bathroom floor. My mother and her girlfriend joked and laughed as they talked about their shopping trip. The smoke from their cigarettes irritated my eyes. I watched in fear as my mother put Vaseline on the end of an enema pipe. They seemed to barely notice that I was there. I wanted to sink into the floor and disappear. My mother held me up by the ankles and her friend pushed the tube up my rectum. They told me I needed help "to get me to go." As they filled me with water, I was terrified I would burst, and begged to be allowed to go to the toilet. "Not until we get all this in you," my Mother told me. "Now come on and be a big boy," she said. "Big boys don't fuss and cry."

"Got to go," I screamed.

"You better not let go and get any shit on me." The other woman's eyes were angry. I fought back my tears and tightened down as best I could to gain control. The pain and shame of the experience were terrible. But even more significant was the forced training in self-control. I learned early on that I must control my feelings and even control my body functions at another person's command.

It wasn't the only enema I was given by my mother and her girlfriend. I never even remembered it happening until I was an adult going through recovery. Even when I remembered, it took me a long time to re-feel the terror, shame, fear, and guilt I had buried. On a conscious level, I'm sure my mother felt that I was constipated and needed an enema to help me. I'm sure her friend thought she was helping my mother with an unpleasant but necessary task "for the child's own good." The lessons being administered—that boys need to develop self-control, learn not to cry, and give over their bodies to meet others' needs—were well hidden below the level of consciousness

The poison that so many of us were forced to swallow is that we were abused in the name of love. As a result, it's very difficult to remember exactly what was done, to recognize that we were violated by those we love, to express feelings we were forced to suppress, and to heal our wounds.

Miller shows how parents abuse their children, justify it as being for the child's own good, and repress the real reasons that drive them. Without being aware of it, they are finally expressing their rage about what happened to *them* as children.

"In beating their children," says Miller, "they are struggling to regain the power they once lost to their own parents. For the first time, they see the vulnerability of their own earliest years, which they are unable to recall, reflected in their children. Only now, when someone weaker than they is involved, do they finally fight back, often quite fiercely."

We begin to heal during this phase of our recovery as we recognize that we were raised on poison. We need to learn what we swallowed before we can learn to spit it up. You may believe the poison to have been so destructive that you'll never be able to lead a healthy life. But I have found that, no matter what was done to you, no matter how traumatic, the core of your being can still heal. But first you must remember.

Acknowledge Your Family Secret and Accept the Truth About Your Origins.

I was sitting in the room listening to the speaker tell her story when I noticed that the room was becoming hot. I wanted to go out for some air, but the speaker's words mesmerized me. "My name is Dorothea," she said, "but my parents always called me 'Dolly.'" When she said that, the hairs on the back of my neck began to tingle and my mouth went completely dry. I didn't understand it consciously, but my body recognized truth for me in her words. "That's how my parents treated me, like their little doll." Her voice was a mixture of rage and grief. I didn't realize the extent to which her words had affected me until I touched my cheek and found tears there.

That was how my mother had treated me: I was her special little doll, very precious and fragile, and all hers. Sitting in the audience, I had flashes of memory of my mother telling me she was so afraid that something would happen to me that she wouldn't let anyone else touch me, not even my father. She bathed me, she held me, she comforted me.

"I never felt that I had a separate self," Dorothea continued. "It was as though there was a zipper down the front of my body that anyone could unzip at will and reach inside me." When I heard those words I burst into tears. That was precisely the experience I had. My mother touched me when *she* needed comforting, but not necessarily when I did. She stroked me when she was scared, hurt, lonely, or in need of love. Her touching was only inadvertently connected to meeting my needs.

For the first time, I understood why I became so uncomfortable when I saw little girls talking to their dollies, admonishing them to be good, and stroking them with words of love. I could also understand my father better. I had always seen him as the "bad guy" who abandoned his family. From another perspective, which I was only now beginning to see, he was pushed out. Having my own children now, I could understand what it must have felt like to be told that it was too dangerous for him to hold his own son. I can feel his anger, confusion, and pain at seeing the loving little diad of mother and son that would never include him.

I began to look back into my family history, and found that in each generation, as far back as I could get information, the father was absent. Some of the fathers died young, others divorced or were thrown out. The children and the mom remained a tightly knit unit. I had only recently heard of the term "covert incest." But this certainly described my family. I was not touched in overtly sexual ways, but the relationship with my mother always had a sexual air to it. I was always her "little man" and I knew I had replaced my father in her eyes and in her heart.

It wasn't until I was well into recovery that I realized I had never done "kid" things with my mother. I never remember her taking me to the zoo, or to an amusement park. We went out to expensive restaurants and to the movies. It was a shock when it hit me that we went out on "dates," just the two of us. Many boys today grow up with absent fathers. The result is almost inevitably a distorted relationship between mother and son.

The family secret that thrived in my family for generations was just this: sons became their mother's soul companions, and fathers were forced out of the picture. I was taught in many subtle ways by my mother that my father wasn't much of a man, but that I could make up for his failure by becoming the man my mother would have liked to have married.

Uncovering the family secret created a lot of turmoil in me; but, ultimately, it was a necessary step in my healing. Every man has a family secret. Going into the black hole to uncover it, and bringing it into the light of our conscious awareness, moves us one step ahead on our path to recovery.

Confront the Social/Cultural Trauma That Creates the Background for Our Addictions

In her pioneering work on childhood and culture, Alice Miller shows that our whole western tradition of raising children, particularly boys, is abusive at its core. This is not an aberration affecting only a few unfortunate children, but is something that molds us all. At this phase in our recovery, we need to recognize that our individual trauma is part of a larger social trauma built into our culture. Yet this social trauma is so common and so pervasive that we don't recognize the harm that it does. This is the phase of recovery when truth begins to dawn.

From the moment we are born, we enter a world where basic human needs are thwarted. We are conditioned to believe that modern methods of childbirth provide for the health and well-being of the mother and child, but nothing could be further from the truth. In her book *Birth as an American Rite of Passage*, cultural anthropologist Robbie Davis-Floyd shows how, from the very beginning, people are treated more like objects than human beings. "In the hospital, a woman's reproductive tract is treated like a birthing machine by skilled technicians working under semi-flexible timetables to meet production and quality-control demands."

Dr. Davis-Floyd quotes a fourth-year obstetrics resident to illustrate her point: "We shave 'em, we hook 'em up to the IV and administer sedation. We deliver the baby, it goes to the nursery and the mother goes to her room. There's no room for niceties around here. We must move 'em right on through. It's hard not to see it like an assembly line." Davis-Floyd points out that this method of treatment is the first rite of passage that prepares children to fit into modern society—into what she calls the "technocracy," where technology, hierarchy, bureaucracy, separation, and domination are the rule.

It is only when we contrast these practices with those carried out by so-called primitive peoples for the last two million years that we recognize how traumatic our childhoods really are. In her book *The Continuum Concept*, author Jean Liedloff documents the child-rearing practices of the Yequana tribe, hunter-gatherers who live in the upper Caura River basin near the Venezuelan/Brazilian border.

"The worlds of infants in arms in Stone Age and in civilized cultures are as different as night and day," she says, "From birth, continuum infants are taken everywhere. Before the umbilicus comes off, the infant's life is already full of action. He is asleep most of the time, but even as he sleeps he is becoming accustomed to the voices of his people, to the sounds of their activities, to the bumpings, jostlings, and moves without warning, to lights and pressures on various parts of his body as his caretaker shifts him about to accommodate her work or her comfort, and to the rhythms of day and night, the changes of texture and temperature on his skin, and the safe, right feel of being held to a living body."

Yequana children, like children in all hunter-gather cultures, are nursed until they are four years old, and are never out of reach of their mother's touch. They don't sleep alone and are never put in playpens. They are never left while mother goes off to work or out to dinner. "Every nerve ending under his newly exposed skin craves the expected embrace, all his being, the character of all he is, leads to his being held in arms," says Leidloff. "For millions of years newborn babies have been held close to their mothers from the moment of birth."

This is precisely what we have lost in our modern world. As children we weren't touched enough, and as adults we continue to crave what we never received. This causes the hunger that fuels our addictions. Our technocratic culture teaches us not to trust our two-million-year-old instincts for raising children. It tells us that fathers are clumsy and don know how to take care of infants; and that doctors and other technological experts know better than mothers how to give birth and raise healthy children.

It is time we recognized that the norms of our modern child-rearing practices are traumatic and unhealthy. We need to take our power back from the hands of the technocracy and re-assert our ability to nurture infants. "The maternal role, the only role which can relate to an infant in the earliest months," says Liedloff, "is instinctively played by fathers, other children, and anyone else who deals with the infant, even for a moment. Distinguishing sex or age groups is not the business of a baby."

Child Sexual Abuse: An Integral Part of Dominator Cultures

Just as the physical abuse and neglect of children is built into the our dominator culture, so too is sexual abuse. As we began to use the animals and the land to fulfill human needs without regard to the needs of nature, so too did adults begin to use children. Just as the land and what lived on the land became the property of those strong enough to hold it with violence, so too were children seen as the property of their parents to be used in any way they chose.

Men, cut off from the core of their own healthy sexuality, become users of those who were weaker. Often these were the women and children they controlled in their family. Susan Brownmiller in *Against Our Will* presents this historical analysis:

> The unholy silence that shrouds the intra-family
> sexual abuse of children and prevents its realistic
> appraisal is rooted in the same patriarchal philoso-
> phy of sexual private property that shaped and
> determined the historic male attitude towards
> rape. For if a woman was man's corporal prop-
> erty, then children were and are a wholly owned
> subsidiary.

Child sexual abuse, in fact, is built into our Judeo-Christian religion. "The Bible and the Talmud encouraged sex between men and very little girls in marriage, concubinage and slavery," says therapist and historian Florence Rush in *The Best Kept Secret: Sexual Abuse of Children*. "The Talmud held that a female child of 'three years and one day' could be betrothed by sexual intercourse with her father's permission."

According to Jewish folklore, a woman came before the renowned and revered second-century Rabbi Akiba ben Joseph. She complained that sexual intercourse had been forced upon her before she reached the age of three. After pondering the problem, the Rabbi compared the situation to a baby who submerges his fingers in honey: "The first time he cries about it, the second time he cries about it, but the third time he sucks it. He ultimately enjoys the experience."[7] We still use this rationale to justify many of our modern forms of sexual exploitation.

The sexual abuse of children by adult family members did not only exist in the past; nor is it restricted to the Judeo-Christian traditions. It is a universal experience affecting children growing up today in countries throughout the world.

Even with my years of experience working with survivors of sexual abuse, I was shocked when I read a recent study on the extent of abuse worldwide. Rates of abuse in our own country are unbelievably high. As part of a review of studies made throughout the world, author Lloyd Demause concluded that the rates of sexual abuse in the United States are at least 60 percent for girls and 45 percent for boys. He noted that the studies from which these figures were derived did not include common sexualized traumas, such as forced and frequent enemas or regular sexualized beatings. He also mentions that statistics on the sexual abuse of boys are widely under-reported.

Demause found similar rates of abuse in other regions, including Canada, Latin America, and Europe—although reliable statistics are difficult to obtain. He also examined studies of countries in the Far East, Middle East, and Asia. His conclusion was: "However high the rates of childhood molestation may turn out to be in contemporary Western countries, the incidence in countries outside the West is likely to be much higher."[8]

As widespread as sexual abuse is in civilized society, it is difficult to accept the truth that it is virtually absent among hunter-gatherer cultures. The sexual abuse of children, we must conclude, is a worldwide phenomenon, and is a consequence of living in our modern dominator societies.

As we confront the social trauma that is built into our dominator culture, we begin to reclaim the power we have lost. We can stop feeling guilty for what was done to us. We can recognize that our abuse is meant to break our will, to keep us in line. We can join together for mutual support, and begin opposing the practices that continue to keep us chained to our dysfunctional past.

Return to Where We Got Off Track and Find the Path Back Toward Our True Selves

As we relive and heal the psychic wounds that we experience going into the black hole, we also encounter what I call the "golden thread." This is the golden thread that connects us to the core of our being, to our true selves. It was this connection we were forced to give up in order to survive in our abusive families. As children we were forced to make a choice. Either hold on to the golden thread and stay connected to our true selves—and face death. Or let go of the golden thread and be the obedient children our parents wanted us to be—and live. From the point of view of a child, the choice was easy. We dropped the golden thread and hoped that if we were "good enough," our parents would keep us alive.

At this phase in our recovery, we can now retrieve what we were forced to abandon. This entails a process of recognizing that when we let go of our true selves and became dutiful children, we lost the deep joy of feeling alive. Regaining our connection with life occurs as we symbolically reconnect the golden thread from the center of our being to our higher power.

Many of us are afraid that if we remember what happened to us, the horror will overwhelm us. Not only are we afraid to find some deformed freak at the center of our being; but we fear that our deformity is permanent. As we begin to remember what happened to us, we are sure that nothing beautiful could have survived our own particular neglect, abandonment, or abuse.

For me, the tears of joy were boundless when I realized that I could still remember and survive intact. Whatever happened to you, no matter how horrible, did not permanently damage the core of your being. Let me say it again: WHATEVER HAPPENED TO YOU, NO MATTER HOW HORRIBLE, DID NOT PERMANENTLY DAMAGE THE CORE OF YOUR BEING. The truth is you were conceived in perfect beauty, and you are still perfect. For the sake of survival you had to let go of the golden thread that connected you with your perfection. But the thread was neither destroyed nor lost. It has been waiting for you to pick it up again

In reclaiming the golden thread, we are able to once again see the path to our true selves. But it is a different kind of seeing than most of us are used to, different from trying to force ourselves to "see" into the void. Before we confronted the black hole, fear and mental chatter would have obscured our ability to keep to the path. The kind of seeing we are capable of now comes from a sense of quiet watchfulness. In Aikido energy awareness training, we call this "seeing with soft eyes."

Seeing with soft eyes can only occur when we have been able to recognize and heal our childhood traumas and quiet our fearful minds, allowing ourselves to rest in what biologist and philosopher John Lilly calls the center of the cyclone. For the first time in our lives, there is no need to hurry, no need to force our mind to find solutions, no need to fight against veils of blindness. All is gentle now. Having released our darkest secrets and shined light into the black hole, we become aware that all our fears are of our own making. We have been running from demons that don't exist. As we illuminate the darkest corners of our mind, we begin to feel at home with ourselves. We begin to remember the things that bring us joy.

Robert Bly describes the experience this way in *Iron John:*

> We notice the turns of thought, or language, that
> please us. One remembers at forty or fifty what
> sort of woman or man we really like. What were
> the delights we felt in childhood before we gave
> our life over to pleasing other people, or being
> nurses to them, to doing what they wanted done.
> Mythologically, catching hold of the end of the
> golden thread is described as picking up a single
> feather from the burning breast of the Firebird.

Once we recognize the abuse we survived, and can grasp again the golden thread that leads to our true self, we can feel how the journey through the wound has strengthened us. This is why addicts in recovery can truly say that they are grateful, not only for their recovery, but for the addiction itself and all that caused it.

As the philosopher Friedrich Nietzsche reminds each of us, "That which does not kill me makes me stronger."[9] All of us have survived, and all of us have grown stronger. We have spent a lifetime trying to avoid remembering what happened to us. As we move in and through the black hole, we have reclaimed our life experience. Rather than avoiding our wounds, we have come to embrace them. It is only on the other side of the wound that the path continues—back to our true selves, back to the gift we have to offer the world. We are now ready to embark on the final stage of our journey, returning to the true self.

Notes

1. Goble, Frank (1971) *The Third Force: The Psychology of Abraham Maslow—A Revolutionary New View of Man*. New York: Pocket Book.

2. Peck, Scott. Lecture at Community Congregational Church, Berkeley, CA, September 19, 1987.

3. Crime Prevention Center, Office of the Attorney General (1988) *Child Abuse Prevention Handbook*, Sacramento, CA.

4. Patterson, James, and Peter Kim. (1991) *The Day America Told the Truth: What People Really Believe About Everything That Really Matters*. New York: Prentice-Hall.

5. Matousek, Mark, "America's Darkest Secret," in *Common Boundary*, March/April 1991.

7. Edwardes, Allen, and R. E. L. Masters (1970) *The Cradle of Erotica*. London: The Odyssey Press.

8. Demause, Lloyd. "The Universality of Incest," in *The Journal of Psychohistory*, Fall 1991.

9. From *Twilight of the Idols*.

9

Returning to the True Self

 "Men do not face enemy machine guns because they have been treated with kindness," says Sergeant Toomey in Neil Simon's *Biloxi Blues.* "They face them because they have a bayonet up their ass."

Task 9: Explore the Origins of Our Violence and Change Our Destructive Behavior

It was an unusually warm night for San Francisco. Sheila and I were walking from our apartment to the apartment of one of our friends, a student at the San Francisco Zen Buddhist Center. Walking through the darkened streets, an approaching Zen student in black robes stopped us. "Be very careful," she said. Her voice was calm but the look in her eyes told me that something terrible had happened. "Chris Persig was just killed around the corner."

I felt shocked, a little sick, and wanted to get away. I also wanted to see for myself what had happened. Cautiously we walked the block and a half to the death scene, the same corner where I got off the bus every evening. Chris was lying face-up at the edge of the street. Police were doing their work, taking pictures, checking pockets, waiting for the ambulance. Zen students stood close by. Everyone was silent, but somehow very peaceful, a circle of love protecting a fellow student even in death.

"That could have been me lying there," I thought. I felt overwhelmed with apprehension and sadness. Later that night, safe in our apartment, I tried to relax and meditate. "How do I make sense of this?" My heart pounded and the tears flowed. "Do I buy a gun, a knife, mace? How do I protect myself? What really happened?"

As I opened my mind, my heart, my spirit, I got a clear message that Chris' death was tied to his "being a man." Maybe he didn't scream for help because men don't scream. Maybe he didn't run because only girls run away. Or maybe he was "too nice," a reaction to having been told that all men are bad. I also felt the presence of his murderer. The image was of a man, also conditioned by the male code: "Be strong, be cool, don't let anyone push you around. Take what you need: Love and compassion are for sissies." I felt a sense of identification with both men. I saw myself lying dead on the sidewalk and also running away with a knife in my hand.

As we move now into the final stage of recovery and begin to get comfortable with our true selves, our final task involves understanding and healing our violence. For most of us, violence is either something we have just accepted as a necessary part of being male, or something we were ashamed of and tried our best to hide. The night of Chris's murder, I realized that I had spent my whole life trying to protect myself and those I loved against the "reality" that at the core of my being was a violent monster who, if let out, would destroy everything I cared for. My fear was that if I got down to my true self, I would find a deadly killer.

I tried to be a nice guy, and kept what I feared was a killer core tightly controlled. As I learned to allow myself to express my feelings, I hoped I could let out all the good stuff—the love, compassion, and empathy—while keeping a lid on the killer rage I knew to be buried deep inside. I remember the sense of being besieged by the women who loved me, who wanted me to open up and let them know how I felt. The few times when I let a little of the real stuff out, they recoiled in horror. There were times when I knew it was all I could do to keep myself and them safe from my violence.

Often I would be accused of being cold, beady-eyed, and unfeeling. I wanted to scream, "Don't you understand that if I let out my real feelings you'd know how I want to rip you to shreds, tear off your breasts, crush you into dust? Is that what you really want to hear? Don't you know that I'm terrified that if I let it out at all, I might lose control and kill you? Don't you know that the only way I can protect you is to kill off my feelings?"

Living with Sheila finally drew me into and through what I thought was my inherent violence.

I always tried to avoid fights with Sheila, on the surface because I felt that fighting was beneath me. In truth I was afraid that I might hurt her; and, beneath that fear, I felt that she could and would kill me if provoked. She often seemed like a wounded animal with so much rage and hurt from her past that she was quite capable of hurting me if she felt threatened.

After we met, I was sure that with a lot of love I could calm Sheila down and heal her wounds. It didn't work out that way. We seemed to feed on each other's fear and rage, and our fights often lasted for hours. Usually I got the worst of the deal. She had hit me, bitten me, broken my glasses, destroyed my property, and threatened to stab me more than once. I was afraid to fight back, afraid if I did I wouldn't stop. During one of our fights, I had retreated to my room for safety. I knew I was approaching my edge and needed to cool off. She followed me in.

"Don't you walk out on me!" she screamed in my face.

I felt my face redden and my blood rise.

"Get the fuck out of my room, now!" I screamed. I knew that if she didn't leave I was going to hit her. She turned to leave and I breathed a sigh of relief. But she turned back, got right in my face and began poking me in the chest with her finger.

"You fucking bastard! You are so cold and uncaring."

I lost it. The many months I had tried to keep my rage under control exploded. The years of self-restraint disappeared. I didn't care what happened anymore. My brain was on fire. All I could see was her finger, feeling like it was poking holes in me. I knew I was going to hit her, and I knew when I started I wouldn't stop until she was dead. I had spent a lifetime trying to protect myself and those I loved from the killer I knew lurked inside me, and I had given up the battle. I just wanted peace.

Yet as my hand came up to hit her—all restraint gone, the killer let out of its well-constructed cage—I didn't hit her. In that moment of passion I realized for the first time in my life that I was not a killer at the core of my being. I knew I was a warrior, that the essence of my being was to protect, not to kill. It was a lesson that was well worth the broken hand that resulted when I hit the wall instead of Sheila. What I received in recompense was a gift of my true self.

Men and Violence

Confronting my own violence has been a long and difficult process. Part of the difficulty lies in the pervasiveness of violence in our society. Though we deplore the rising tide of violence, we have come to accept it as a necessary reality, like death and taxes.

Gang warfare in our inner cities makes life precarious for many. Robbers don't ask for "your money or your life" any more. Increasingly they take both. Neither are we safe in our suburbs and small towns. The late 1980s and early 1990s brought us machine-gun killings of school children, mass murders of people in the workplace, the killing of parents by their sons, vengeful killings of ex-wives and girlfriends, and increases in racist and anti-Semitic acts of violence.

We hear increasingly of crimes committed out of boredom, or "for fun," or out of curiosity—like the boys in a small Missouri town who wanted to see what it would feel like to kill someone, so they bludgeoned one of their schoolmates to death. We cringe in horror when we hear of the young Brooklyn boy who was set on fire by a 13-year-old "to see what it was like," or the Central Park jogger raped and beaten by a group of boys out "wilding."

We shake our heads in disbelief when we hear about another soldier surviving war in the Middle East only to return home to be killed in some senseless crime. We hide from the reality that our nation has become so violent that people are actually *safer* going off to war than living in many of our American cities.

After documenting extensive research on violence, a recent study concluded, "The United States is the most violent country in the world." In support of their conclusions, the researchers offer the following statistics: The homicide rate per 100,000 people was 18.0 in the U.S, compared to 4.1 for Canada, 3.9 for Australia, 2.4 for France, 2.2 for West Germany, 1.5 for Japan, and 1.4 for the United Kingdom. Some of their major findings are summarized as follows:

- The United States has 20 times the number of rapes reported in Japan, England, and Spain.

- Young males in Harlem are less likely to survive to the age of 40 than are their counterparts in Bangladesh.

- The homicide rate among young American males is 20 times that of Western Europe and 40 times the Japanese rate.[1]

Although we don't often talk about violence as a men's issue, we don't need a thorough statistical analysis to convince us that most of the violence we see is being perpetrated by males, not females. The statistics back this up. Women are also capable of violence—living with Sheila taught me that lesson, and Sheila isn't unique in her capacity for violence. The number of women arrested for violent crimes went up by 42 percent between 1985 and 1989. But the baseline for female violence was so low to begin with that 88.6 percent of persons arrested for violent crimes in 1989 were nevertheless male.[2]

To heal our violence and return to our true selves, we need to work through the following issues:

- Understanding and preventing violence

- Healing our violence toward women

- Healing our violence toward children
- Healing our violence toward other men
- Healing our violence toward the environment

Understanding and Preventing Male Violence: Getting to the Core of Healing

As we approach the year 2000, it seems that the world is on the brink of destruction. Nationalistic wars threaten the peace of the planet. Violence at home creates war zones in most of our major cities. Our addictive desire to use more and more of the earth's resources places the poor peoples of the earth on the brink of starvation while the rich choke in their own waste. Though we deplore violence, we don't seem to be able to get a handle on what causes it.

The following story told to me by Richard Heckler, and recounted in his book *In Search of the Warrior Spirit*, can help us begin to understand the roots of our violence:

> I'm in line at the post office waiting to mail a
> package to the East Coast. A young mother steps
> up to the long counter with her two-year-old boy.
> He's cranky and fidgety, she tells him to quiet
> down as she rummages through her purse. He
> puts his hand into her purse and she tells him to
> stop. He looks curiously into the purse reaching
> for something inside. Turning abruptly she slaps
> him hard across the face. "I told you to stop!"
> she shrieks. The two people in front of me drop
> their heads, the clerk at the desk acts as if noth-
> ing had happened. Anger surges through me. The
> child grows red in the face. He begins to howl.
> The mother turns towards him raising her hand,
> threatening to strike. "Don't pull that on me," she
> hisses. The boy trembles and holds his sounds
> back in sucking gasps. I was outraged.
>
> I wanted to pull her teeth out with my bare
> hands. I walked around the block twice until I
> was collected enough to drive my truck.

Heckler continues:

Reading an article about a bar in Dearborn, Michigan, now transforms the episode in my mind. In this establishment men are given black plastic miniature Uzi submachine guns. The miniature Uzis are built to shoot hard streams of water, not bullets. The evenings they hand out the water Uzis are called Rambo Wet-Panty Nights. On these particular nights women go on stage dressed in skimpy T-shirts and G-strings. Rock music blares out, men begin to shoot at the women's crotches. There's a lot of yelling and stamping. The bar's night manager exhorts the men on, "Shoot those guns! If you guys were like this in Vietnam, we would have won the war!" The woman who does the best job getting shot at wins one hundred dollars.

The comments of shooters are certainly explicit: "I got her. She's hot; I know she likes it. She likes it, and she knows that I know she likes it," says a computer marketing specialist.

"You work hard all day, and this is a release. I worked twelve hours today, and this is a way to get some aggression out," says a worker at a plastics manufacturing company.

"You don't get to do something like this every day ... how many times do you get to shoot a girl in the pussy? This is great," says an auto worker.

"This gives you a feeling of power and authority. The ultimate machoism. I'm aiming at her clitoris. She knows I'm shooting at her crotch and she knows it's me and she gets stimulation from it," says a batch processor in a chemical plant.

"Maybe they don't like it at first, but when they get all wet they've got to like it. They've got to like it," the auto worker says.

It's as though the boy in the post office will someday grow up and go to a bar like this and shoot Uzis at women's crotches and not know

why. His wife will be angry at him for being out
without her and she'll take her anger out on their
son. This son will grow up and take it out on
other women.... Where does the cycle of violence
end?

I've read this passage a number of times. Each time I do, I
get tears in my eyes. It touches home on so many levels.

It shows us that the roots of male violence go back to the
abuse we experienced as children. The often covert abuse that parents visit on their sons in the name of child-rearing leaves a deep
reservoir of rage. As boys grow up, the rage gets expressed at
other women, and is often tied in with sexual violence disguised
as "men just out having fun."

There is a suggestion that the men now shooting at the women are Vietnam vets who were not good enough to win and
must now redeem their honor by becoming better at violence and
domination. What isn't said explicitly is that many of the men
will drink a few too many and get into fights in the bar, passing
on the violence to other males. The young boy in the post office
will grow up to shoot Uzis, go home after an evening's fun, and
with anger and shame will likely beat up his wife and probably
his son as well.

The connection between male violence and our child-rearing practices is borne out by a great deal of recent research. Children reared in violent homes often grow up to become violent
adults. Violence begets violence. According to psychologists B. F.
Steele and C. B. Pollock, "Without exception in our study group
of abusing parents, there is a history of having been raised in the
same style which they have re-created in the pattern of rearing
their own children."[3]

Alice Miller shows us that boys who are raised violently
and come to power in a society are more likely to take their country to war. Those who look into the origins of Hitler's and Stalin's
destructiveness, for instance, will find that both came from extremely abusive childhoods. It isn't just the historical murderers
of the past who were brutalized as children. Saddam Hussein's
father died before Saddam was born. He was raised by a step-
father who brutalized him. In our "war of liberation," more than
200,000 Iraqis were killed: how many more sons will now be
raised by raging, violent stepfathers?

Pleasure and Nurture: The Antidotes to Male Violence

There is compelling evidence that the principal cause of human violence is the lack of bodily pleasure during the formative periods of life. Individuals and societies that experience and promote physical pleasure are also peaceful. As a nation we can reduce crime and violence in the future by stopping our abuse of children, and giving infants and young people the physical nurturing they need.

The evidence for these findings was developed by neuropsychologist James W. Prescott, who conducted his research while at the National Institute of Child Health and Human Development. First published in 1975, Prescott's findings are so clear and unequivocal that they could only be ignored by a society in which child abuse and violence were deeply ingrained in the social fabric.

Prescott found that societies that provide infants with a great deal of physical affection ("tender loving care") are later characterized by relatively nonviolent adults. In 36 of the 49 cultures he studied, a high degree of infant physical affection was associated with a low degree of adult physical violence. Conversely, a low degree of infant physical affection was associated with a high degree of adult physical violence. When Prescott investigated the 13 exceptions, he found that *all* provide adolescents with a great deal of sexual freedom, thus allowing them to compensate for the lack of physical affection during infancy.

Prescott also found that there was a correlation between a lack of physical affection and other characteristics of what I have been calling a dominator culture: women's status is inferior to men's, children are treated more roughly, male prisoners of war are more often killed or tortured, personal crime is high, class stratification is high, and the gods are seen as being more aggressive.

Prescott concludes with these words: "If we strive to increase the pleasure in our lives this will also affect the ways we express aggression and hostility. The reciprocal relationship between pleasure and violence is such that one inhibits the other; when physical pleasure is high, physical violence is low. When violence is high, pleasure is low. This basic premise of the somatosensory pleasure deprivation theory provides us with the tools necessary to fashion a world of peaceful, affectionate, cooperative individuals."[4]

Men Caring for Children: The Best Prevention for Male Violence and Abuse

Sociological studies of delinquent boys indicate that a high percentage of them come from families in which either there is no father in the household, or the father is on hand but abusive or violent. Cross cultural anthropological studies suggest that violent behavior is often characteristic of male adolescents and adults whose fathers were absent or played a small role in their sons' early rearing.[5]

Dorothy Dinnerstein, professor of psychology at Rutgers University, believes there to be a link between male violence and the fact that so many boys are reared almost exclusively by women. Without a healthy model of masculinity, men forever feel unmanly and inadequate, and often become hypermasculine in order to compensate.

Many of us feel that women are natural nurturers, that they possess some inherent knowledge about how to take care of babies. It's true that women possess this ability. But so do men. The natural ability to nurture children has been built into all members of the human species over our two-million-year-old history. Some of us have just forgotten.

Jean Liedloff spent two-and-a-half years deep in the South American jungle living with Indians who still practiced the ways of their hunter-gatherer ancestors. She found that not only were children reared with a degree of love and care that far surpassed our "civilized" ways, but nurturing was naturally practiced by all in the tribe. Her conclusion in *The Continuum Concept: Allowing Human Nature to Work Sucessfully* leaves no doubt about what is natural for us. "Every man, woman, girl, and boy of us, possess a minutely detailed knowledge of baby-care technique."

Psychologist Diane Ehrensaft and psychiatrist Kyle Pruett have done extensive studies on families in which the father is the primary caregiver or in which caregiving is equally shared with the mother. Both agree that when fathers nurture babies, it is not only good for the development of the children, but for the fathers as well.

Both are convinced that tending babies puts men in touch, at the deepest level, with feelings of vulnerability, dependency, love, and forgiveness, feelings they learned to repress at an early age. In *Parenting Together: Men and Women Sharing the Care of Their Children*, Ehrensaft describes nurturing fatherhood as a "corrective emotional experience." It permits us to make contact with the lost boy within ourselves and thus connect with our own lost humanity. We no longer have to pretend to be men. We feel it from the inside, sometimes for the first time in our lives.

As we get to the roots of male violence, and begin to embrace our true warrior spirit, we see that the essence of our journey at this stage is to replace violence with pleasure and nurture. To do that we must end our violence toward women, children, other men, and the environment.

Healing Our Violence Toward Women

A report from the Senate Judiciary Committee depicted violence against women as one of the fastest rising crimes in the nation, with 29 states reporting record numbers of assaults.[6] Although our fears of violence conjure up images of assaults by violent strangers, in fact most violence occurs between people who know each other. Domestic violence and date rape are two of the most prevalent forms of violence against women.

Twenty percent of the women interviewed in a recent survey reported that they had been raped on a date, although fewer than five percent reported the crime. As one woman says, "I never told anyone I was raped. I would not have thought that was what it was. It was 'unwilling sex.' I just didn't want to, and he did. Today, at 29, I know it was rape."[7]

Most date-rapists are not Jack-the-Ripper types. Many women report that the men who raped them had at first seemed intelligent, attractive, and kind. There was nothing about their exterior behavior that would have indicated a tendency toward sexual violence. What does not show on the surface, is true of most date-rapists, is that they grew up in violent families. Their training led them to believe that sex is a form of combat: women who resist a man's advances need to be subdued with force.

Once men and women pass the dating stage, violence does not decrease. Sociologist Myriam Miedzian reports in *Boys Will Be Boys: Breaking the Link Between Masculinity and Violence* that 1.8

million women a year are physically assaulted by their husbands or live-in boyfriends.

Why are men so violent toward women? The situation that most often fosters battering in a relationship is one in which a man comes to expect service and obedience from a woman. For a relationship like this to develop, there has to be a certain amount of collusion—a sort of shared illusion—that both the man and woman buy into. Many women learn as part of their social development that their primary role in life is to please a man. A man in this type of relationship comes to expect to be served. He becomes so emotionally dependent on this servitude that any deviation is seen as a threat to his very existence.

This can perhaps begin to account for the extreme overreaction men may have to what are certainly trivial occurrences. A woman burns her husband's toast and he goes into a rage. She is a half-hour late and he wants to kill her. A date says, "No, I want to go home now," and a man rapes her instead.

For men to heal their violence toward women, first we need to name our behavior correctly: When we yell at the top of our lungs at our partner, we are being verbally violent. When we grab her by the arms "to shake some sense into her," we are being physically violent. When we force her to have sex, telling ourselves that she just needs to be warmed up, we are being sexually violent.

We must also take full responsibility for our violence: No one but the individual is responsible for his own violence. There are *no* justifications for verbal, physical, or sexual assault. We can no longer accept the excuses that she "provoked me," or "brought this on herself," or "pushed me over the edge," or even that "the alcohol made me do it."

We need to stop the violent behavior: The only way to stop violence is to stop violence. For those men who have difficulty stopping on their own, a support group led by men who understand male violence can be very helpful. There are an increasing number of programs throughout the country that focus on male violence; many are connected with centers that work with abused women.

We need to recognize that our violence is linked to our feelings of weakness and powerlessness: Men often hit women when the woman is being emotional. She gets angry, or begins to cry, and that triggers our violent response. What is not often recognized is that men do to women what the men had done to them as children. No man abuses a woman who wasn't himself abused as a child. Recognizing and healing the abuse from the past allows men to end their violence in the present.

Healing Our Violence Toward Children

A recent issue of *Mother Jones* carried the headline, "America's Dirty Little Secret: WE HATE KIDS." The authors backed up their belief with statistics, including the following:

- Every 8 seconds of the school day, a child drops out.

- Every 26 seconds of each day, a child runs away from home (1.2 million a year).

- Every 67 seconds, a teenager has a baby.

- Every 7 minutes, a child is arrested for a drug offense (79,986 a year).

- Every 53 minutes, a child dies due to poverty (10,000 a year).

- Every day 100,000 children are homeless.

- Every school day, 135,000 children bring guns to school. A child is safer in Northern Ireland than on the streets of this country.[8]

"Living in the wealthiest, most advanced society on the earth," says Marian Wright Edelman, founder and president of the Children's Defense Fund, "we have consigned millions of our next generation to poverty, drugs, violence, and despair. Most Americans still don't know that our immunization rates against polio among black infants lag behind those of Albania and Botswana. They don't know that infant-mortality rates among minority children in some U.S. cities rival the overall rates of Third World nations." She goes on to say, "Rich kids snorting cocaine suffer the same sense of drift—for different reasons—as poor kids smoking crack.... Physical poverty is killing our children's bodies, but spiritual poverty is squashing their souls."[9]

Ending our violence toward children will require a massive shift in our social priorities. But the healing must begin at home.

The most difficult admission I ever had to make was telling my support group that I had been violent with my kids. For years I hid that fact from my awareness. I told myself that they needed to be disciplined. I rarely used physical force, but often yelled and screamed. I told myself yelling wasn't violent. Occasionally, when I would lose control, I would throw my daughter, who was two or three at the time, on the bed. I knew that if I didn't get her out of my face, I might hurt her. I told myself that throwing a child was not a violent act. Even after recognizing my behavior as violent, it still took me a long time to stop. In talking with hundreds of men, I know I am not alone.

One man I spoke to said, "When my infant son cried, I thought it meant he didn't love me. I'd get mad and hit him." There are many of us who didn't get the love *we* needed as children who take out our anger on our own babies.

"Sometimes I get so mad at my son Jason I want to hurt him." Ron had that look of pain and confusion I had seen so often looking into the mirror. "I don't know why I do it. He's so precious and innocent, but sometimes a rage comes over me that I don't understand. It seems to happen most often when Jason is acting wild, full of childish exuberance, totally out of control. I'm pretty sure I'd never hit him, but the fear keeps me from being as close to him as I would want. I feel I have to protect him from me. When I look deeply inside, I'm afraid I want to kill his spirit. It sickens me to acknowledge that, but I know it's true." Ron began to cry. His tears were my own and they were the tears of so many other men.

The first steps of this stage of healing are similar to those we must follow to end our violence toward women. We must first name what we are doing. We have to call violence violence. The difficulty is that most of us are so ashamed of our behavior, we feel so bad about harming our innocent children, that we deny both the behavior and its meaning. I found it very helpful to be in a group with other men who all were dealing with their violence toward women and children. It helped me recognize that I wasn't the only one who did this, and helped me see the destructiveness of my behavior without seeing myself as a horrible monster.

Once we've named our behavior, we can go on to take responsibility for it, and to stop it. Violence comes from our own fear. The one act for which children are punished more than any other is disobedience. When our child won't obey us, it triggers feelings of loss of control. There is an irrational fear that if I can't make them obey me, I'm going to die.

It was extremely helpful in my own recovery from violence to recognize that I had internalized my abusive parent, that I was doing to my children what had been done to me. As long as I repressed my own childhood, I found myself passing on the legacy of violence. I would yell and scream at my children, feel guilty and ashamed, publicly hold that they "needed" to be yelled at, and privately tell myself that I would never do it again. I would "be good" until the next time. Only when I began to heal my own abuse could I begin to stop being violent to my children. It also helped to recognize that I had internalized the values of a 10,000-year-old dominator culture: change would not come about immediately.

Healing Our Violence Toward Other Men

When we think about male violence, we often think about men as the perpetrators, with women and children as the victims. Because as a culture we see men as expendable, we are blind to the violence we inflict on men and boys. When we think of date rape, for instance, we often think about what men do to women. In the same study revealing that a surprising 20 percent of women had been date raped, it was found that 37 percent of homosexual or bisexual men had been raped by men they knew.[10]

Proving ourselves manly often means doing harm to other men. If you are poor and live in one of the big city ghettos, proving you are a man might involve a willingness to rob, assault, or kill another man. Homicide is the major cause of death among young African-American males.[11] If you come from a middle- or upper-class family, it might mean showing your buddies how well you can handle a car at high speeds even after a few drinks. Automobile accidents are the major cause of death among young white males.

Although women are often hurt and killed by men, the most likely victims of male violence are other men. Each year about three times as many men as women are murdered.[12] All men are not at equal risk, however. For every white male killed each year, seven African-American males die violent deaths.[13]

If men survive the violence on the streets, they often end up facing more violence in prison. The U.S. has the world's highest rate of incarceration. At present there are one million people in our prisons, the great majority of them men. Most of the men in prison are from racial minorities. It's a sad commentary on American society to recognize that we send black males to prison at four times the rate of South Africa.[14]

In order to decrease male violence toward men, we have to explore the roots of the training which taught us to win at all costs, separate "us" from "them,"and "get him before he gets me." We need to go into the football locker rooms and Little League dugouts of our American childhood.

Sports: When Winning Is the Only Thing, Violence Will Not Be Far Away

Even in such "peaceful" sports as baseball, we accept that pitchers will throw 90-mile-per-hour fastballs at the heads of opposing players to "brush them back" from the plate. We accept, and even look forward to, the brawls that often ensue. One boy was depicted by his teammates, with some pride, as "a real kamikaze on the basepaths" because he specialized in "taking out" opposing fielders, even when this was not entirely necessary.[15]

The lessons are learned early. When "60 Minutes" did a program on youth football, they found that the emphasis was very much on winning. When one boy on a Hollywood, Florida, youth football team was asked if he was ever scared when he went into a ball game, he replied, "Yes, scared of losing." We all remember the remarks of the late Vince Lombardi. "Winning isn't everything, it's the only thing."

A study of 10 relatively warlike and 10 relatively peaceful societies revealed that in most of the warlike societies young men engaged in combative sports. In the more peaceful societies such sports were rare.[16] Myriam Miedzian says, "The prevalent view in the United States is that violent sports operate as a catharsis, allowing athletes and spectators to release hostile, aggressive energy in a relatively harmless way, thus cutting down on crime, domestic violence, or warfare. Research reveals that the facts are actually quite the reverse."

Healing involves our willingness to see the truth about the ways we are prepared to dominate, hurt, and kill other men. In order to do that, we need to recognize how our traditional sports instill values that make it easier for us to cut off our feelings of love and caring in favor of feelings of competition and anger. We need to stop cheering on men who do damage to others. As author Warren Farrell reminds us, "Violence against women we protest; violence against men we call 'entertainment'—westerns, war movies, boxing, football, wrestling, etc."[17] We need to say "no" to the social attitudes that tell us that hurting other men or watching them be hurt is fun.

Healing Our Violence Toward the Environment

It's becoming increasingly clear that the violence we direct at women and children is the same violence we direct at other men and ourselves. Sadly, what we do to others is also what we are doing to the environment.

As Sri Lankan writer and psychotherapist Anuradha Vittachi reminds us in *Earth Conference One: Sharing a Vision of Our Planet*, "When we (who are merely a part of creation) see ourselves as 'the be-all and end-all of the universe' we make two kinds of mistakes: first, we behave with greedy destructiveness; and second, because we are linked to everything else in the web, we set in motion a chain reaction of ecological catastrophe."

Our childish egotism coupled with the power of modern technology makes for a deadly combination. In his book, *In The Absence of the Sacred: The Failure of Technology & the Survival of the Indian Nations*, Jerry Mander shows how our modern technologies have not lived up to their promise. Instead technology has contributed to the destruction of the planet as well as the indigenous peoples who have tried to protect it.

Though technology has done its best, it has not destroyed those who carry on the traditions of our hunter-gatherer ancestors. According to *The Gaia Atlas of First Peoples*, there are 250 million or more members of indigenous tribes in the world today, and over a thousand indigenous political organizations worldwide, most established in the last 20 years.[18] These people not only won't be eliminated, but as they fight for their survival and the survival of the land, they call us back to our true roots. "At first," said Chico Mendez, the environmental activist who was murdered in Brazil, "I thought I was fighting to save rubber trees, then I thought I was fighting to save the Amazon rain forest. Now I realize I am fighting for humanity."[19]

The Fourth World is a term used by the World Council of Indigenous Peoples to distinguish their way of life from the life-style of those who have tried to conquer the earth—the highly industrialized countries of the First World, the Socialist bloc countries of the Second World, and the developing countries of the Third World.

It is the Fourth World that is calling us down to do the grief work that we have avoided. Out of the ashes of our grief, we have an opportunity to build a new world, one in which we can all join with the Fourth World in creating a sustainable society in which all can live freely in balance with the earth. The inhabitants of the First, Second, and Third Worlds believe that the land belongs to the people; the keepers of the Fourth World believe that the people belong to the land. "We are on the one hand the most oppressed people on the globe," says John Mohawk, a Haudenosaunee writer. "On the other hand, we are the hope for the future of people on the planet."[20]

There are many stages of recovery at which it seems to us that the task ahead is impossible. Yet over and over again we find that "taking one step at a time" allows us to move through our fear. Now we are at the threshold of a new challenge. We are called upon to extend our recovery to the whole planet. Once again we are afraid, and once again we have the opportunity to move beyond our fear. "I will act as if what I do makes a difference," says the philosopher William James.

We all know the recovery benefits of "acting as if." It has helped us move ahead in the darkness when we've felt lost and alone. We don't have to wait until there is a ground swell of support before we take on the problems of the world. "Never think that a small group of committed people can't change the world," says Margaret Mead. "Nothing else ever has."

Though we may have gotten off track, I believe we are all, in our hearts and souls, Fourth World people. For 99 1/2 percent of human history, it has been so. Our brief detour has not changed that fact. It is time for the Fourth World to lead the return to the One World.

The hope for our future lies in the willingness of men and women who have the courage, strength, and compassion to wake up from our slumber and fight for the life of our planet. One man who has awakened to the call is Dave Foreman, co-founder of Earth First! "I am alive!" cries Foreman. "I am not a machine, a mindless automaton, a cog in the industrial world, some New Age android. When a chain saw slices into the heartwood of a 2000-year-old Coast Redwood, it's slicing into my guts. When a bull-dozer rips through the Amazon rain forest, it's ripping into my side. When a Japanese whaler fires an exploding harpoon into a great whale, my heart is blown to smithereens. I am the land, the land is me."[21]

Notes

1. Patterson, James, and Peter Kim (1991) *The Day America Told The Truth: What People Really Believe About Everything That Really Matters*, New York: Prentice Hall.

2. Miedzian, Myriam (1991) *Boys Will Be Boys: Breaking the Link Between Masculinity and Violence.* New York: Doubleday.

3. Steele, B.F., and C.B. Pollock, "Psychiatric Study of Abusing Parents," pp. 111-112, in *The Battered Child* (1966), edited by Ray E. Helfer and C. Henry Dimpe. Chicago: University of Chicago Press.

4. Prescott, James, "Body Pleasure and the Origins of Violence," *The Futurist*, April 1975.

5. See Miedzian, *Op. cit.*

6. From Gennett New Service, reported in Marin Independent Journal, March 22, 1991.

7. From Patterson and Kim, *Op. cit.*

8. "America's Dirty Little Secret: We Hate Kids," *Mother Jones*, May/June, 1991.

9. *Ibid.*

10. Patterson and Kim, *Op. cit.*

11. Miedzian, Myriam, *Op. cit.*

12. *Ibid.*

13. Uniform Crime Reports (UCR), Federal Bureau of Investigation, U.S. Department of Justice, 1989. Statistical Abstract of the United States (SA), U.S. Bureau of the Census, 1985, 1990.

14. Reported in Miedzian, Myriam, *Op. cit.*

15. *Ibid.*

16. Sipes, Richard G., "War, Sports and Aggression: An Empirical Test of Two Rival Theories," *The American Anthropologist*, 75, 1973.

17. Interview with Warren Farrell, "Feminism, Men's Rights, and the Inner Male," *Man!* magazine, a Journal of the Austin Men's Center, Issue No. 11, Summer 1991, Austin, Texas.

18. Burger, Julian (1990) *The Gaia Atlas of First Peoples: A Future for the Indigenous World*, New York: Anchor Books.

19. *Ibid*.

20. *Ibid*.

21. Foreman, Dave (1991) *Confessions of an Eco-Warrior*. New York: Harmony Books.

10

Warriors Without War: Separating the Soldier From the Warrior

 A Cree Indian legend says that when the Earth is sick and the animals disappear, there will come a tribe of people from all creeds, colors and cultures who believe in deeds, not words and who will restore the Earth to its former beauty. This tribe will be called the Warriors of the Rainbow.[1]

Task 10: Return to the Spirit of True Warriors

It is almost six o'clock, and the sun is setting over the beautiful waters of the Pacific. Esalen, the legendary center for the exploration of consciousness, is bathed in pink light. I am participating in a weekend workshop called The Discipline of Harmony: Warrior Virtues Without War, taught by Richard Strozzi Heckler. We have been practicing Aikido and other energy awareness techniques for the entire day. Although the work has been exhilarating, it's all been within the range of my experience. But it is clear from Richard's instructions that something very different will take place after dinner.

"When you return at eight o'clock, Richard says, his voice calm and serious, "you will be engaged in an experience in which most of you will die. This will be a simulation, but can feel very real to those who engage wholeheartedly. If you choose to play, you will learn a great deal about life and death, and about what it means to be a warrior."

Richard proceeded to give us the outline of what was to be a life-transforming experience for me. We would "become" Samurai in fifteenth century Japan, joining one of two armies, each led by a daimyo or warlord. If killed, a warrior would immediately fall; later he would be carried to the burial ground to await the end of the war. Richard would play the part of the War God who directed the battle by giving instructions to each daimyo. He represented the uncontrollable forces of the universe and could act capriciously. Looking in the eyes of the War God was cause for instant death. It was implied that there were other ways we might die, not all of which we could anticipate.

"Go now and prepare yourselves," Richard said. "In two hours, we will meet again here, and the battle will begin. Do whatever is right for you in preparing over these next few hours, knowing that they may be the last ones you will have on this earth." This exercise was already beginning to feel real.

I walked out of the hall just as the sun was setting over the ocean. I began to feel what it would be like if this were my last sunset. The colors seemed particularly vivid, the sounds of the birds clear and poignant. I sat on a rock overlooking the cliffs and thought back on my life. I was surprised to find how good I felt.

I thought of my accomplishments, but they seemed to pale as my thoughts were drawn to my family. Tears washed down my face as I thought of saying goodbye, of things that had not been said.

What would I want to say if my time were short? I began to write to my wife:

> Dear Carlin,
> This could be my last night alive, and I want you to know that my sadness at not having years to love you and play with you and adventure together is overwhelming.

The tears poured down and I had to wait until I could see again.

> Yet what we have had in our 10 years would satisfy many lifetimes. Each moment has been precious, each minute, just one, would make my stay here worthwhile.
>
> I know we will always be together, and who we are and have been will expand through the years. Hold me in your heart as you hold your love of life. Celebrate us.
> With joy overflowing,
>
> > Jed

I thought about my children and my men's group, and said a prayer to my mother and father. It was getting dark and I was aware that I didn't have much time to say what was in my heart. Damn, I wished I had more time.

To my 15-year-old stepson, Aaron, I wrote:

> It doesn't seem right that life should end so suddenly. Perhaps I will have many years ahead, but we never know.
>
> You have been a special presence in my life since I first met you in Oregon. I remember you sleeping so soundly—I marveled at your peacefulness.
>
> You are a fine young man and I am very proud of you—privileged to see you grow more into being your own special self. You are sensitive, feeling, strong, enduring.

> You have already done great things in your
> young life and you will do more. Know that I
> love and cherish you.
>
> Jed

With each child I thought about and wrote to, my heart
seemed to be breaking wide open, and the tears flowed and
flowed. I hadn't seen Jemal in six months. He was away at college
in St. Louis. I thought of the times we had missed with him growing up apart from me.

> Jemal, my firstborn, the joy of my life. You've
> taught me how to love. From the moment I came
> back into the delivery room even though the doc-
> tor told me to leave, I have felt the power of
> your presence.
>
> You are a wise soul and I have learned
> much from you. You see through illusion and are
> not afraid to feel the sadness and joy of life.
>
> Keep in touch with those feelings. They are
> the salvation of all that is good in the world.
>
> There hasn't been a moment when I haven't
> loved you. I pass on some of my spirit to you.
> Just as you have passed some of yours to me.
>
> I'll be with you in your silent times, in your
> poetry, and in your dreams.
>
> Love, Dad

The feelings kept pouring out and I felt compelled to go
on.

> Angela, my precious daughter. I've had a special
> connection with you since I first held you at the
> adoption agency when you were two-and-a-half
> months old and you fell asleep in my arms.
>
> Your aliveness and joy were wonderful to be-
> hold. I'm sorry I wasn't able to honor it as much
> as I would have wanted.
>
> You are a fighter. You have courage and
> strength and the compassion to love children and
> animals.

You've been a gift in my life. I will love you
always,

Dad

Saying goodbye to my wife and children felt devastating, but freeing. When I thought of my men's group, still together after 12 years, I felt a smile come over me. In my wildest dreams I could never have conceived of a men's group lasting longer than any of my marriages. It never occurred to me that at the moment of my death I might care enough about a man to remember him, no less eight men—John, Tom, Tony, Dick, Denis, Ken, Norman, and Kellie.

> This may be my last night to live and I'm think-
> ing of you all with love and affection, a sly smile,
> and a deep sense of gratitude for all you have
> meant to me.
> You are my brothers, my friends, my teach-
> ers, my playmates. Think of me with fondness
> once a year on the anniversary of my passing.
> Get together, share stories and wine and beer and
> laughs and tears. I honor you and us and our
> group. I love you.
>
> Jed

After finishing the letters, I felt cleansed and peaceful. I walked in the darkness and felt united with all that is and was and will be. As I got ready to return to the lodge, I felt uneasy. The thought struck me that the only person I didn't feel at peace with was my ex-wife, the mother of Jemal and Angela. It had been over 10 years since we divorced, but there was still some hurt and anger between us. I decided to write to her as well.

> Candace, know that I hold you close in my heart.
> I care about you and honor the time we were to-
> gether. You were a good friend and companion.
> Our early times together were joyous. You taught
> me to frolic and you shared your soul.
> Our children were a gift to us and I'm glad
> we are parents together. I hoped we could heal
> our hurts and fears and anger toward each other.

I think of you fondly on this my last night.

Jed

With the possibility of death only hours away, it seemed so easy to let go of my anger, of all the ways in which I had justified our emotional distance. All the hurts seemed trivial. As I walked back into the workshop room, now transformed into an open battlefield, I felt an aliveness I'd never known.

People were sitting along the edge of the rug. Their faces were serious. The room was in semidarkness. A voice quietly told us, "When the sun comes up, it will be the day of the battle." My heart pounded and my mouth was dry. This was all feeling very real. We were told to move through the room and allow ourselves to be drawn to one side or the other, either to the army of the North or the army of the South.

I moved North. We were told to select a *daimyo*, but could not use words. Any talk or indication that a decision was being made "democratically" would result in death. This was clearly a different world than the one I had left only a few hours ago. Did I want to be the leader and take responsibility for people's lives, or be one of the group? As I decided I wanted to lead, someone thrust my arm up in the air. Could I get people to follow me? What if they turned away? I would be disgraced and kill myself. Slowly the group turned to me and one by one bowed as a show of allegiance.

As I spoke to my warriors I felt a connection to all the true warriors of the past. Their thoughts seemed to flow through me. "There is no need to be afraid," I began, and found that I was actually calm. "We are all connected. Life and death are the same. There are no mistakes and you can't fail. Your job is to be yourself, to be present wholeheartedly. The army of the South is not your enemy; they offer only opportunities for you to confront yourself. Their job is to send us energy and hone us to our true form, like a flint napper, chipping off bits of superfluous stone, to make us strong and useful. You must be serious on the outside, but joyful on the inside. All that matters is that you move more closely to the center of your being, where you will feel connected to all that is. You must honor all life, and you must honor death as well, for without death there can be no life. We go into battle in the service of the planet, to nourish and protect it."

But all the philosophy drained away when the War God called each of the *daimyos* to send out a Samurai to face the first confrontation. Now I had to decide who would go into battle, who would face death. My throat became dry. When I pointed to one of the men, I could feel his fear and also his excitement. I was elated when he returned victorious and felt the pain of death as I watched the Samurai of the South fall on the battlefield. Some of the battles were over in an instant, others went on for 15 or 20 minutes.

The shorter battles involved two Samurai confronting each other at the center of the battlefield, shouting a war cry, then "fighting" with paper, rock, and scissors. (This is the children's game in which you face each other while pounding your right fist into your left hand. On the third pound, you extend either a flat hand—paper, a closed hand—rock, or two fingers—scissors. The winner is decided by the result: paper covers rock, rock breaks scissors, scissors cut paper.)

The longer battles involved balance and endurance. Two Samurai might face each other standing on only one leg with their eyes closed. The loser was the one who toppled over first.

Whoever lost the battle would immediately fall to the ground as though killed with a sword. He would remain on the battlefield until he was carried by his comrades to the burial ground, where he would spend the rest of the time experiencing what it was like to be dead.

By the end of the "war," only one person was left alive, the surviving *daimyo*. It wasn't me.

Afterwards, we shared insights and understanding long into the night and again the next morning. Most everyone agreed that the game felt very real. Many who died said that they had profound experiences of death and were no longer afraid of dying. That was certainly my experience. On some deep level I know now that death is not the end, that there is a spirit that lives on; and I suspect that we may come back to continue our spiritual growth. I also learned some profound lessons about the warrior spirit.

I felt deeply that the essence of the warrior spirit is love: there are no distinctions between enemy and friend. We really are one. I found that peace is not the absence of conflict—it isn't some gushy paradise where there are no disagreements and everyone loves everyone else. Rather, peace comes through loving confrontation.

As a peace activist in the 1960s, I had the rather naive view that we could achieve peace if we would just learn to love each other. I believed that conflict should be avoided at all cost. Now I recognize that we must be willing to deal with conflict, to confront our rage and fear, to have courage to put our lives on the line for what we believe in.

Richard said that even combat veterans who had engaged in the Samurai experience felt it was real. Many of them had profound experiences that they had only associated, in the past, with combat. There may be something important and valuable for men in the experience of battle. But battles need not be destructive. Hunter-gatherer peoples seemed to understand what we have long forgotten—that ritual war can satisfy needs that soldierly killing never can.

In our most recent war in the Persian Gulf, America rejoiced at our victory and at the fact that only 376 U.S. soldiers died in operation Desert Storm. Our government has, thus far, awarded 47,000 medals for valor and achievement. Yet there is a darker reality we wish to deny: as many as 200,000 Iraqi soldiers died during the war. According to a Harvard Medical School team of physicians, 55,000 children also died during the war, and as many as 170,000 died after the war as a result of our destruction of the Iraqi electrical and water systems.[2]

Perhaps through experiences like the Samurai War and other ritual practices, we can recapture the essence of the warrior spirit that was so much a part of our hunter-gatherer roots and which we have so completely lost in our modern world. Perhaps we can eventually make war obsolete.

Understanding the Difference Between Being a Soldier and Being a Warrior

In moving into the final stage of recovery, reclaiming our warrior spirit, it is crucial that we understand the difference between the warrior and the soldier. Until we separate the two in our hearts and souls, men will continue to be lured into becoming soldiers by those who would play on our basic needs to become warriors.

The soldier is the addictive shadow of the warrior. What drives both is the need to experience the mystery of life and death. When we stopped being hunters who felt one with all life, and became domesticators who dominated life, something in us atrophied—something that needs to be nurtured before it can be received.

The alienation that began 10,000 years ago is now reaching its climax. We have become so cut off from the life force, so insulated, so closed down that we are like zombies, just barely alive. We need more and more extreme forms of stimulation to let us know that we exist. The soldier's sense of the life force that is sparked by danger and deprivation, his feeling of love for a buddy only when both are facing death—these are the last gasps of manhood about to expire.

Men turn to addictive relationships with drugs and other substances or behavior in an attempt to find what is missing in them. So, too, do men become soldiers hoping to find the magic that will bring them back to life. But war, like any addiction, never brings life, only death.

What the soldier is looking for, but can never find, is what our warrior ancestors found in their daily lives—the feeling of an "I" connected with a "thou." Where soldiers in war thrive on mindless hate and violence, hunter-warriors thrive on love and communion. Where the soldier must separate himself from and dehumanize the enemy, the hunter merges with and honors the spirit of the animal he will kill. Where the soldier disregards his inner knowing in favor of the voice of external authority, the hunter-warrior acts on the truth he finds within. Where the soldier must deaden his feelings in order to survive the horrors of war, the hunter-warrior is in touch with all the emotions that make up the mystery of life and death.

Both hunters and soldiers kill; but the meaning that each brings to that ultimate act are worlds apart. The hunter kills only to live, and he does so with love and reverence. The soldier kills only to destroy, and he does so with fear and hatred.

We are at a turning point in history. Either we will continue to follow the ways of our 10,000-year-old dominator society, in which men are trained to be soldiers, or we will begin to develop a new partnership society in which men will bring the ancient practices of the hunter-warrior into the modern world. Continuing on the first path will lead to the end of life as we know it on the earth. Embarking on the second can open us all to a life of spiritual renewal. The choice is ours.

From Soldier to Warrior: John Dunbar to DancesWith Wolves

As we move toward the twenty-first century, the warrior ideal is beginning to emerge clearly from the ruins of our past preoccupation with soldiering, although the process is still slow and uncertain.

Nineteen-ninety was the year in which actor/director Kevin Costner brought *Dances With Wolves* to the screen and swept the Academy Awards. Though the film has all the flaws of a Hollywood epic movie, it also touched something very deep in the collective consciousness of the country, particularly among men.

The movie begins with Lieutenant John J. Dunbar, sick of the killing of the Civil War, trying to commit suicide by riding back and forth in front of Confederate gunfire. Mistakenly viewed as a hero by his superiors, he is granted his request to be posted out West to a frontier fort.

For Dunbar, the trip West is a rebirth. He is transformed from Lieutenant John J. Dunbar, the archetypal soldier preoccupied with death and destruction, into Dances With Wolves, a warrior dedicated to protecting the land, the animals, and the indigenous peoples from the ravages of civilization.

I still remember that wonderful final scene at the end of the movie, with Wind in His Hair proclaiming his brotherhood to Dunbar, the man he once hated. It made me believe that it was possible to unite those who carry the traditions of the hunter-gatherer peoples with those of us who recognize the bankruptcy of our present addictive civilization.

Dunbar is a symbol for all men as we approach the end of the twentieth century. It is time to end our 10,000-year-old addiction to domination. It is time for men to forge a new identity, which is actually a reemergence of a very old identity based on service to the earth, rather than use and destruction of the earth. As Dunbar says, "The first time I really knew who I was was when I was called by my Sioux name—Dances with Wolves."

Returning Home to Our Warrior Roots

The ideal of a new identity for men which I call the warrior is just now beginning to emerge. The essence of this new man is still in the germination phase. In order to get a feel for him, let's listen to what a number of contemporary explorers are saying about the warrior.

"Is now the time," asks Matthew Fox, author of *Creation Spirituality: Liberating Gifts for the Peoples of the Earth*, "when the Earth yearns and humankind yearns for the end of war—to take back the archetype of the spiritual warrior from the Pentagon and bastions of militarism?"

He asks, who is a warrior today? "A warrior is one who is alert, who concentrates, who contemplates, who centers oneself fully. If the warrior is not well grounded he or she may die. The warrior is one who faces death. The warrior is also one who is committed to a goal that is larger than the individual ego."

George Leonard, author of many books including *The Ultimate Athlete* and *Mastery*, has spent many years developing an understanding of what humans are like when they live fully, with passion and commitment. "The Modern Warrior," says Leonard, "is not one who goes to war but rather one who exhibits integrity in every aspect of living, one who seeks to attain control then act with abandon. For the Modern Warrior, life is vivid, immediate, and joyful. He or she lives each day to the full, and is fulfilled in serving others. To achieve peace in the world and harmony in daily life, it might well be necessary for men and women to reown the warrior ideal."[3]

Anthropologist Joan Halifax has worked with shamans and healers the world over. She feels strongly that our culture is in need of the warrior's way if we are to survive. "The warrior's way," Halifax tells us, "is to recognize that everything is sacred. All life and death.... It is the warrior, the true warrior, who understands the location of the battlefield. The battlefield is not somewhere outside of us, but it's within. So the warrior's way leads toward the interior." She quotes Krishnamurti, who said that "the only revolution is the revolution within. The only war that has *meaning* is the inner war. It is absurd to pursue any fight outside of one's soul."[4]

This is the same view of those who practice the martial art Aikido, which was developed by Morihei Ueshiba. In his book,

Aikido and the New Warrior, Richard Heckler gives this description of Ueshiba's gift to contemporary society: "Master Ueshiba developed a martial form that empowered human beings from the inside out, without categories and contests to determine who is best. He said that the 'opponent is within' and that we must first work with our own minds and bodies instead of trying to correct others. He established dignity and integrity as a priority to greed and the acquisition of fame and power. Through the techniques developed in Aikido he brought to the world an alternative to our current form of heavy-handed militarism and turn-the-other-cheek pacifism."

As "New Warriors" we must do battle with our own inner demons. This does not have to do with fighting others. Yet we would be wrong to view the men who are practicing this new ideal as merely self-reflective. The battles of the warrior may be interior, but the work of the warrior involves taking responsibility for *all* our relationships. Such a sense of social responsibility is exemplified by Danaan Parry, a former physicist with the Atomic Energy Commission, who decided that the world needed to learn about conflict resolution more than it needed nuclear technology. He now travels throughout the world to such trouble spots as Northern Ireland, using the warrior ideals to help bring about peace.

"Our world needs women and men who are willing to walk the Warrior path today," says Parry. In his book *Warriors of the Heart*, he offers an invitation "for all those who know (maybe not understand, but know) that they have somehow chosen to be a part of something very new, something that could bring our species from the brink of destruction to the doorway of an entirely new concept of human relationships."

Bill Kauth, author of *Men's Friends* and a leader in the New Warrior Training Program, offers his description of the new warrior. "We believe the word 'Warrior' best describes the spirit of the masculine psyche. The New Warrior knows who he is, what he wants and where he is going. Simply put, he is a man without guilt, shame, or apology. He has integrity. He holds himself accountable for his own actions. He is wild and gentle, tough and loving, fierce and perceptive. He comes from a tribe of men. He is not a savage. He is a Warrior of the Heart."

The Warrior's Journey Home

One of the major social problems we face in this country is home-lessness. We see it every day as we pass men in the street who ask us for a quarter, or block the sidewalks. Usually we try to ignore them because we don't know what to do and feel vaguely uneasy, but don't exactly know why. Homelessness is really a met-aphor for our times. The men we see on the street are simply the outer manifestation of a much deeper problem. As men today, we don't feel at home with ourselves. We don't feel at home with our families. We don't feel at home at work. We don't feel at home on the earth.

In our fear and loneliness, we have insulated ourselves ever more strongly from the healing community that could save us. As all addicts, we have become hooked on the very things that cause us pain, while we push away the things that could heal us.

In recovery we have been on a journey home to our male spirit. As we come to the final stage of the journey (though, in truth, the journey never ends), we return to the essence of our hunter-warrior selves which we left so long ago.

There are a number of things we must do if we are to return to our roots and develop into modern-day warriors:

- Develop physical practices
- Develop mental practices
- Develop love practices
- Develop healing practices

Physical Practices of the Warrior

For modern warriors, exercise will become a natural part of our lives, not simply something we do on weekends or for a few weeks after making our New Year's resolutions. Exercise will become something we do regularly to allow our minds to rest, and allow us to integrate our physical selves with the spirit within and around us.

I envision three types of physical practices that the new warrior will engage in: a non-competitive martial art, a practice that allows us to develop strength and stamina, and a practice that allows us to feel connected to the non-human world. For me the three practices have been Aikido, running, and walking.

Aikido. I changed into my newly bought *gi* (white pants and jacket tied with a belt—the practice gear for Aikido) and self-consciously took my place at the end of the mat. I was terrified but acted calm. It hurt to sit with my weight on my knees and feet and I was glad when we bowed and stood up. We did some strange warm-up exercises, turning and stretching ankles, wrists, knees, and back. The instructor called to a student who bowed and quickly came out on the mat. They then demonstrated a strike by the *uke* and response by the *nage,* repeating it a number of times. I tried to watch carefully and dissect the moves so I could repeat them.

Before my mind could begin to comprehend what I had seen, there was a loud handclap and we paired up to practice. I was hopelessly confused. The more I tried to figure out the physical moves, the more anxious and lost I became. "Forget your mind," said my partner, "just let your body move. It knows what to do." His voice broke my concentration. It would be many months before I began to understand what he was talking about.

After another demonstration, we paired up again with a new partner. This guy was huge, and scared the shit out of me. I tried hard to get the wrist hold right. "Relax—you don't have to use your strength to do this." His words seemed to come from far away. "I am relaxing," I told him. He just smiled and looked down at his wrist. As I followed his gaze I realized that I was holding him in a death grip. My hand was white, the veins and tendons stood out like ropes, and I was twitching from the tension. It was clear that I had a lot to learn about relaxing.

After we finished the class, I felt physically sick. I was sure I could never learn the subtleties of this art. But I stayed to watch the advanced class, and then I was hooked. It was like nothing else I had ever seen or even imagined. The movements were at once powerful and graceful, swordlike strikes turned into a circular blend and finally resolved peacefully and returned to the earth. It really seemed possible to be strong and gentle at the same time, to have a martial art without competition or violence.

Running. Having taken on many aspects of the "speed and greed" mentality of our addictive society, I found it easier to run than to walk. But getting started as a runner was not easy either. I was too busy with work and family to take time to exercise. It wasn't until I encountered an unusual physician that I was able to begin a regular program of exercise.

I had gone to my allergist to get some pills to help me through the spring pollen season. Instead of giving me a prescription, he asked about my life. "Are you under any stress?" he wanted to know. "Nothing unusual," I replied, "eighty- to ninety-hour work week, worries about money, a daughter who needs multiple surgeries. You know, the regular." And those were only the things I was willing to talk about! "Are you getting any exercise?" he wanted to know. "Well, I joined the YMCA about a year ago, but I don't really have time to get down there very often." He looked concerned and leaned forward in his chair. "You know what's going to happen if you don't get some regular exercise and reduce the stress in your life?" I felt like this was all a big joke. For God's sake, I was only coming for some allergy pills. "No," I smirked, "what's going to happen?" What he said wiped the crooked little grin right off my face. "You're going to die." His answer was simple and direct and I knew he was right. He ended up giving me a prescription, but not the one I had expected. "Get into some regular program of exercise. Try it out for six weeks. Then come back if you're still having problems."

I joined the Y's running program. I never went back for medications. My allergies gradually went away, as did my life-long problems with asthma. A year later, I saw the doctor running in the park. I was running the other way. We jogged in place as I thanked him for saving my life. He just smiled and waved as he continued his practice.

Walking. I've been running regularly for over 20 years, but have just now begun to slow down enough to get the benefits of walking. When running I felt blessed to see and feel things that I never felt while I whizzed by in my car. I'm now in touch with things I never saw or heard when I was running. I see the natural world more clearly. Birds and animals that held no interest for me before now are fascinating and wonderful. I notice the wind blowing through the boughs of the trees, and stop to wonder about the tracks I see in the sand.

When I'm walking I often think about the ancient hunters who walked the Earth and got to know the animals, trees, plants, stones, air, and water. When I walk I can feel the earth on my feet. I've begun to walk barefoot more often, and remember the wonder I felt as a child, excited at the first warm day when I could take off my shoes and begin to feel the mud between my toes again.

Mental Practices of the Warrior

Whenever I would feel overstressed, which was often, my mind would seem to go on "red alert." It was as though a thousand terrified technicians would be running around all screaming at the top of their lungs for my attention. Trying to figure out what they were saying, and deciding what I should do, would be overwhelming. My description for my state of mind was "spaghetti-brained."

The solution, I found, was to learn to meditate. The problem was that I couldn't sit still. Before I could meditate, I had to learn the physical practices I described earlier. Running and Aikido helped me concentrate my mind. Walking helped me slow it down. Having slowed down my mind, I would learn to sit still and let the spaghetti in my mind untangle itself.

Meditation helped me learn to think differently. I realized that the way in which the human mind had functioned over the last two million years had to change if we were to survive in the world today. The brain of our hunter-gatherer ancestors evolved to register short-term changes that were obvious to the senses, and to overlook the backdrop against which these changes took place. Environmental change took place over centuries and was slight enough not to require my individual's attention. It was much more important to pay attention to the movement of wild animals, the approach of storms on the horizon, and the distribution of wild edibles. To survive we needed to act quickly. We needed to escape the tiger before we were eaten, and spear the deer before he ran away.

Now when we need to be patient and assimilate the events of the day or week, our mind tells us to "do it now." There are many who believe that the death and destruction we created in Iraq were caused by this compulsion for action at the expense of reflection. In a world on the brink of devastation, we need to cultivate a mind that can wait. The warrior mind will develop watchful waiting instead of wasteful action.

On the other side of the coin, we can no longer ignore the environmental backdrop. Our life-support system is slipping away; but because our mind is trained to deal with short-term crises, we don't register the problem. We are like the frogs in a science experiment. If they are put in a pan of hot water, they jump out. When they are put in cold water and the temperature is slowly raised, they happily sit in the "hot tub" until the boiling water kills them. Like these frogs, many of us are unable to detect the gradual but lethal changes in our environment.

It's as though our minds suffer from a disorder that causes us to misread the "temperature" of our collective situation. Our thermostats are defective. As the temperature rises, we think it's still too cold, and we turn the heat up even higher. It is the nature of addiction that as the problems in our lives get worse, we "do" even more of the drug that is killing us, and ignore the very things that could save us.

The old mind is geared to the "news." It only springs into action when something unusual happens. The new warrior mind will be able to keep its focus on the problems in the background and recognize that they are much more serious than the latest crisis reported in today's news.

The evolved warrior mind will be keener to our environment. It will cultivate new levels of awareness and hone the four senses to be more aware of subtle changes in our world. The fact that we don't see the hole in the ozone layer or taste acid rain, or hear the cries of animals being slaughtered in factory farms, does not mean that these things don't exist. The new warrior mind will have an expanded sensitivity.

Love Practices of the Warrior

For many of us, learning to love is the graduate school of warrior training. It's where all our hopes and fears come together, where our defenses come down, and our shadows come up, and we must face our greatest challenges. Our dominator culture teaches that love is a coming together of opposites, an interaction in which someone wins and someone loses. "If one judges love by the majority of its effects," said La Rochefoucauld, "it is more like hatred than friendship."

Often the greatest lessons come to us when we stop trying, when we surrender. I had decided that I didn't really know how to love another person, and thought I'd concentrate instead on trying to develop a spiritual relationship with my higher power, and to begin to practice by loving myself.

I spent a lot of time hugging trees, having discovered that trees reminded me of my connection to the spirit that moves through all things. Hugging trees also taught me to love and accept myself, just the way I am. I found that trees never say to themselves, "Damn, I wish I was taller," or "My nobs are too small," or "I'm getting a little too fat around the trunk."

Hugging trees taught me that there are two core experiences of love. One comes from the soul. The other comes from the heart. Soul love is gender-based. It is the experience of loving ourselves as men. We must love our male soul *before* we can love another. Loving another comes from the heart.

To learn about soul love, I practiced treating myself the way I was longing to be treated by a lover. I began to take myself out to nice restaurants, buy romantic music just for me, and look at myself nude in the mirror and practice seeing myself as beautiful. I even learned to masturbate without fantasizing about a woman.

To learn about heart love, I stopped looking for "my type of woman." For the first time in my life, I felt complete without a woman in my life. That's when I met Carlin. A friend introduced us at the Aikido dojo. She was on vacation from her home in Portland, Oregon, and was passing through California on her way to Mexico. She seemed pleasant enough, but I was busy getting to know myself and wasn't interested in a "relationship." More importantly, she wasn't my "type." All the women I had previously gotten involved with were short, dark, young, and "perky."

Carlin is taller and older than I am, traits that in the past had eliminated women immediately from my list of possible partners. Her hair was brown with blond and red highlights, not the dark black I remembered from my Jewish childhood. She was beautiful, quiet, and elegant. No one would ever call her perky.

If it hadn't been for her persistence, I probably would have walked the other way. Instead, she pursued me in spite of her training that told her to wait for the man to take the initiative. I allowed myself to be open to a woman who "wasn't my type." In the process, we got to know each other, became friends, then lovers, and finally life partners.

Having reconnected with the mysteries of spirit, I could be more comfortable with the mystery of a woman. Like my hunter-gatherer ancestors, I could appreciate the difference between my male being and Carlin's female being. There was less need to judge or change her. Fifteen years into the relationship, I am still discovering more about the way a warrior loves. It is as different from what I had known in the past as night is from day.

Healing Practices of the Warrior

 The radical vision of the future rests on the belief that the logic that determines either our survival or our destruction is simple:

1. The new human vocation is to heal the earth.
2. We can only heal what we love.
3. We can only love what we know.
4. We can only know what we touch.

—Sam Keen

The final phase of the warrior's journey ends where it began, with our coming home to the land we left so long ago. This homecoming is not that of the agriculturist or farmer returning to the land as a commodity to be used, but is the homecoming of the ancient warrior-hunters returning to the land as living, breathing parent—earth mother, earth father.

Place becomes crucial in our lives now, and we make a commitment to a particular part of the planet. We come to accept a warrior's love and responsibility for a piece of land. Whether in the city, suburbs, or country, we put down roots. As Sam Keen suggests, there are four things we must do. We must touch the earth. We must come to know the earth. We must love the earth. We must heal the earth.

Touching the Earth.   How long has it been since you touched the earth? We cover the earth with cement. We cover our feet for protection. We spend most of our hours within artificial boxes. Then we wonder why we don't feel connected. We can begin with something as simple as taking off our shoes and feeling the earth under our feet. We can plant a flower and feel the earth with our hands. We can even go out and lie on the ground, heaven forbid, without a blanket underneath us looking up at the sky.

Knowing the Earth.   We need to talk to the earth as a friend and listen to the earth's response. We can take a day and go out on the earth and, instead of doing something, just relax. "Don't just do something, sit there," as someone wise once said. We can listen to the sounds of the earth, watch the changes in light as the day progresses. We can feel the natural forces of the earth, appreciate the way in which gravity supports us. We can taste the abundance of the earth, pluck a berry off a bush and savor the flavor. It's like becoming a child of the earth once again.

Loving the Earth.   To love the earth, we need to love all the players in earth's magic theater. We can begin by picking an animal species that seems special to us, get to know it, learn to love it. We can make it our business to protect that animal in the same way we make it our business to protect the children in our lives.

We might pick a species of trees that we are drawn to, and again learn to love it and protect it as we would a member of our family. "If we lived a life that valued and protected trees," says Anuradha Vittachi at the First Earth Conference, "it would be a life that also valued and protected us—and gave us great joy. A way of life that kills trees, our present way of life, kills us too, body and soul."

Healing the Earth.   Healing the earth will require the birth of a new partnership society. The original partnership society ended 10,000 years ago with the birth of the dominator-domesticator cultures. During the reign of the dominator society, we have done everything possible to wipe out the descendants of the original hunter-gatherers who see themselves as the guardians of the earth. Yet the hunter-warrior tradition carries on. I found it in an unlikely place, from the stories of a man named Tom Brown.

Tom Brown: A Voice for the Earth

Meeting Tom Brown was the result of two years of searching. I had felt lost. After spending 45 years of my life trying to understand and survive in the human world, I felt drawn to the nonhuman world. I wanted to become comfortable with the earth and the animals, but I didn't have a clue where to begin.

As a kid born in New York City, who grew up in Los Angeles, and was living in the San Francisco Bay Area, wilderness was foreign to me. I wanted a guide, someone I could trust to teach me the skills of relating to the natural world. I talked in my men's group and asked for help in my meditations. Somebody told me I should get a book by Tom Brown. I wasn't inspired by the name. Tom Brown sounded too much like white bread. I wanted someone with more grit. Drawing on my fantasies of mountain men from my childhood, I wanted someone with a name like Jim Bowie or Davey Crockett, or someone with "Chief" appended to his name.

But meeting Tom changed the way I looked at my life. My friends laughed when I told them I was going back to New Jersey to Tom's wilderness survival school. "Wilderness in New Jersey?" They laughed. "Learn to survive in the urban jungle?" When I and my fellow students arrived Sunday evening, we were picked up at the bus-stop in Asbury, a small town near the Pennsylvania border, and taken to an old farmhouse just out of town.

Called for the evening introduction, the 50 students from all over the U.S., with a few from Europe, were crammed onto wooden benches. I felt like I was back in school, and my hopes for an experience of the wildman-warrior dimmed ... that is, until Tom walked into the room. A strongly built, darkly tanned man, Tom Brown commands your attention. If there is anyone who can be said to possess animal magnetism, it is Tom. Although he looks like Hollywood's depiction of a Marine drill sergeant, he exudes the feel of the wild. Looking into his eyes, I saw a deep sadness. He seemed to embody the pain of what we are doing to the earth.

Much of his love for the earth, Tom told us, came from his experiences with Stalking Wolf, an old Apache shaman and scout whom Tom referred to as "Grandfather." According to Tom, "Grandfather was as mystical as his past, an anachronism wandering in modern society. He was an Apache, raised by his great-grandfather in the mountains of the deep Southwest to be a warrior, a scout, and eventually a shaman and healer. It was his destiny, however, to be a wanderer, and for the better part of his lifetime he traveled from Canada to Mexico, Oregon to Virginia, always learning, always searching, living with the old ones—Native American, black, and white alike—learning all he could about the ancient ways, the ancient medicine, herbs, and shamanism."

Tom remembers their first encounter in the Pine Barrens of western New Jersey. "When I met him by the river, Grandfather was then eighty-three and I was seven. The age and cultural differences had little effect on our friendship. Though he could hardly speak English, we understood each other well. For most of the ten years that followed, he taught me to survive in the wilderness lavishly, making all my own tools, shelter, clothing, and gathering food. He taught me how to track and observe the wilderness and to become part of its life force, a process he called 'oneness.' Most of all, he taught me the spiritual laws of creation. His lessons every day taught the things of the unseen and eternal, to the degree that the spiritual life became more real than the life of the flesh."

Tom was 18 in 1968, and like many young men faced the prospect of becoming a soldier. "I remember it as a time of great personal confusion," says Tom. "I knew that I could be effective in war, up to a point. I could track, stalk, camouflage, and evade— but I couldn't kill. When men kill, it should be for survival. Man should kill for no other reason, and he should never kill another human being."

Tom's simple yet eloquent statement offers clear guidance for true warriors. He goes on to describe the issue all men wrestle with, for the first time in adolescence and often throughout our lives. "There is in every 18-year-old boy the desire to face death. We all want to be tested. We all want to know for sure whether or not we are cowards or heroes.... We think the only way we can prove our manhood is through some life-or-death situation on the battlefield."

Yet manhood has little or nothing to do with physical prowess or cowardice or our ability or inability to kill. "Our manhood," says Tom, "can be understood through our relation to the earth and its creatures, and survival is not to kill or be killed, but to understand our place, our part in nature, and play it out."

As I spent more time in Tom's class, I learned a great deal about the animals and the earth and my place in the great mystery of life. But while I felt more comfortable, Tom seemed to be getting increasingly anxious. He reminded me of a caged animal wanting desperately to get back home to the wild. I wondered why he was here with us rather than in the wilderness he loved so much. On the last morning of the training we heard the story.

It had begun with the birth of his son, Tommy, in November 1978. "I was beside myself with joy and wonder," Tom said as he began the story. "More than ever I had to get back to the wilderness, especially for my new son's sake. I went to the woods to pray that day, to give thanks to the Creator for my son, my wife, and my kids and ask Him to direct our lives toward the wilderness. It was then that I remembered what Grandfather had once asked me to do: In the moon of purification, January, after my son's birth, I was to bring him into the Pine Barrens to give thanks. I was to take little Tommy to Medicine Creek, to the sacred grounds, where I was to raise my pipe in thanksgiving as Grandfather once requested so very long ago."

"I remember vividly the cold and clear January day. I drove to the Pine Barrens with little Tommy and my pipe, so happy, so at peace, and so excited to be going back to the purity of wilderness. I had not seen the sacred area for nearly a decade and was thrilled to be headed back, especially with my baby. I parked the car, bundled little Tom up in one arm, carried the pipe in the other, and wandered down the trail to the sacred area, deep in prayer.

"My heart truly soared with the eagles, that is, until I rounded the bend in the trail that led to Medicine Creek. I was stopped dead in my tracks, and my spirit trembled with sickness, for there, so far as the eye could see, was a sea of garbage. The area had been plowed for development and abandoned, and had now become an illegal dump site. Piles of garbage and chemicals were strewn all around, the stream was glazed with oil, and what few trees were left had been burned.

"I had to lay my baby down on that pile of garbage, for no earth showed through anywhere. Trembling and crying, I raised my pipe to the Creator." As Tom spoke, I cried too, feeling the pain at the destruction of a once sacred and beautiful wilderness. I wept for my own son and all the children of the earth who would live a life surrounded, not by beauty, but by garbage. Tom continued, his voice almost choking with emotion.

"I now knew why Grandfather had asked me to bring my baby here. He knew that it would forever change my life and begin my living Vision, which I had so long denied.

"I realized at that moment that my own son would never taste the wilderness I had once known. I saw the results of a society that gives no thought to the survival of its grandchildren. I was more shaken that I had ever been in my life. I felt even more helpless than the baby lying at my feet.... I raised my pipe again and swore to the Creator that I would no longer run, that I would give up everything else in my life to save what was left of the wilderness, for I had to now teach, reeducate, so that my own child could run free and wild as I once did."

Many of us were still crying openly by the time Tom concluded. "So that's why I'm here, that's why I do nothing else but teach or write. The only thing that will work is reeducation." Tom paused and shook his head slightly. "I lied to you. I brought you here under the guise of learning survival and tracking." Tom took a deep breath and continued. "Brothers and sisters, that was not my underlying motive. I brought you here to make you into warriors."

In the silence that followed I felt something moving inside me, a reawakening of some soul wisdom long buried. The birds singing in the background seemed to be affirming our journey back home to the natural world. "If you leave here," Tom continued, the look of intense concentration back on his face, "and do nothing with these skills, then Grandfather's vision dies." Tom leaned back and I felt the call of the ancient hunter-warriors. "But if you lead one person back to the earth, then that vision lives. It is that simple." Tom looked out the window as though feeling the presence of the spirit that moves through all things and then looked back at us.

"There is a voice out there, the voice you can only hear with your heart. It's the voice of the earth." Once again tears were running down my cheeks, as I too began to hear that voice. I knew that my warrior's journey was bringing me back to my roots, back to my ancestors. "She's crying," Tom said quietly, the anguish unmasked. "She's dying. If her flesh dies, our grandchildren will die as well." Tom's voice was almost a whisper now, but it spoke directly to our hearts. "If you love her, if you love them, then do *something* ... anything." Tom's voice broke, a last plea for the earth, for our mothers, fathers, children, grandchildren, and for ourselves. "But don't run away, *please*, don't run away."[5]

Notes

1. Dell, Twyla (1990) *Call of the Rainbow Warrior: An Environmental Fable.* Overland Park, KS: Foresight Institute.

2. Statistics on war casualties from Sam Keen in a lecture given at College of Marin, March 6, 1991.

3. Leonard, George, "The Modern Warrior," a description of a workshop given at the Esalen Institute in Esalen catalogue, Big Sur, CA, May-October, 1990.

4. Halifax, Joan. "The Way of the Warrior," in Toms, Michael (1991) *At the Leading Edge: New Visions of Science, Spirituality, and Society.* New York: Larson Publication.

5. Tom Brown's class notes and from his books *The Vision* and *The Search.* Reprinted by permission of The Berkley Publishing Group.

Resources

When I began working in the field of addiction and recovery 28 years ago, the problem was a lack of resources. The good news was that you didn't have to worry about making choices. Now the problem is that, with so many resources, it's difficult to know how to find what is appropriate for you. The following compendium is a list of resources I have found particularly helpful. It is by no means exhaustive. A full citation for each book mentioned can be found in the Bibliography.

Since things change rapidly in this field, and there is a time gap between my writing this list and your reading it, some listings may be out of date. Please let me know if a resource is no longer available, or if the address or phone number has changed. Also let me know if you have found a particularly good resource you think should be added to the list. People helping people is our best resource. Thanks for being part of the network.

Recovery Resources

The American Academy of Health Care Providers in the Addictive Disorders, 260 Beacon Street, Somerville, MA 02143. (617) 661-6248. This group certifies professionals who are treating addictions to alcohol, drugs, eating, gambling, and sex. If you're looking for a counselor who specializes in these areas, this is a good place to begin.

The Recovery Resource Book by Barbara Yoder. Published in 1990 by Simon & Schuster, it is still the most valuable single resource for recovery. In it you will learn about the differences between recovery and treatment, about self-help groups, and programs that charge for their services. Resources are listed for help with the following: Alcohol, nicotine, caffeine, sugar, food, prescription drugs, street drugs, marijuana, cocaine, codependency, love and sex, money, work, dual disorders, incest and abuse, and AIDS. In addition, the book lists the major self-help clearinghouses where you can learn about groups in your area.

The American Self-Help Clearinghouse, (201) 625-7101, 9 AM to 5 PM, Monday-Friday, Eastern Standard Time. Write: American Self-Help Clearinghouse, St. Clares-Riverside Medical Center, Denville, NJ 07834.

There are actually a number of national clearinghouses, as well as regional resources in most states. I've found the American Self-Help Clearinghouse to be the most responsive and helpful. They maintain a computer listing of groups for people facing a variety of illnesses and life problems, including addictions. They also publish a directory of resources in the U.S. and Canada. If an appropriate support group exists in your area, the clearinghouse will know about it. If no appropriate group exists, clearinghouse staff members can help you start one.

Sober Times: The Recovery Magazine, P.O. Box 40259, San Diego, CA 92164, (619) 295-5377. A fine recovery magazine. The purpose of *Sober Times* is to promote sobriety as a means of attaining a happy, healthy lifestyle. In addition, *Sober Times* helps to provide a sense of community among recovering individuals.

Recovering: The Adventure of Life Beyond Addiction, 490 Sixth Avenue, Suite 202, San Francisco, CA 94118, (415) 752-2246. *Recovering* is an independent nonprofit magazine written by and for people recovering from addictive diseases, and is published monthly. One of the real values of this magazine is that it deals with all aspects of recovery. I highly recommend it.

The Phoenix, 2464 Arona Street, Roseville, MN 55113, (612) 722-1149. *The Phoenix* is a monthly publication for people actively working on their physical, mental, emotional, and spiritual well-being, and that of those around them. One of the oldest and best publications on recovery.

Co-Dependence: Healing the Human Condition—A New Paradigm for Helping Professionals and People in Recovery, by Charles L. Whitfield, M.D., Health Communications, Deerfield Beach, FL, 1991. I list Dr. Whitfield's book here because of it's extensive resource listing (over 100) and huge Bibliography (747 entries). If you can't find what you need here, it probably hasn't been discovered yet.

Resources for Preventing Violence and Abuse

Parents Anonymous (PA), 6733 South Sepulveda Blvd., Los Angeles, CA 90045, 1-800-421-0353. A crisis intervention program, founded in 1970 to help potentially abusive parents build better relationships with their children. PA also sponsors groups for abused children, and operates an information and referral hotline.

Incest Survivors Anonymous, P.O. Box 5613, Long Beach, CA, 90805-0613, (213)428-5599. A national self-help recovery program for incest and ritual abuse survivors based on the 12 steps of Alcoholics Anonymous. Members are committed to changing negative behavior patterns and healing the pain of past abuse.

National Clearinghouse on Child Abuse and Neglect, P.O. Box 1182, Washington, DC 20013, (703)385-7565. Provides referrals, information, and publications on all aspects of child abuse and neglect.

National Organization of Circumcision Information Resource Centers (NOCIRC), P.O. Box 2512, San Anselmo, CA 94979-2512, (415) 488-9883. NOCIRC provides parents, health-care professionals, lawyers, and other concerned individuals with information on the practice of routine infant circumcision of males and genital mutilation of females. The clearinghouse has sponsored two international conferences on circumcision and is planning a third. The proceedings of the first conference were published in 1989, with the descriptive title "Crimes of Genital Mulilation." If you care about children, I highly recommend that you send for their literature.

National Organization to Halt the Abuse and Routine Mutilation of Males (NOHARM), P.O. Box 460795, San Francisco, CA 94146. NOHARM is a national direct action network of men organized against routine infant circumcision. If you want to know more about what can be done to end this practice, write them for more information.

Men's Resouces

Having emerged most recently, the information on men is more diverse and less unified, so I have included a wider selection of resources. Although the media highlights a certain aspect of men's work, the real lifeblood of the movement takes place out of the spotlight at local and regional gatherings. I recommend that you sample a number of these resources and enjoy the different flavors.

- Tom Brown's books (listed in bibliography) and Tracker School, Box 173, Asbury, NJ 08802, (908)479-4681.

- Touch the Earth: Wilderness Skill Workshops, Bob Hemenger, Box 2136, Pagosa Springs, CO 81147. Bob was an instructor in Tom Brown's school for a number of years. His workshops are excellent.

Publications

Wingspan Journal of the Male Spirit, Published quarterly, with plans for bi-monthly issues later this year. A fine publication. Write to: *Wingspan*, P.O. Box 23550, Detroit, MI 48223.

The New Warrior Journal. Hear from men who have completed the New Warrior Training Adventure. Write to: *The New Warrior Journal*, 3873 North 67th St., Milwaukee, WI 53216

Seattle M.E.N.—Men's Evolvement Network, 602 W. Howe St., Seattle, WA 98119, (206)285-4356 One of the fine regional centers that publishes an excellent newsletter.

Mentor, The Oregon Resource for Men, P.O. Box 10863, Portland, OR 97210. Another excellent regional resource, a newsletter for men interested in learning about manhood and sharing their discoveries with other men.

Resource, Redwood Men's Center, 705 College Ave., Santa Rosa, CA 95404, (707)546-4636. *Resource* is printed quarterly by the Redwood Men's Center and is provided at no cost to readers. Contributions are appreciated.

Men's Council Journal, P.O. Box 385, Boulder, CO 80306. Published quarterly by the Men's Council of Boulder, Colorado, this offers an excellent perspective on men emerging today.

Man, Alive!: A Journal of Men's Wellness, P.O. Box 40300, Albuquerque, NM 87196. *Man, Alive!* is an independent journal published in support of men's wellness worldwide.

Men Talk ... A Source for Emerging Male Expression, 3255 Hennepin Ave. S., Suite 45, Minneapolis, MN 55408, (612) 822-5892. One of the oldest and best of the men's journals. *Men Talk* is the official, informal, regional publication of the Twin Cities Men's Center, and is published quarterly.

Changing Men: Issues in Gender, Sex, and Politics, 306 North Brooks St., Madison, WI 53715. This journal has been publishing excellent material for the past 13 years.

Journeymen, 513 Chester Turnpike, Candia, NH 03034. Publishes excellent articles on a broad range of men's issues.

White Crane Newsletter. P.O. Box 170152. San Francisco, CA 94117. Explores the world of gay men's spirituality.

The Green Man. P.O. Box 641. Pt. Arena, CA 95468. Publishes articles on Earth-based spiritulaity.

Ardell Wellness Report Don Ardell, 9901 Lake Georgia Dr., Orlando, FL 32817. For many years Don Ardell has been a leader in promoting men's health. This is an excellent newsletter.

The Santa Barbara Institute for Gender Studies. P.O. Box 4782, Santa Barbara, CA 93140, (805)963-8285. Directed byAaron Kipnis and Elizabeth Hingston co-authors of *Gender War/Gender Peace: The Quest for Love and Justice Between Women and Men* the Institute offers excellent workshops and classes for men and women on gender reconcilliation.

Understanding the Men's Movement: The Myth of Male Power, Simon & Schuster, 1993, and *Why Men Are the Way They Are,* Berkley Books, 1988, both by Warren Farrell. These two books offer a wealth of information on men. Reading them is an education in self-discovery, and offers an in-depth understanding of healing relationships and healing the planet.

What Makes a Man a Man? by Dan Jones, Mandala Books and Tapes, P.O. Box 5892, Austin, TX 78763. A wonderful little book on men. I include it here for its extensive bibliography of men's stories from throughout the world.

Contemporary Perspectives on Masculinity by Kenneth Clatterbaugh, Westview Press, Boulder, CO, 1990. I like to think of the men's movement as being made up of different streams. Sometimes they flow together; most often they follow their own course. This is the best single source for understanding the various ways in which the movement flows. Not only does Clatterbaugh identify six major perspectives in the men's movement today, he shows how they developed historically, how they relate to each other, and what their strong and weak points are. The six perspectives he identifies are: conservative, profeminist, men's rights, spiritual, socialist, and group-specific. I've had direct involvement with three of the six, and would like to list the following resources for further exploration.

- National Organization for Men Against Sexism (NOMAS) represents the profeminist stream. They can be contacted at 794 Penn Avenue, Pittsburgh, PA 15221.

- Men's Rights Incorporated is one of the organizations representing the men's rights stream. They can be contacted at P.O. Box 163180, Sacramento, CA 95816.

- Ally Press keeps up on many of the activities in the spiritual stream. They focus on the mytho-poetic work of spokesmen like Robert Bly, Michael Meade, James Hillman, and Robert Moore. This is an organization in the same way in which the Grateful Dead is an organization. You don't join, you go and participate. For information on upcoming gatherings, and listings of books and tapes, contact Ally Press, 524 Orleans St., St. Paul, MN 55107, 1-800-729-3002.

The National Men's Resource Center, P.O. Box 800, San Anselmo, CA 94960-0800. In addition to providing an updated directory of resources in the San Francisco Bay Area, this organization offers an excellent current bibliography on men's issues.

Sounds True, 1825 Peal St., Boulder, CO 80302, 1-800-333-9185, ext. 275. This company has an excellent catalogue of men's audiotapes for sale, as well as interviews with leaders such as John Lee and Michael Meade.

Resources for Planetary Healing

There are thousands of excellent resources that could be listed here. I suggest that you follow your own passion in seeking ways you can support the healing of the planet. I'll list a few organizations that have drawn me.

EarthSave, 706 Frederick Street, Santa Cruz, CA 95062-2205, (408) 423-4069. Started by John Robbins as a result of the world-wide interest in his book *Diet for a New America*, EarthSave is a nonprofit environmental and health educational organization dedicated to helping the Earth restore its delicate ecological balance. EarthSave publishes a quarterly newsletter that I highly recommend.

The New Road Map Foundation, Box 15981, Seattle, WA 98115. One of the greatest difficulties of modern life is our addictive search for "more." The New Road Map Foundation was started by Joe Dominguez to help people find out how much is really enough. His course "Transforming Your Relationship With Money and Achieving Financial Independence" pays off in what it promises. It will teach you how to "have a clear, relaxed relationship with money. Do the work you love. Spend time with the people you care about. Volunteer on projects that inspire you and serve others. Learn, grow, explore. Know and achieve your purpose in life."

In the Absence of the Sacred: The Failure of Technology & the Survival of the Indian Nations, by Jerry Mander, Sierra Club Books, San Francisco, 1991. After reading Jerry's wonderful book (he also wrote *Four Arguments for the Elimination of Television)*, I told my men's group that it was the most important book I had read in over 20 years. (The last one that came close to moving me this much was Alvin Toffler's *Future Shock* written in 1970. I list Jerry's book here for its fine bibliography and resource list.

How To Reach the Author

For further information on other books and booklets I've written, tapes, workshops and training sessions (or if you would like to sponsor a workshop in your area), write to: Jed Diamond, 34133 Shimmins Ridge Rd., Willits, CA 95490.

Bibliography

The following works were helpful in writing *The Warrior's Journey Home*. Those marked with an asterisk were particularly valuable to me.

Adams, S., ed. (1992) *The Best Man: Selections from the First Three Years of MAN! Magazine.* Austin, TX: Mandala Publications.

Allen, J. (1985) *Picking on Men: The First Honest Collection of Quotations About Men.* New York: Ballantine Books.

Allen, M. (1993) *In the Company of Men.* New York: Random House.

Arcana, J. (1983) *Every Mother's Son: The Role of Mothers in the Making of Men.* New York: Doubleday.

Armstrong, L. (1978) *Kiss Daddy Goodnight.* New York: Hawthorn Books.

Aronson, E. (1976) *The Social Animal.* San Francisco: W.H. Freeman.

*Arrien, A. (1993) *The Four-Fold Way: Walking the Paths of the Warrior, Teacher, Healer and Visionary.* San Francisco: Harper San Francisco.

*Arrien, A. (1990) "The bridge of healing: Discovering the universal themes of human culture." *Magical Blend*, no. 28, October.

*Arrien, A. (1993) "The four-fold way." *New Realities*, May/June.

*August, E. R. (1993) *The New Men's Studies: A Selected and Annotated Bibliography.* Englewood, CO: Libraries Unlimited.

*Augustine Fellowship, Sex and Love Addicts Anonymous (1986) *Sex and Love Addicts Anonymous.* Boston: Augustine Fellowship of Sex and Love Addicts Anonymous.

Austin, B. L. (1971) *Sad Nun of Synanon.* New York: Holt, Rinehart, & Winston.

Baber, A. (1992) *Naked at Gender Gap.* New York: Carol Publishing Group.

Beattie, M. (1987) *Codependent No More: How to Stop Controlling Others and Start Caring for Yourself.* San Francisco: Harper/Hazelden.

Berry, T. (1988) *The Dream of the Earth.* San Francisco: Sierra Club Books.

*Biesele, M. (1993) *Women Like Meat: Ju'hoan Bushman Folklore and Foraging Ideology.* Bloomington: Indiana University Press.

*Bigelow, J. (1992) *The Joy of Uncircumcising! Restore Your Birthright and Maximize Sexual Pleasure.* Aptos, CA: Hourglass Book Publishing.

Bly, R., and B. Moyers (1990) "A gathering of men." New York: Public Affairs Television.

*Bly, R. (1990) *Iron John.* Reading, MA: Addison-Wesley.

Boyd, B. R. (1990) *Circumcision: What It Does.* San Francisco: Taterhill Press.

Bradshaw, J. (1990) *Homecoming.* New York: Bantam Books.

Brower, D. (1990) *For Earth's Sake: The Life and Times of David Brower.* Layton, UT: Gibbs-Smith Publisher.

Brown, S. (1985) *Treating the Alcoholic: A Developmental Model of Recovery.* New York: John Wiley & Sons.

*Brown, T., Jr. (1991) *The Quest.* New York: Berkley Books.

*Brown, T., Jr. (1988) *The Vision.* New York: Berkley Books.

*Brown, T., Jr. (1980) *The Search.* New York: Berkley Books.

*Brown, T., Jr. (1978) *The Tracker.* New York: Prentice-Hall.

Brownmiller, S. (1975) *Against Our Will.* New York: Simon & Schuster.

Broyles, W., Jr. (1984) "Why men love war." *Esquire*, November.

Buber, M. (1958) *I and Thou.* New York: Charles Scribner.

*Burger, J. (1990) *The Gaia Atlas of First Peoples: A Future for the Indigenous World.* New York: Anchor Books.

Cahalan, D., and B. Treiman (1976) *Drinking Behavior, Attitudes, and Problems in Marin County, California.* Berkeley: Social Research Group, School of Public Health, University of California.

Cahalan, D., and R. Room (1974) *Problem Drinking Among American Men.* New Brunswick, NJ: Rutgers Center for Alcohol Studies.

Caldicott, H. (1985) *Missile Envy: The Arms Race and Nuclear War*. New York: Bantam Books.

Campbell, J. (1988) *The Power of Myth*. New York: Doubleday.

*Campbell, J. (1959) *The Masks of God: Primitive Mythology*. New York: Viking Press.

Cancian, F. (1987) *Love in America*. Cambridge, England: Cambridge University Press.

Canetti, E. (1966) *Crowds and Power*. New York: Viking Press.

*Carnes, P. (1991) *Don't Call It Love: Recovering from Sexual Addiction*. New York: Bantam Books.

*Carnes P. (1991) *Out of the Shadows: Understanding Sexual Addictions*. Minneapolis: CompCare Publications.

Castaneda, C. (1972) *Journey to Ixtlan: The Lessons of Don Juan*. New York: Simon & Schuster.

Catton, W. R. (1982) *Overshoot: The Ecological Basis of Revolutionary Change*. Urbana: University of Illinois Press.

Cermak, T. L., M.D. (1988) *A Time to Heal: The Road to Recovery for Adult Children of Alcoholics*. Los Angeles: Jeremy P. Tarcher.

Chodorow, N. (1978) *The Reproduction of Mothering: Psychoanalysis and the Sociology of Gender*. Berkeley: University of California Press.

Cirese, S. (1977) *Quest: A Search for Self*. New York: Rinehart & Winston.

*Cohen, M. N. (1989) *Health & the Rise of Civilization*. New Haven, CT: Yale University Press.

Coleman, E. (1987) "Sexual compulsivity: Definition, etiology, and treatment considerations." *The Journal of Chemical Dependency Treatment* 1(1).

*Coon, C. (1971) *The Hunting People*. London: Jonathan Cape.

Coon, C. (1954) *The Story of Man: From the First Human to Primitive Culture and Beyond*. New York: Alfred A. Knopf.

*The Dalai Lama of Tibet (1989) *Ocean of Wisdom: Guidelines for Living*. Santa Fe, NM: Clear Light Publishers.

Dale, S. (1992) *My Child, My Self: How to Raise the Child You Always Wanted to Be*. San Mateo, CA: Human Awareness Publications.

Davis-Floyd, R. E. (1992) *Birth as an American Rite of Passage*. Berkeley and Los Angeles: University of California Press.

Dell, T. (1990) *Call of the Rainbow Warrior: An Environmental Fable*. Overland Park, KS: Foresight Institute.

*Diamond, C. (1985) *Love It, Don't Label It: A Practical Guide for Using Spiritual Principles in Everyday Life*. Willits, CA: Fifth Wave Press.

*Diamond, Jared. (1992) *The Third Chimpanzee: The Evolution and Future of the Human Animal*. New York: HarperCollins.

Diamond, Jed (1990) *Healing Male Co-Dependency: From Isolation and Rage to Intimacy and Joy*. Willits, CA: Fifth Wave Press.

Diamond, Jed (1989) *Fatal Attractions: Understanding Co-Dependency, Sex, Romance, and Relationship Addictions*. Willits, CA: Fifth Wave Press.

Diamond, Jed (1988) *Looking for Love in All the Wrong Places: Overcoming Romantic and Sexual Addictions*. New York: Putnam & Sons.

Diamond, Jed (1983) *Inside Out: Becoming My Own Man*. Willits, CA: Fifth Wave Press.

Diamond, Jed (1973) "Our anti-drug abuse programs: Pathologies of defense." *Ex-Change*, 1:6, August.

Diamond, S., ed. (1969) *The Primitive Views of the World*. New York: Columbia University Press.

Dinnerstein, D. (1977) *The Mermaid and the Minotaur: Sexual Arrangements and Human Malaise*. New York: Harper & Row.

*Dobson, T., and V. Miller (1978) *Giving In to Get Your Way*. New York: Delacorte Press.

*Dominguez, J. (1986) *Transforming Your Relationship With Money and Achieving Financial Independence*, Audio Cassette and Workbook. Seattle: The New Road Map Foundation.

*Dominguez, J., and V. Robin. (1992) *Your Money or Your Life: Transforming Your Relationship with Money and Achieving Financial Independence*. New York: Viking Penguin.

Druck, K., with J. C. Simmons. (1987) *The Secrets Men Keep*. New York: Ballantine Books.

*Durning, A. (1992) *How Much Is Enough? The Consumer Society and the Future of the Earth*. New York: W.W. Norton & Co.

Earll, B. (1988) *I Got Tired of Pretending*. Tucson, AZ: Stem Publications.

Easthope, A. (1986) *What a Man's Gotta Do: The Masculine Myth in Popular Culture*. Winchester, MA: Unwin Hymus.

Edwardes, A., and R. E. L. Masters. (1970) *The Cradle of Erotica*. London: Odyssey Press.

Ehrensaft, D. (1987) *Parenting Together: Men and Women Sharing the Care of Their Children*. New York: Free Press.

*Eisler, R. (1988) *The Chalice & the Blade*. San Francisco: Harper & Row.

Endore, G. (1967) *Synanon*. New York: Doubleday.

Eliade, M. (1963) *Myth and Reality*. New York: Harper & Row.

Erikson, E. (1963) *Childhood and Society.* New York: W.W. Norton & Co.

*Fagan, B. M. (1987) *The Great Journey: The Peopling of Ancient America.* London: Thames & Hudson.

Fanning, P., and M. McKay (1993) *Being a Man: A Guide to the New Masculinity.* Oakland, CA: New Harbinger Publications.

*Farb, P. (1968) *Man's Rise to Civilization: The Cultural Ascent of the Indians of North America.* New York: E.P. Dutton.

*Farrell, W. (1993) *The Myth of Male Power: Why Men Are the Disposable Sex.* New York: Simon & Schuster

*Farrell, W. (1986) *Why Men Are the Way They Are.* New York: McGraw-Hill.

Ferencz, B., and K. Keyes, Jr. (1991) *Planethood.* Coos Bay, OR: Love Line Books.

Fields, R. (1991) *The Code of the Warrior: In History, Myth, and Everyday Life.* New York: HarperCollins.

Fine, G. A. (1987) *With the Boys: Little League Baseball and Preadolescent Behavior.* Chicago: University of Chicago Press.

*Foreman, D. (1991) *Confessions of an Eco-Warrior.* New York: Harmony Books.

*Fossum, M. (1989) *Catching Fire: Men Coming Alive in Recovery.* San Francisco: Harper & Row.

Fossum, M., and M. Mason (1986) *Facing Shame: Families in Recovery.* New York: W.W. Norton & Co.

*Fox, M. (1991) **Creation Spirituality: Liberating Gifts for the Peoples of the Earth.** San Francisco: Harper San Francisco.

*Friedan, B. (1981) *The Second Stage.* New York: Summit Books.

Friedan, B. (1963) *The Feminine Mystique.* New York: Dell Publishing Co.

Gerzon, M. (1982) *A Choice of Heroes: The Changing Face of American Manhood.* Boston: Houghton Mifflin.

*Gilmore, D. (1990) *Manhood in the Making: Cultural Concepts of Masculinity.* New Haven CT: Yale University Press.

Glover, J. M. (1986) *A Wilderness Original: The Life of Bob Marshall.* Seattle: The Moutaineers.

*Goble, F. (1971) *The Third Force: The Psychology of Abraham Maslow.* New York: Pocket Books.

Goldberg, H. (1976) *The Hazards of Being Male.* New York: New American Library.

*Gray, J. G. (1967) *The Warriors: Reflections on Men in Battle.* New York: Harper & Row.

*Gray, J. (1984) *What You Feel, You Can Heal: An Illustrated Guide to Enriching Your Relationships.* Mill Valley, CA: Heart Publishing Co.

Green, J. (1991) *The Male Herbal: Health Care for Men and Boys.* Freedom, CA: Crossing Press.

Halberstam, D. (1969) *The Best and the Brightest.* New York: Penguin Books.

Halifax, J. (1991) "The way of the warrior." In *At the Leading Edge: New Visions of Science, Spirituality and Society* by Michael Toms. New York: Larson Publications.

*Harding, C. (1992) *Wingspan.* New York: St. Martin's Press

Hardinge, M. (1962) "Nutritional studies of vegetarians: dietary fatty acids and serum cholesterol levels." *American Journal of Clinical Nutrition* 10:522.

*Heckler, R. (1990) *In Search of the Warrior Spirit.* Berkeley, CA: North Atlantic Books.

*Heckler, R., ed. (1985) *Aikido and the New Warrior.* Berkeley, CA: North Atlantic Books.

Hendrix, H. (1988) *Getting the Love You Want.* New York: Harper & Row.

Hill, P. (1981) "Environmental factors of breast and prostatic cancer," *Cancer Research* 41:3817.

Hill, S. (1988) *A Man Thinks About Pornography: Beauty, Images, and Totalitarianism.* Bellingham, WA: Tow Hill.

Hite, S. (1981) *The Hite Report on Male Sexuality.* New York: Alfred A. Knopf.

Hoebel, E. A. (1964) *The Law of Primitive Man.* Boston: Harvard University Press.

*Hoffman, E. (1988) *The Right To Be Human: Biography of Abraham Maslow.* Los Angeles: Jeremy P. Tarcher.

Hunter, M. (1990) *Abused Boys: The Neglected Victims of Sexual Abuse.* New York: Ballantine Books.

Hunter, R. (1970) *Warriors of the Rainbow: A Chronicle of the Greenpeace Movement.* New York: Holt, Rinehart & Winston.

Huxley, E. (1957) *The Red Rock Wilderness.* New York: William Morrow & Co.

*Janeway, E. (1971) *Man's World, Woman's Place: A Study in Social Mythology.* New York: Dell Publishing Co.

*Johnson, R. (1987) *Ecstasy: Understanding the Psychology of Joy.* San Francisco: Harper & Row.

*Jong, E. (1990) *Any Woman's Blues.* New York: Harper & Row.

*Kasl, C. D. (1992) *Many Roads, One Journey: Moving Beyond the 12 Steps.* New York: HarperCollins.

*Kasl, C. D. (1988) *Woman, Sex, and Addiction: A Search for Love and Power.* New York: Ticknor & Fields.

Kauth, B. (1992) *Circle of Men.* New York: St. Martin's Press.

Kazantzakis, N. (1952) *Zorba the Greek*. New York: Ballantine Books.

*Keen, S. (1991) *Fire in the Belly: On Being a Man*. New York: Bantam Books.

*Keen, S. (1986) *Faces of the Enemy: Reflections of the Hostile Imagination*. San Francisco: Harper & Row.

Kellogg, T. (1991) "Talking with Terry Kellogg." *The Phoenix:* 11, no. 1, January, Cambridge, MI.

*Keyes, R. (1980) *The Height of Your Life*. Boston: Little, Brown & Co.

Kimball, G. (1987) *50-50 Parenting*. Lexington, MA: Lexington Books.

*Kipnis, A. (1991) *Knights Without Armor: A Practical Guide for Men in Quest of Masculine Soul*. Los Angeles: Jeremy P. Tarcher.

Kohn, A. (1986) *No Contest: The Case Against Competition*. Boston: Houghton Mifflin.

Kolata, G. B. (1974) "!Kung hunter-gatherers." *Science* September 13, 174.

Kramer, J., and D. Dunaway (1990) *Why Men Don't Get Enough Sex and Women Don't Get Enough Love*. New York: Pocket Books.

Kundtz, D. J. (1990) *Managing Feelings: An Owner's Manual for Men*. Albany, CA: Insight Editions.

*Kurtz, E. (1981) *Shame and Guilt: Characteristics of the Dependency Cycle*. Center City, NM: Hazelden Foundation.

*Kurtz, E. (1979) *Not-God: A History of Alcoholics Anonymous*. Center City, MN: Hazelden Foundation.

*LaChapelle, D. (1978) *Earth Wisdom*. Silverton, CO: Finn Hill Arts.

*Laibow, R., M.D. (1991) "Circumcision and its relationship to attachment impairment." Presentation given at The Second International Symposium on Circumcision, NOCIRC, April 30–May 3, in San Francisco.

Lapchick, R. E. (1986) *Fractured Focus: Sports as a Reflection of Society*. Lexington, MA: D. C. Heath & Co.

* Leaky, R. E., and R. Lewin. (1977) *Origins*. New York: E.P. Dutton.

*Lederer, W., M.D. (1968) *The Fear of Women: An Inquiry into the Enigma of Woman and Why Men Through the Ages Have Both Loved and Dreaded Her*. New York: Harcourt Brace Jovanovich.

*Lee, J. (1992) *At My Father's Wedding: Men Coming to Terms With Their Father's and Themselves*. New York: Bantam Books.

*Lee, R. B. (1993) *The Dobe Ju-'hoansi: Case Studies in Cultural Anthropology*. New York: Harcourt Brace Publications.

*Lee, R. B., and I. De Vore, eds. (1968) *Man the Hunter*. Chicago: Aldine.

*Leonard, L. S. (1989) *Witness to the Fire: Creativity & the Veil of Addiction*. Boston: Shambhala Publications.

*Levinson, D. (1978) *Seasons of a Man's Life*. New York: Ballantine Books.

*Lew, M. (1988) *Victims No Longer: Men Recovering from Incest and Other Sexual Child Abuse*. New York: Nevraumont Publishing.

Liebowitz, M. R. (1983) *The Chemistry of Love*. New York: Little, Brown & Co.

*Liedloff, J. (1975) *The Continuum Concept: Allowing Human Nature to Work Successfully*. Reading, MA: Addison-Wesley.

Littleton, J. (1988) "A comparison of the quality of life in hunter-gatherer and present day societies." Unpublished manuscript.

*Love, P., with J. Robinson. (1990) *The Emotional Incest Syndrome: What to Do When a Parent's Love Rules Your Life*. New York: Bantam Books.

Luthman, S. G. (1980) *Collection, 1979*. San Rafael, CA: Mehetabel & Co.

Madhubuti, H. R. (1990) *Black Men Obsolete, Single, Dangerous? The AfricanAmerican Family in Transition*. New York: Third World Press.

Mailer, Norman (1966) *Cannibals and Christians*. New York: Dial Press.

Maimonides, M. (1972) *The Book of Women*. New Haven, CT: Yale University Press.

Maimonides, M. (1956) *Guide for the Perplexed*. New York: Dover Publications.

Maltz, W. (1992) *The Sexual Healing Journey: A Guide for Survivors of Sexual Abuse*. New York: Harper Perennial.

Maltz, W., and B. Holman (1987) *Incest and Sexuality: A Guide to Understanding and Healing*. Lexington, MA: Lexington Books.

*Mander, J. (1991) *In the Absence of the Sacred: The Failure of Technology & the Survival of the Indian Nations*. San Francisco: Sierra Club Books.

*Maslow, A. H. (1962) *Towards a Psychology of Being*. New York: Van Nostrand.

Masters, W., V. Johnson, and R. Kolodny (1988) *Masters and Johnson on Sex and Human Loving*. Boston: Little, Brown & Co.

Masters, W., V. Johnson, and R. Kolodny (1985) *Human Sexuality*. Boston: Little, Brown & Co.

Matousek, M. (1991) "America's darkest secret." *Common Boundary* March/ April.

McClellan, D. (1987) "Womanizers." *This World*, August 16.

McClelland, D. (1961) *The Achieving Society*. New York: Van Hostrand.

*McDougall, J. (1985) *McDougall's Medicine*. New York: New Century Publishers.

Meade, M. (1993) *Men and the Water of Life*. New York: HarperCollins.

Meggessey, D. (1970) *Out of Their League*. Berkeley, CA: Ramparts Press.

Meggit, M. J. (1960) *Desert People*. Chicago: University of Chicago Press.

*Messner, M. (1990) "When bodies are weapons: Masculinity and violence in sports." *International Review of Sociology of Sport*, August.

Meth, R. L., and R. S. Pasick, with B. Gordon, J. A. Allen, L. B. Feldman, and S. Gordon (1990) *Men in Therapy: The Challenge of Change.* New York: Guilford Press.

*Miedzian, M. (1991) *Boys Will Be Boys: Breaking the Link Between Masculinity and Violence.* New York: Doubleday.

*Milkman, H. B., and S. G. Sunderwirth (1987) *Craving for Ecstasy: The Consciousness and Chemistry of Escape.* Lexington, MA: Lexington Books.

*Miller, A. (1990) *Banished Knowledge: Facing Childhood Injuries.* New York: Doubleday.

*Miller, A. (1984) *Thou Shall Not Be Aware: Society's Betrayal of the Child.* New York: Farrar, Straus, Giroux.

*Miller, A. (1983) *For Your Own Good: Hidden Cruelty in Child-Rearing and the Roots of Violence.* New York: Farrar, Straus, Giroux.

*Miller, A. (1981) *The Drama of the Gifted Child: How Narcissistic Parents Form and Deform the Emotional Lives of Their Talented Children.* New York: Basic Books.

Montagu, A. (1968) *The Concept of the Primitive.* New York: Free Press.

Moore, R. (1990) "Decoding masculine initiation." *Wingspan* Spring.

Moore, R., and D. Gillette (1992) *The Warrior Within.* New York: William Morrow.

*Moore, R., and D. Gillette (1990) *King, Warrior, Magician, Lover: Rediscovering the Archetypes of the Mature Masculine.* San Francisco: Harper San Francisco.

National Association on Sexual Addiction Problems of Colorado. *Twelve Step Resources for Sexual Addicts & Co-Addicts.* P.O. Box 3348, Boulder, CO 80307.

Neitlich, A. (1985) *Building Bridges: Women's and Men's Liberation.* Cambridge, MA: Building Bridges.

Nietzsche, Freidrich (1990) *Twilight of the Idols.* New York: Viking Penguin.

Nin, A. (1966) *Diary, 1931-1934.* New York: Harcourt, Brace & World.

*Norwood, R. (1985) *Women Who Love Too Much.* New York: Pocket Books.

Olin, W. (1980) *Escape from Utopia: My Ten Years in Synanon.* Santa Cruz, CA: Unity Press.

*Ornstein, R., and P. Ehrlich (1989) *New World, New Mind: Moving Towards Conscious Evolution.* New York: Simon & Schuster.

Ornstein, Y. (1991) *From the Hearts of Men.* Woodacre, CA: Harmonia Press.

*Ortega, Gassett, J. (1972) *Meditations on Hunting.* Translated by Howard Wescott. New York: Charles Scribner

*Osherson, S. (1986) *Finding Our Fathers: The Unfinished Business of Manhood.* New York: The Free Press.

Paige, K. E. (1978) "The ritual of circumcision." *Human Nature* May.

*Parry, D. (1989) *Warriors of the Heart.* Coopertown, NY: Sunstone Publications.

*Patent, A. M. (1989) *Death, Taxes, and Other Illusions.* Piermont, NY: Celebration Publishing.

*Patent, A. M. (1984) *You Can Have It All: The Art of Winning the Money Game and Living a Life of Joy.* Piermont, NY: Celebration Publishing.

*Patterson, J., and P. Kim (1991) *The Day America Told the Truth: What People Really Believe About Everything That Really Matters.* New York: Prentice-Hall.

*Pearson, C. (1986) *The Hero Within: Six Archetypes We Live By.* San Francisco: Harper & Row.

Peck, S. (1978) *The Road Less Traveled.* New York: Simon & Schuster.

Pedersen, L. (1991) *Dark Hearts: The Unconscious Forces That Shape Men's Lives.* Boston: Shambhala.

Peele, S. (1975) *Love and Addiction.* New York: NAL

Phillips, D. (1983) "The impact of mass media violence in U.S. homicides." *American Sociological Review*, August.

*Pleck, J. (1984/85) "Healing the wounded father." *The Men's Journal* Winter.

*Pleck, J. (1981) *The Myth of Masculinity.* Cambridge: MIT Press.

*Prescott, J. (1989) "Genital pain vs. genital pleasure: Why the one and not the other?" *The Truth Seekers*, vol. 1, no. 3, July/August.

*Prescott, J. (1975) "Body pleasure and the origins of violence." *The Futurist* April.

Pruett, K. D. *The Nurturing Father.* New York: Warner Books.

*Quinn, D. (1993) *Ishmael.* New York: Bantam Books.

Rappaport, R. A. (1979) *Ecology, Meaning, and Religion.* Berkeley, CA: North Atlantic Books.

*Ravenholt, R. (1984) "Addiction Mortality in the United States 1980: Tobacco, alcohol and other substances." *Population and Development Review* 10(4).

*Rifkin, J. (1991) *Biosphere Politics: A New Consciousness for a New Century.* New York: Crown Publishers.

*Ritter, T. J., M.D. (1992) *Say No to Circumcision! 40 compelling reasons why you should respect his birthright and keep your son whole.* Aptos, CA: Hourglass Book Publishing.

*Robbins, J. (1992) *May All Be Fed: Diet for a New World.* New York: William Morrow & Co.

*Robbins, J. (1987) *Diet for a New America.* Walpole, NH: Stillpoint Publishing.

Robertson, N. (1988) *Getting Better: Inside Alcoholics Anonymous.* New York: William Morrow & Co.

*Romberg, R. (1985) *Circumcision: The Painful Dilemma*. South Hadley, MA: Gergin & Garvey Publishers.

*Roszak, T. (1992) *The Voice of the Earth*. New York: Simon & Schuster.

*Rubin, L. (1983) *Intimate Strangers: Men and Women Together*. New York: Harper & Row.

*Rush, F. (1980) *The Best Kept Secret: Sexual Abuse of Children*. New York: PrenticeHall.

Rutter, P., M.D. (1989) *Sex in the Forbidden Zone: When Men in Power— Therapists, Doctors, Clergy, Teachers, and Others—Betray Women's Trust*. Los Angeles: Jeremy P. Tarcher.

*Sahlins, M. D. (1972) *Stone Age Economics*. Chicago: Aldine Atherton.

Saitoti, T. O. (1986) *The Worlds of a Maasai Warrior: An Autobiography*. Berkeley, CA: University of California Press.

*Samuels, M., M.D., and H. Z. Bennett. (1983) *Well Body, Well Earth*. San Francisco: Sierra Club Books.

*Satir, V. (1973) *Peoplemaking*. Mountain View, CA: Science & Behavior Books.

*Satir, V. (1964) *Conjoint Family Therapy*. Mountain View, CA: Science & Behavior Books.

*Schaef, A. W. (1988) *Escape from Intimacy—Untangling the "Love" Addictions: Sex, Romance, Relationships*. San Francisco: Harper & Row.

*Schaef, A. W. (1987) *When Society Becomes an Addict*. San Francisco: Harper & Row.

*Schmookler, A. B. (1989) *Sowings and Reapings: The Cycle of Good and Evil in the Human System*. Indianapolis: Knowledge Systems.

*Schmookler, A. B. (1988) *Out of Weakness: Healing the Wounds That Drive Us to War*. New York: Bantam Books.

*Schmookler, A. B. (1984) *The Parable of the Tribes: The Problem of Power in Social Evolution*. Boston: Houghton Mifflin.

Schneider, J. (1991) *Sex, Lies, and Forgiveness: Couples Speaking Out on Healing from Sex Addiction*. Center City, MN: Hazelden Foundation.

*Schneider, J. (1988) *Back From Betrayal: Recovering From His Affairs*. San Francisco: Harper & Row.

Schor, J. B. (1991) *The Overworked American: The Unexpected Decline of Leisure*. New York: HarperCollins.

*Service, E. (1966) *The Hunters*. Englewood Cliffs, NJ: Prentice-Hall.

Shanor, K. (1978) *The Shanor Study: The Sexual Sensitivity of the American Male*. New York: Dial Press.

Sheehy, G. (1987) "The road to Bimini." *Vanity Fair*, September.

*Shepard, P. (1982) *Nature and Madness.* San Francisco: Sierra Club Books.

*Shepard, P. (1972) *The Tender Carnivore and the Sacred Games.* New York: Charles Scribner.

*Siegel, R. (1989) *Intoxication: Life in Pursuit of Artificial Paradise.* New York: E.P. Dutton.

Simon, N. (1986) *Biloxi Blues.* New York: Random House.

Sipes, R. G. (1973) "War, sports, and aggression: An empirical test of two rival theories." *The American Anthropologist* 75.

Slater, P. (1991) *A Dream Deferred: America's Discontent and the Search for a Democratic Ideal.* Boston: Beacon Press.

*Slater, P. (1983) *Wealth Addiction.* New York: E.P. Dutton.

Small, J. (1991) *Awakening in Time: The Journey From Codependence to Co-Creation.* New York: Bantam Books.

Smith, B. (1991) "Bob Smith shares his memories of dad—The co-founder of AA." *Sober Times,* July.

*Snyder, G. (1990) *The Practice of the Wild.* Berkeley, CA: North Point Press.

Snyder, G. (1969) *Turtle Island.* New York: New Directions Publishing Co.

Spock, B., M.D. (1989) "Circumcision—It's Not Necessary." *Redbook,* April.

Starhawk (1987) *Truth or Dare: Encounters with Power, Authority, and Mystery.* San Francisco: Harper & Row.

Steele, B. F., and C. B. Pollock (1966) "Psychiatric study of abusing parents." edited by R. E. Helfer, and C. H. Kempe. In *The Battered Child.* Chicago: University of Chicago Press.

Stevens, J. (1985) "The Founder, Ueshiba Moriehi." In *Aikido and the New Warrior,* edited by R. S. Heckler. Berkeley, CA: North Atlantic Books.

Stokes, J. (1990) "Finding our place on earth again." *Wingspan,* Summer.

Strick, A. (1978) *Injustice for All.* New York: Penguin Books.

*Szasz, T. (1985) *Ceremonial Chemistry: The Ritual Persecution of Drugs, Addicts, and Pushers.* Holmes Beach, FL: Learning Publications.

Talese, G. (1980) *Thy Neighbor's Wife.* New York: Doubleday.

*Tennov, D. (1979) *Love and Limerence: The Experience of Being in Love.* New York: Stein & Day.

Thomas, T. (1989) *Men Surviving Incest.* Walnut Creek, CA: Launch Press.

de Tocqueville, A. (1945) *Democracy in America.* New York: Random House.

*Toffler, A. (1970) *Future Shock.* London: Pan Books Ltd.

*Trungpa, C. (1984) *Shambhala: The Sacred Path of the Warrior.* Boston: Shambhala Publications.

Van Der Post, L. (1962) *Patterns of Renewal.* Pendle Hill Pamphlet no. 121. Wallingford, PA: Pendle Hill Publications.

*Van Der Post, L. (1961) *The Heart of the Hunter: Customs and Myths of the African Bushman.* New York: Harcourt Brace Jovanovich.

*Van Der Post, L. (1958) *The Lost World of the Kalahari.* New York: Harcourt Brace Jovanovich.

Vittachi, A. (1989) *Earth Conference One: Sharing a Vision of Our Planet.* Boston: Shambhala Publications.

Vonnegut, K. (1989) "Weapons junkies." *Recovering Magazine.* San Francisco, August/September.

*Walker, A. (1992) *Possessing the Secret of Joy.* New York: Harcourt Brace Jovanovich.

Walker, E. E. (1972) *The Emergent Native Americans.* Boston: Little, Brown & Co.

*Wallerstein, E. (1980) *Circumcision: An American Health Fallacy.* New York: Springer Publishing.

Watson, E. (1990) "Can the fast track be a round trip to nowhere?" *The Seattle Times,* January 28.

*Watzlawick, P., J. Weakland, and R. Fisch (1974) *Change: Principles of Problem Formation and Problem Resolution.* Palo Alto, CA: Science and Behavior Books.

Wegscheider, S. (1981) *Another Chance: Hope and Health for the Alcoholic Family.* Palo Alto, CA: Science and Behavior Books.

*Weil, A., and W. Rosen (1983) *Chocolate to Morphine: Understanding Mind-Active Drugs.* Boston: Houghton Mifflin.

Wetcher, K., M.D., A. Barker, and F. R. McCaughtry (1991) *Save the Males: Why Men are Mistreated, Misdiagnosed, and Misunderstood.* Washington, D.C.: Psychiatric Institutes of America.

*Wheelis, A. (1987) *The Doctor of Desire.* New York: W.W. Norton & Co.

Wheelis, A. (1971) *The End of the Modern Age.* New York: Basic Books.

White, L. (1959) *The Evolution of Culture: The Development of Civilization to the Fall of Rome.* New York: Grove Press.

*Whitfield, C., M.D. (1991) *Co-Dependence—Disease of Humankind: The New Paradigm for Helping Professionals and People in Recovery.* Deerfield Beach, FL: Health Communications.

*Whitfield, C., M.D. (1989) "Co-dependence—our most common addiction: some physical, mental, emotional and spiritual perspectives." *Alcoholism Treatment Quarterly* 6, no. 1.

Whitfield, C., M.D. (1987) *Healing the Child Within: Discovery and Recovery for Adult Children of Dysfunctional Families*. Deerfield Beach, FL: Health Communications.

Whiting, J. W. M., and S. Gunders. (1968) "Mother-infant separation and physical growth." *Ethnology*, 7.

Wilber, K. (1978) *No Boundary*. Boston: Shambhala Publications.

*Williams, T. (1989) *Cocaine Kids: The Underground American Dream*. New York: Addison-Wesley.

*Wilson, P. (1988) *The Domestication of the Human Species*. New Haven, CT: Yale University Press.

*Yablonsky, L. (1965) *The Tunnel Back: Synanon*. New York: The Macmillan Co.

*Yoder, B. (1990) *The Recovery Resource Book*. New York: Simon & Schuster.

*Zinberg, N. E. (1984) *Drug, Set, and Setting: The Basis for Controlled Intoxicant Use*. New Haven, CT: Yale University Press.

Index

Jed Diamond lives in Willits, CA, with his wife Carlin, a fellow writer and counselor and his partner in leading workshops throughout the country. He and Carlin have five children ranging in age from 19 to 34. As Jed says, with wisdom and humor earned through experience, "Being a husband and father has been a key element in my own healing journey."

For the last 28 years Jed has been one of the most respected leaders in the Recovery and Men's Movements. John Bradshaw describes him as "one of the best teachers around." His book *Inside Out: Becoming My Own Man* was an inspiration to author John Lee, who said it gave him, "tears of joy and healing."

Warren Farrell says Jed's last book, *Looking For Love In All The Wrong Places: Overcoming Romantic and Sexual Addictions,* is "a time-tested map for helping us to find love in all the right places."

According to Diamond, "Addiction is the dis-ease of lost selfhood. Whether people get hooked on drugs, food, gambling, sex, romance, or any other substance or activity that produces a 'rush,' they are cut off from themselves, desperately trying to escape the pain of their present life. Addicts are people who want to go home, yet like confused homing pigeons.they fly ever faster in the wrong direction." *The Warrior's Journey Home* will help thousands of people find their way again.

Other Books and Tapes by Jed Diamond

	Price	Quantity	Total
Books			
The Warrior's Journey Home	$12.95		
Looking for Love in All the Wrong Places	$10		
Inside Out: Becoming My Own Man	$10		
Love It, Don't Label It (by Carlin Diamond)	$10		
Booklets			
The Lazy Person's Guide to Relationships	$10		
The Adrenaline Addict: Hooked on Danger and Excitement	$10		
"Love" Addictions: For Women Only	$10		
Healing Male Co-Dependency	$10		
Sex and "Love" Addiction & Chemical Dependency	$10		
Fatal Attractions: Understanding Sex and "Love" Addictions	$10		
When Men Stopped Being Warriors and Became Killers	$10		
Cowboys, Killers, Wimps, and Sex Addicts	$10		
Beyond Drug Wars	$10		
Audio Tape Sets			
Looking for Love In All the Wrong Places (4-tape set)	$20		
Understanding Co-Dependency and the "Love" Addictions (3-tape set)	$15		
Sex: Escape, Intimacy or Addiction? (2-tape set)	$12		
Agony or Ecstasy: Changing Sex and "Love" Addiction to Healthy Intimacy (2-tape set)	$12		
Sex and Love Addiction Recovery for Men vs. Women (2-tape set)	$12		
Addiction Free in the 90's (2-tape set)	$12		
Close Yet Free: How to Have Intimate Relationships (2-tape set)	$12		
The Warrior's Journey Home (2-tape set)	$12		
The Way of the Peaceful Warrior (2-tape set)	$12		
Recovering the Deep Masculine (2-tape set)	$12		
Yoga (by Carlin Diamond)	$12		
Meditation (by Carlin Diamond)	$12		
Subtotal			
Tax (California residents add appropriate tax)			
Shipping: $3.80 for the first item and 75¢ for each additional item			
TOTAL			

Send order form and checks to: New Harbinger Publications, Inc., 5674 Shattuck Ave., Oakland, CA 94609.

Ship to:

Name: _____

Address: _____

City: _____ State: _____ Zip: _____

Country: _____

Other New Harbinger Self-Help Titles

The Warrior's Journey Home: Healing Men, Healing the Planet, $12.95
Weight Loss Through Persistence, $12.95
Post-Traumatic Stress Disorder: A Complete Treatment Guide, $39.95
Stepfamily Realities: How to Overcome Difficulties and Have a Happy Family, $11.95
Leaving the Fold: A Guide for Former Fundamentalists and Others Leaving Their Religion, $12.95
Father-Son Healing: An Adult Son's Guide, $12.95
The Chemotherapy Survival Guide, $11.95
Your Family/Your Self: How to Analyze Your Family System, $11.95
Being a Man: A Guide to the New Masculinity, $12.95
The Deadly Diet, Second Edition: Recovering from Anorexia & Bulimia, $11.95
Last Touch: Preparing for a Parent's Death, $11.95
Consuming Passions: Help for Compulsive Shoppers, $11.95
Self-Esteem, Second Edition, $12.95
Depression & Anxiety Mangement: An audio tape for managing emotional problems, $11.95
I Can't Get Over It, A Handbook for Trauma Survivors, $12.95
Concerned Intervention, When Your Loved One Won't Quit Alcohol or Drugs, $11.95
Redefining Mr. Right, $11.95
Dying of Embarrassment: Help for Social Anxiety and Social Phobia, $11.95
The Depression Workbook: Living With Depression and Manic Depression, $13.95
Risk-Taking for Personal Growth: A Step-by-Step Workbook, $11.95
The Marriage Bed: Renewing Love, Friendship, Trust, and Romance, $11.95
Focal Group Psychotherapy: For Mental Health Professionals, $44.95
Hot Water Therapy: Save Your Back, Neck & Shoulders in 10 Minutes a Day $11.95
Older & Wiser: A Workbook for Coping With Aging, $12.95
Prisoners of Belief: Exposing & Changing Beliefs that Control Your Life, $10.95
Be Sick Well: A Healthy Approach to Chronic Illness, $11.95
Men & Grief: A Guide for Men Surviving the Death of a Loved One., $11.95
When the Bough Breaks: A Helping Guide for Parents of Sexually Abused Childern, $11.95
Love Addiction: A Guide to Emotional Independence, $11.95
When Once Is Not Enough: Help for Obsessive Compulsives, $11.95
The New Three Minute Meditator, $9.95
Getting to Sleep, $10.95
The Relaxation & Stress Reduction Workbook, 3rd Edition, $13.95
Leader's Guide to the Relaxation & Stress Reduction Workbook, $19.95
Beyond Grief: A Guide for Recovering from the Death of a Loved One, $10.95
Thoughts & Feelings: The Art of Cognitive Stress Intervention, $13.95
Messages: The Communication Skills Book, $12.95
The Divorce Book, $11.95
Hypnosis for Change: A Manual of Proven Techniques, 2nd Edition, $12.95
The Chronic Pain Control Workbook, $13.95
Visualization for Change, $12.95
Videotape: Clinical Hypnosis for Stress & Anxiety Reduction, $24.95
My Parent's Keeper: Adult Children of the Emotionally Disturbed, $11.95
When Anger Hurts, $12.95
Free of the Shadows: Recovering from Sexual Violence, $12.95
Lifetime Weight Control, $11.95
The Anxiety & Phobia Workbook, $13.95
Love and Renewal: A Couple's Guide to Commitment, $12.95
The Habit Control Workbook, $12.95

Call **toll free, 1-800-748-6273**, to order. Have your Visa or Mastercard number ready. Or send a check for the titles you want to New Harbinger Publications, Inc., 5674 Shattuck Avenue, Oakland, CA 94609. Include $3.80 for the first book and 75¢ for each additional book, to cover shipping and handling. (California residents please include appropriate sales tax.) Allow four to six weeks for delivery.

Prices subject to change without notice.